A General Introduction to
Institutional Investment

To Joan and Family
with love and best wishes
from Alan.

March 1987

David P. Hager.

also of interest
An Introduction to the Mathematics of Finance

A General Introduction to Institutional Investment

A. J. FROST, BSc., FIA
and
D. P. HAGER, MA, FIA, FPMI

Published for the
Institute of Actuaries and
the Faculty of Actuaries

HEINEMANN: LONDON

*This book replaces an earlier
work by J. G. Day and A. T.
Jamieson which is one of a series
of volumes entitled Institutional Investment*

William Heinemann Ltd
10 Upper Grosvenor Street, London W1X 9PA

LONDON   MELBOURNE   JOHANNESBURG   AUCKLAND

First published 1986
© The Institute of Actuaries and
the Faculty of Actuaries in Scotland

British Library Cataloguing in Publication Data
Frost, Alan J.
  A general introduction to institutional investment
  1. Financial institutions – Great Britain –
  Investments
  I. Title   II. Hager, David P.
  332.6'7154'0941   HG5432

ISBN 0 434 90582 8

Set by Keyset Composition, Colchester
Printed in Great Britain by
Redwood Burn Ltd, Trowbridge

CONTENTS

PREFACE

The word 'investment' means different things to different people. Those who observe the actions of the City of London from an uninformed aspect often wonder what is the difference between gambling and investment as practised by, say, pension funds. The *Shorter Oxford English Dictionary* reads as follows:

'Invest':   To employ (money) in the purchase of anything from which interest or profit is expected.

'Speculate': To engage in the buying and selling of commodities or effects in order to profit by a rise or fall in their market value; to undertake, or take part or invest in, a business enterprise or transaction of a risky nature in the expectation of considerable gain.

'Gamble':   To stake money on some chance; to speculate recklessly.

There appears to be a distinction between the three definitions indicating a clear hierarchy. The difference may be one of time scale; or of motivation; or of 'risk' in the colloquial sense; or even a distinction by reference to social approbation. The buying and selling of shares falls within the definition of speculation. Is this then what a financial institution such as a life assurance company does? The 'investment' of money in venture capital projects (essentially, the provision of capital to a company with no proven financial history but great prospects) is dangerously close to the definition of 'gambling'. For the purposes of this book we assume that investment is the responsible placing of funds by certain financial institutions who comprise the 'savings market' in the U.K. The savers themselves would probably differentiate between investment, speculation and gambling by some subjective feeling for risk and reward. This scale of riskiness, however defined, is mirrored in the activities of the investing institutions whose breadth of operations stretches from simple overnight transactions with the (totally safe) Bank of England to investment in seedcorn capital in new high-risk industries.

This book deals predominantly with the investment activities of long-term investment funds such as life assurance companies and pension funds and the authors' day-by-day pre-occupation with these institutions will be evident throughout. The emphasis is on what is termed fundamental analysis, although reference to chart or technical analysis and modern portfolio theory (MPT) is made. As long-term funds life assurance companies and pension funds require long-term performance. This can be only a succession of short-term performances. The changing product mix of the institutions and increasing competition within the savings market has led over the last decade or so to increasing emphasis on short-term performance. In some ways the forces of competition and increasing demands for short-term published performance figures make the task of providing risk capital in the longer term extremely difficult. The dangers of concentrating on short-term performance cannot be over-estimated.

The decision-making process for selecting individual stocks and shares is discussed later in the book. It is useful to reflect, however, at this early stage on how decisions are made in general. The investment manager has at his disposal an enormous number of facts. Having marshalled the facts he will be required to make certain assumptions based on his opinions. He will then make a judgement about the investment. Thus a decision to buy or sell the shares of a high street store will begin with an analysis of the facts of past performance of the company, its trading record, its position within its industry and so on. Assumptions will then have to be made about the future growth of the industry and the relative growth of the company compared with its competitors within the industry. The final judgement as to whether the shares should be bought or sold will to some extent reflect the investment manager's confidence in his assumptions but it is a considered judgement based on experience of similar investments in similar companies. The process used by chartists or exponents of MPT is similar in its assessment of past facts. These techniques, however, make no judgement about the future and attempt to predict the future mathematically or graphically. They are unable to cope with a discontinuity at the present caused by, say, a takeover or death of a significant executive. It is the judgement required by the investment manager that justifies his existence and sets him apart from the man who uses a 'system' to win at roulette.

The long-term savings institutions of which life assurance companies and pension funds are examples are in turn part of the total population of the 'City'. The 'City' comprises a number of institutions including clearing banks, accepting houses, merchant banks, discount houses, the trustee savings banks, national savings banks, licensed deposit takers, finance houses, building societies, unit trusts, investment trust companies, insurance companies, pension funds, leasing companies, factoring companies, special finance agencies (Investment in Industry, Equity Capital for Industry, Commonwealth Development Finance Company etc.) and public sector finance agencies (National Enterprise Board, Export Credits Guarantee Department etc.).

These institutions are the members of a series of interlocking financial communities. There is the banking system with the Bank of England at its head; leading from it is the money market, the foreign exchange market, and the discount market, which in turn is closely connected with the gilt-edged market of the Stock Exchange. There is the insurance market which includes Lloyd's and its famous international business, and also includes insurance companies transacting general and life business. There are also the commodity markets, the metal exchange and the markets in sugar, cocoa, rubber and other important commodities, including oil. There are also the services for importing or exporting, usually with short-term specialized finance. The most recent member of this community is the financial futures market which trades in gilts, equities, currency and other money instruments on a formal basis. It is known as the London International Financial Futures Exchange (LIFFE).

The book begins by examining briefly the economic framework within which investment decisions are made. It includes a brief discussion on the Wilson Report, in view of its importance as a milestone in the life and development of the City. Chapter 2 describes the mechanisms for raising capital and the nature of the securities markets. In Chapter 3 the types of investment are reviewed. We follow with elementary accounting for investors and the mechanics of new issues. Chapter 6 outlines the elements of portfolio theory and planning. This is followed by a consideration of the special problems of investment in inflationary conditions and the relevance of real rates of return. We conclude with an account of practical fund management and indicate the methodology of performance measurement.

This work inevitably draws upon existing published works which are noted in the references. The book was commissioned by the Institute of Actuaries in order to replace Volume I of *Institutional Investment* by Day and Jamieson which needed extensive revision after more than a decade of useful life. We owe an enormous debt of gratitude to Gilfrid Day and Andrew Jamieson whose book has formed the foundation for this current volume. We also thank Terry Arthur and David Bays for kind permission to use extracts from their work in Chapters 1 and 5 respectively. To our understanding wives, our patient secretaries, and our colleagues within the actuarial profession and elsewhere, who have all helped to bring our work to fruition, we give immense thanks. The final product reflects, however, our own style, thoughts and prejudices for which we take full responsibility.

ACKNOWLEDGEMENTS

Figures 6.1 – 6.4 and the material in section 6.21 are reproduced from E. J. Elton and M. J. Gruber (1981), *Modern Portfolio Theory and Investment Analysis* by permission of John Wiley & Sons, Inc., New York.

Appendix 1 is reproduced from the Stock Exchange Yearbook.

Appendix 2 is reproduced by permission of St Ives Group plc and N. M. Rothschild & Sons Limited.

The charts in Chapter 1 are reproduced by permission of James Capel & Co.

CHAPTER ONE

THE ECONOMIC FRAMEWORK

1.1 Introduction

The word 'investment' is capable of being interpreted in several ways. Economists use the phrase 'capital formation' to illustrate the replacement of capital assets that depreciate and become obsolescent. If all existing resources are used to maximize current consumption then capital formation cannot take place. Thus capital formation takes place via abstinence from consumption. The resources released are directed into assets having the capacity to produce – more prolifically – in future.

A purchase, from another investor, of previously issued stock does not in itself produce capital formation, yet it is considered to be an investment. This is the activity with which institutional investors are normally concerned. Portfolio investment can occur without capital formation and is the process by which exchanges in the ownership of assets are made.

For capital formation to occur savings must be made over and above the requirements of asset maintenance (if we assume that all savings are directed via financial institutions). These excess savings will be directed (largely) to the higher order producers (manufacturing for other parts of the production process rather than for consumers). Portfolio investment, taking place via the financial institutions, will include the direction of some of these excess savings (into new share issues, for example), but will also include the exchanging of existing assets on a large scale. This exchange process is a prime means of promoting the efficient use of capital, as well as the source of evaluation of new projects.

In the past fifteen years or so a number of criticisms have been levelled at institutional investors in the U.K. Broadly speaking, there is no legislation which either compels or bans investment in any specific areas. U.K. governments have not (yet?) lightly cast aside the principle of 'freedom with disclosure', a principle which has been accepted for many years by most interest groups.

Government influence has been by less direct means, three of which stand out:

(i) taxation; pension funds enjoy full tax relief on contributions from both members and employers and on investment income and capital gains. Maxima apply to either benefits or contributions, depending on the nature of the arrangements and a large part of the maximum retirement benefits must usually be taken as a taxable pension.

Apart from pensions business, where treatment is the same as that for a direct pension fund, life assurance companies are the subject of a myriad of conflicting tax provisions, but the broad result is to encourage savings via life assurance companies to a greater extent than via most other media.

(ii) Government can ensure receipt of part of the savings of the institutions by issuing stock (on behalf of taxpayers) on attractive terms; of particular interest here is the recent introduction of index-linked Government securities.

(iii) via the mechanism of inflation, in particular unanticipated inflation, Government can distort bargains between suppliers and users of capital.

These basic influences – taxation, competition for funds, and inflation, have recently been considered insufficient by a growing number of critics. The financial institutions are cited as having failed in various areas, prominent among which are the provision of capital for industry, the direction of capital to its most productive uses, and the creation of employment. In addition, they are held to be too important to escape more direct control from the authorities, and fears are voiced that the concentration of capital funds in a relatively small number of gigantic institutions leads to an undesirable oligarchy.

The welter of criticism reached its climax in the mid 1970s following the worst recession for decades and a collapse in stock prices comparable to that of 1929. Trade unions, journalists, and academics vociferously accused the institutions of an investment strike and called for much greater political control. The Wilson Committee, chaired by the former Prime Minister Sir Harold Wilson, was formed by the Government in January 1977 to investigate the situation.

1.2 The Wilson Report

Reviews into the financial system in the U.K. have been undertaken about once every quarter of a century. The Wilson Committee was set up in January 1977, in the same mould as the Macmillan Committee on Finance and Industry (1931) and the Radcliffe Committee on the Working of the Monetary System (1959).

In late 1976 there were severe economic problems. Inflation was increasing, interest rates were high, the exchange rate weak and the Government was forced to implement a package of measures in conjunction with the International Monetary Fund. There were feelings in some quarters that the institutions were not playing their part in improving the economic situation by not providing sufficient finance for industry and because they had not taken up a large issue of gilt-edged stock at the price set by the Government (the so called 'gilts strike'). Nationalization of banks and insurance companies was being suggested at that time.

The Wilson Committee was given very wide terms of reference to look not just at the specific allegations against the institutions but into their role and functioning at home and abroad, their value to the economy, the provision of funds for industry and trade, and the issue of nationalization.

The Committee made a large number of conclusions but we look at those which are relevant to the theme of this book.

The Committee found that the contention that real investment in the U.K. had been unnecessarily constrained by shortages in the supply of external finance could not generally be substantiated. Indeed, one of the main problems was thought to be the reluctance of acceptable borrowers to come forward, rather than a limitation on the amount of available bank credit. Another inhibition on real investment was found to be the price of finance in relation to expected profitability.

In its conclusions on the operations of the capital market the Report concluded that in the context of industrial finance a wide range of financial instruments, with the exception of index-linked securities, was available to savers and borrowers and that the system has a good record in meeting new requirements. The Report noted that it appears that the pricing of securities in the markets is fair, in that differences between companies in expected returns and risks are reflected in prices, although the risks being assessed are in part those related to the holdings of securities rather than to the longer-term prospects for earnings on the underlying real assets. It judged the stock market as not being particularly successful at predicting which companies will show a substantial profit growth, that the level of secondary market dealing may often be more than is required to establish correct relative prices, and that there may be some disadvantages in a high level of secondary market deals, for instance, in fostering a speculative psychology. The Report voiced concern as to whether the growing dominance of the institutions in the securities markets has been a cause of increased market volatility and wondered whether the investment policies of the institutions unduly discriminate against smaller or high-risk companies.

On indexation in the capital market, the Report recommended experimentation in the index-linked market by the corporate sector, the issue of index-linked gilts and the issue of index-linked mortgages. These have occurred since the publication of the Report.

The Report called for more institutional involvement with managements of companies in which they have investments. Institutional shareholders should exercise responsibility in keeping management on its toes, in requiring information and in making contact with management.

The Report expressed concern about the drying up of new issues of long-term industrial bonds. The introduction of index-linked gilts has, in fact, assisted in achieving this since 1981. By avoiding conventional high coupon long gilts in his funding programme the Government Broker has encouraged some corporate bond issues (mainly for financial companies). Nevertheless, even five years after the Report, an issue of industrial debenture or loan stock is still uncommon.

The Report noted the importance of pension funds and insurance companies in the capital market and the way this causes concern. The Report goes on to suggest that the system of marketing government securities was not well adapted to the dominance of the institutions as purchasers in the context (in 1980) of considerable economic uncertainty, a high Public Sector Borrowing Requirement and a commitment to published monetary targets. Finally, it remarked that there was no comprehensive framework for securing the accountability of pension funds.

Regulation of the securities market was also examined, and whilst some strengthening of the methods then in use was recommended, it rejected greater statutory powers for the Takeover Panel, and thought that the British equivalent of the American Securities and Exchange Commission would not be beneficial.

1.3 Long-term investment

The central problems of the recent past have been the effects of structural unemployment (as distinct from short-term cyclical trends); a persistent rise in prices and money incomes; the slow rate of economic growth in the U.K. compared with our competitors overseas; the deepening responsibility of Britain and the other developed countries of the world towards the less developed countries and, in particular, the increased burden of Third World debt. These different forces, often acting in conflict, have provided a highly unstable backdrop for institutional investment. An investment manager is inevitably part of the circular flow of money, receiving as reward for fixed interest investment periodic interest payments as compensation for loss of use of the money; and receiving dividends (or profits) and rents as reward for his 'equity' in other investments. At the micro level considerable analysis is carried out to ascertain the viability of individual proposals or projects. At the macro level a number of features are studied to decide on the propitiousness of investment in different economies or market sectors.

The institutional investment manager has to be aware of the nature of the pension or life assurance contracts that the assets under his control are supporting. In the case of pension funds there will be a need to produce real rates of return in excess of earnings inflation and the manager will be aware of the need for assets that grow in real terms. For certain life assurance contracts it may be necessary to achieve a rate of return on fixed interest securities. The balance between the main classes of investment, namely, real assets such as equities and property, and money-based assets such as fixed interest securities, will be determined by the investment manager and the actuary after discussion of assumed funding rates, the outlook for interest rates, the prospects for inflation, and the assumed returns from the various classes of investment whether money-based or expressed in real terms.

Thus the requirement is for long-term investment in sound money, shares and factors of production in that order, with physical goods and short-term speculation as last resorts.

The users of these preferred investment forms (Government, long-term borrowers, those running long-term projects) will earn sufficient to provide the investors' return only if the funds are put to work to make what consumers want to buy or make use of (including leisure and cultural pursuits). They must make existing goods or services more cheaply, or provide brand-new products at a price the consumer thinks worth paying, or invest in equipment to do these things in future.

All these things will be beneficial to consumers as a whole and there appears to be every reason for a fund's investment policy to harmonize with the common good especially with the interests of long-term manu- facturing projects and eventual consumers.

Investment in goods (hoarding) or short-term financial assets, however, will lead to short-term projects, rising prices, and possibly shortages. The undesirability of this is common to the investors and the public at large.

1.4 Economic indicators

Part of the fund of knowledge available to the managers of assets is historic economic data. This, of course, is used to project future trends. Any study must start with the U.K. economy, but the U.S. is very much the driving force for other world economies and often helps to form sound views on the U.K. The actuary involved in long-term institutions is concerned with the trend of interest rates and the movement of stock markets as well as industrial production and profits. Interest rates in turn may reflect

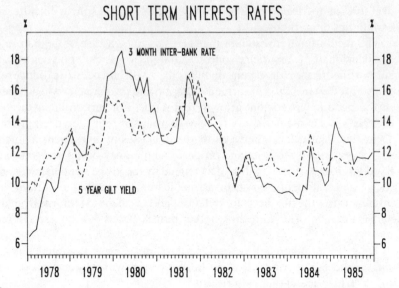

Figure 1.1

government policy and actions. The movement of the gilt-edged market will be influenced by interest rates and these will affect the equity market as well as specific questions about capacity and profitability. Do the national economic figures show a trend and does this indicate lower sales and production or greater activity? Will consumer sales rise or fall? Will capital investment rise or fall? The answers form the background to investigations of specific industries within the economy and specific companies within an industry. The main statistics are now described.

1.5 Economic cycles

Despite the continuing arguments between followers of Keynesian theories and devotees of monetarism it is always useful to consider the position of the economy within its cycle. Kondratieff has forwarded a hypothesis about long-term economic cycles about which opinion is divided, but over the shorter term there is good evidence to show the regular peaks and troughs of economic activity, albeit distorted by the 'Oil Shocks' of the 1970s. The pattern of rising activity, levelling off and then declining activity is noteworthy as a guide to the probable trend of interest rates. The Confederation of British Industry Industrial Trends Survey offers a good guide to the state of the business cycle, and industrial production figures are produced monthly.

1.6 Unemployment statistics

Traditionally, published figures of unemployed and unfilled vacancies have given a fair indication of the extent to which 'labour' capacity is being used and they have reflected the pattern of the economic cycle. The current levels of unemployment and the forecasts by many commentators that these high levels will persist do suggest that a change of thinking may be required. The dramatic fall in the proportion of the economy involved in manufacturing since the Second World War and the impressive rise in productivity during the early 1980s confirm this suggestion. The fund manager's use of employment statistics is now limited and the most profitable projection to be drawn is a forecast of the areas of the economy remaining which will need to add to labour resources rather than make capital investment in computers and the like.

1.7 Capital investment

Although consumer expenditure does rise and fall, it has been the case in the past that changes in the economic cycle have had the most effect on capital investment. The comments in 1.6 are as relevant here. The structural changes in the U.K. economy do not lead nowadays necessarily to massive investment in heavy industries – many are declining or have

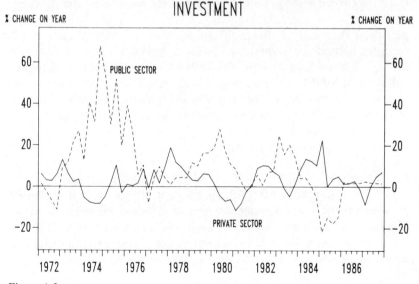

Figure 1.2

Figures in 1.2 are actual to 1985 and estimates thereafter.

naturally disappeared. Of more relevance is the investment in computer hardware and software including all sorts of automation and robots. Nevertheless, the building industry may show where this capital investment begins through the construction of new factory buildings, industrial units and so on. The graph in Figure 1.2 shows the change in levels of capital investment in recent years.

1.8 Money supply

Monetarists claim that many economic problems, including inflation, can be traced to an excess in money supply. Many governments have espoused the tenets of monetarism as a fundamental part of economic management. The so-called 'monetarist' school of economists, the leading exponent of which is Professor Milton Friedman, believe that the supply of money (and its rate of increase) is the main determinant of the level of demand. They argue, therefore, that a government must control the rate of growth of the money supply: if it grows too fast, so will aggregate demand, with consequent inflationary and balance of payments problems. The implication is that a large budget deficit must be financed by borrowing, even if this means a large rise in interest rates, rather than by a rapid expansion of the money supply.

The supply of money undoubtedly affects the fixed interest market, and those concerned with fixed interest investments, particularly the gilt-edged stocks, have to carefully evaluate the money supply figures, and in particular their rate of change. There is, however, no single universally accepted definition of money, and hence money supply. Any definition of money must to some extent be arbitrary and different monetary aggregates will be used for different purposes. There are four main definitions in use for money supply (M0, M1, M2 and M3) and two for private sector liquidity (PSL1 and PSL2). The relationships between each of these definitions can be seen from Figure 1.3.

In 1984 the Government set target ranges for the growth of M3, but in 1985 more official attention seems to be placed on M0. The monetary growth of both M0 and M3 in 1984 and 1985 can be seen from the graph in Figure 1.4.

It is interesting to see from the graph that M0 and M3 give different answers for the levels of monetary growth, and it is important to ensure that the correct measure is used for each particular circumstance. M2 has, for example, been designed to be more directly related to transactions in goods and services than M3 and less sensitive to relative interest rates than M1.

During the period of Conservative government from 1979 a great deal of emphasis was placed on control of the money supply. The combination of

Relationships among the monetary and liquidity aggregates and their components

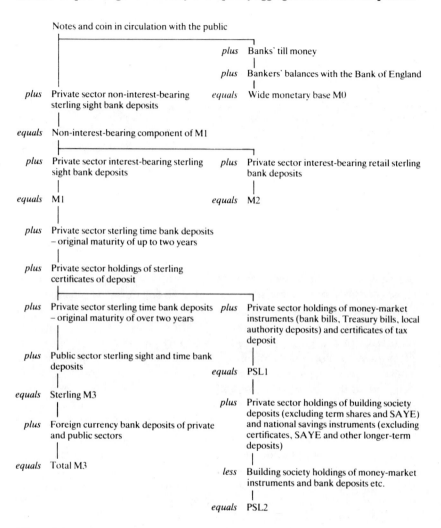

Figure 1.3

Source: Bank of England, *Quarterly Review*

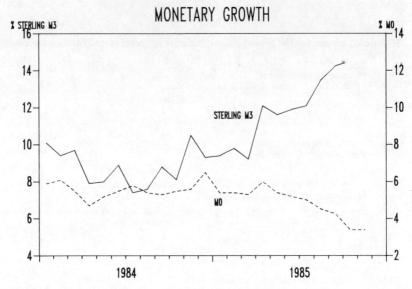

Figure 1.4

our reserves of North Sea oil at a time of rising crude oil prices in the early
stages of this Government together with a strong personal leadership by
Prime Minister Margaret Thatcher and commitment to tight money
control led to a rapid revaluation of sterling. This was one of the consequences of the U.K. open-ended economy and the fact that the City
plays host to 'hot money' as a result of sterling's international appeal.
These inflows of money inflated money supply and paradoxically un-
determined the very resoluteness which had led to the inflows in the first
place.

Two other examples are worth noting. The Federal Reserve Bank of the
United States publishes frequent data on money supply and has shown
that, whatever else, a monetarist doctrine has, until 1985 at least, reduced
inflation whilst the budget deficit has been growing and economic growth
has been high. By contrast, weak monetary control by the left-wing
Government of France soon after it assumed power led to a rapid economic
crisis affecting the currency, inflation and interest rates.

1.9 U.K. eligible liabilities and the public sector and central government
borrowing requirements

There are detailed published figures in the financial sector for money, bank
deposits and bank loans and advances. These can be found in the monthly

publication 'Financial Statistics', published by the Central Statistical Office. Some of these items are used to make up the figures for money supply (see 1.8). The figures for bank loans and advances analyse lending by type of customer and it is possible to study the trend of borrowing by public authorities, local authorities, the corporate sector and individuals. They can reveal or prove the existence of, for instance, a consumer-led

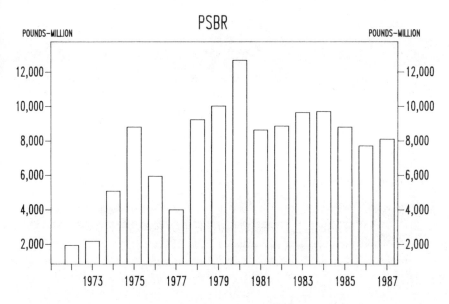

Figure 1.5

Figures in 1.5 are actual to 1985 and estimates thereafter.

boom or substantial investment by industry as orders increase. The different demands of the public, corporate and private sectors for capital if analysed can be of significant use in forecasting. For example, a strong need by the public sector for finance may lead to 'crowding out' i.e. bidding for funds by raising interest rates to levels which cannot be afforded by the corporate sector. The level of new issues can be of interest, suggesting high optimism about business conditions and draining money from investors' pockets with, ironically, usually an adverse effect on Stock Exchange prices. The graph in Figure 1.5 shows the level of the Public Sector Borrowing Requirement since 1972.

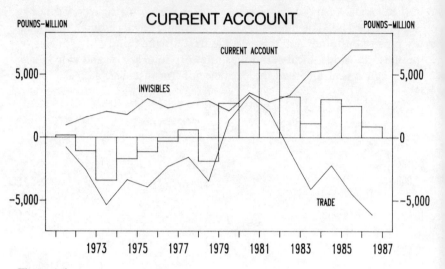

Figure 1.6

Figures in 1.6 are actual to 1985 and estimates thereafter.

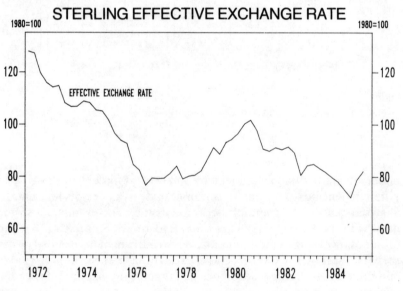

Figure 1.7

1.10 Balance of payments and reserves

Britain is an international trading country and one has to look at the economic statistics which show our trading position and the effect on these of Government policies and international trading conditions. The loss of certain export markets to other developed or developing countries, particularly in the Far East, means that for manufactured goods the balance of payments is in serious long-term decline. Invisible items such as financial services and shipping and our earnings abroad have assumed greater significance recently. Our North Sea oil has improved our position dramatically because not only are we self-sufficient in oil in volume terms but are even net exporters – at least for the time being. The visible balance of trade has been negative for some time. Our invisibles produce a positive figure. Net of oil, however, the position is not a strong one. The trend is important because clearly if a long-term deficit exists there will be pressure on the level of sterling. The balance of payments situation is summarized in the graph in Figure 1.6.

The balance of payments should be looked at in relation to the reserves of a country. A deficit on the current balance of payments can be supported by large reserves or by large involuntary capital inflows but underlying pressure on a currency will always recur. The position of our balance of payments excluding oil is not sufficiently strong to support sterling and there is always an interest in the U.K. Official Reserve figures published monthly by the Bank of England. The published figures indicate an impression that the Bank wishes to give. Full disclosure could be damaging to the national interest and have in some circumstances a disastrous effect on sterling or on our trade. The figures quoted do not show the liabilities which theoretically should be drawn against them.

1.11 Profits

The Financial Times publishes profits and profit margins for listed companies at monthly intervals. Although private companies are not included the published figures give an accurate impression of profit trends historically. The delay in reporting results means that the figures will be out of date and investors are more concerned with current earnings and those of the immediate future. This means that Stock Exchange prices will be discounting future earnings and those of the current period. This is, perhaps, self evident if one regards the purchase of a share as the right to receive future earnings (although in practice it is dividends).

A breakdown of U.K. corporate profits can be seen from the graph in Figure 1.8.

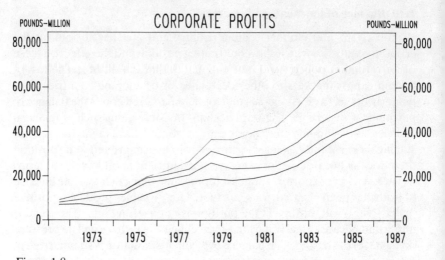

Figure 1.8

Figures in 1.8 are actual to 1985 and estimates thereafter.

1.12 Earnings indices

Figures produced monthly show the rate of increase in earnings for different types of working group. This is a useful indicator to pressures on prices from earnings inflation.

1.13 Price indices

In the U.K. two main series of price indices are published monthly. The first is the Index of Producer Prices which shows the movement of manufacturers' prices against money. Input and output indices are quoted, the first showing the level of inflation being borne by manufacturers who purchase raw materials and the latter indicating the level of 'factory gate' inflation i.e. the rate of increase of prices of wholesale goods. The second series of monthly prices is the index of retail prices, commonly called the cost-of-living index. In the U.S. and Japan this series is known as consumer price inflation.

A Tax and Price Index is also published in the U.K. to show the effect of both tax changes and price inflation on the consumer. In theory this index should be of great interest to the public particularly if there is a change in taxation from direct to indirect taxation. However, the index receives little publicity and attention is focused on the Retail Prices Index. The Tax and Price Index is seen by many to be a political gimmick.

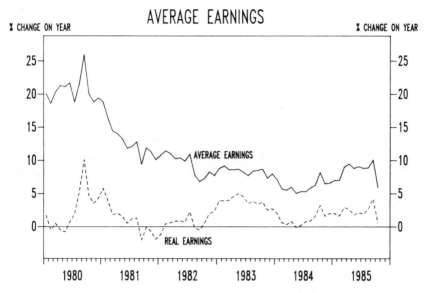

Figure 1.9

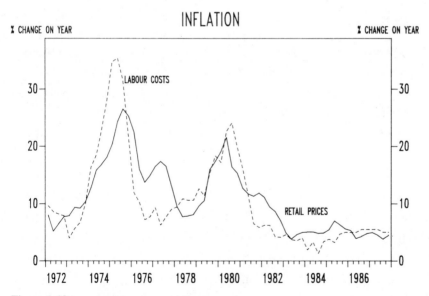

Figure 1.10

Figures in 1.10 are actual to 1985 and estimates thereafter.

The graph in Figure 1.10 shows the change in the Retail Prices Index and in labour costs since 1972.

1.14 Retail sales

The last of the general statistics that should be covered are those for consumer expenditure. Non-durable goods include large elements of food and other items which do not vary very much. Durables include cars, washing machines and so on which may reflect the state of the business cycle, ease of credit and a number of other factors. Because this is an area of large import penetration it is possible that sales may reflect the consequences of dumping by another country anxious to lessen inventories.

1.15 Other statistics

There are naturally many other published figures and analysts for a particular industry will seek out information on that industry. The Monthly Digest of Statistics published by the Central Statistics Office gives detailed figures covering a wide range of activities. It gives figures, for example, on

Figure 1.11

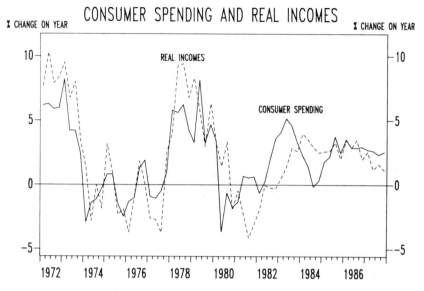

Figure 1.12

Figures in 1.12 are actual to 1985 and estimates thereafter.

labour, for consumption of fuel and power, production of steel, chemicals and other materials through to the production of finished goods such as cars, beer and television sets. There are always time lags between the period to which the figures relate and the date they are released but some industries have Trade Associations who have more up-to-date information.

As well as analysing trends within industries investors must also spot the structural changes within an economy alluded to earlier in respect of the U.K. New industries must be identified, old industries discarded. Automobile production figures are probably more relevant in Japan than in the U.K. – to the investor, at least. Iron and steel production in the Far East or Poland is important as are their order books – are they manufacturing for British clients? Substitution of new materials for old can also lead to clear investment trends. The dividing lines between some industries may become blurred. For example, what used to be called the electrical sector came to contain a number of companies who were recently developed electronic specialists rather than older heavy electrical engineers. Eventually, the two groups were categorized separately. The sector known as 'health care' is not identifiable in the U.K. There are no central statistics and the companies involved are classified in several of the FT-

Actuaries Sectors. Yet it is an important consumer sector worthy of observation.

   In other countries which are of consequence to the investing institutions in the U.K. it is possible to discover more statistics than we are accustomed to have. In particular, inventory figures are published frequently in the U.S. and Japan thus giving a very good guide to the state of an industry or economy. If an industry has a long chain between the primary producer and the eventual retailer, with stocks held at each stage, then these can

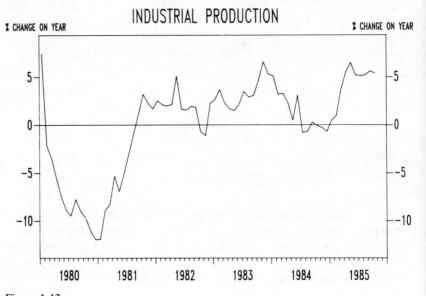

Figure 1.13

acutely accentuate the economic cycle. If sales fall at the retail end; if the wholesaler does not reduce orders quickly enough; and if the manufacturer, at the end of the chain, does not curtail production quickly enough then stocks build up. When this happens orders are cut back more sharply than sales so that as one goes back through the processes to the primary producers, production is affected more and more sharply. A good example of this is in textiles, which is an industry with a large number of processes followed by wholesaling, making up, wholesaling again and retailing. The effect of the economic cycle on textiles was one of the strongest arguments used for the rush of vertical mergers that took place in the 1950s and 1960s. Some figures of stocks are given in the Monthly Digest of Statistics and the Business Monitor.

The last set of relevant statistics are those relating to other markets. *The Financial Times* contains within its pages a mass of figures only some of which relate to the stock market directly. Many of these figures can suggest investment opportunities or have an impact on investment activity. Figures relating to transportation, whether by ship or air, may suggest changes in production in certain industries. The effect of only a small laid-up rate for shipping could have a very large effect on freight rates which may affect a shipping company's profitability. Probably the most significant figures to have emerged during the last decade are those relating to futures markets. The need for information on spot commodity prices is obvious. If one takes, for example, the price of copper, this can be looked at in two ways. First, it affects the income of the copper mines. Secondly, it affects the costs of the large copper users, in particular, cable manufacturers. Similarly, the price of cocoa affects confectionery makers.

Changes in commodity prices are heightened or dampened by the level of stocks and consumption. In the case of metals supplies come from the mines but true figures for consumption of, say, copper are distorted by the recovery of scrap. During a period of low demand the prices of raw materials fall sharply and stocks tend to build up. Once stocks are run down then increased demand will push up the prices substantially. The volatility of commodity markets has encouraged producers to fix prices but in many cases the fixing has collapsed. Producers have also turned to longer-term contracts with their larger consumers as a means of stabilizing income.

Development of futures markets means that there is additional information on other people's views of trends to add to the knowledge of the fund manager. Making a fortune from pork belly futures in Chicago is not easy. Reading the movements in such markets, however, may help in making other decisions.

1.16 Conclusion

This chapter has discussed various economic indicators. In a sense, each is a fact, although in some cases to be taken with a pinch of salt. They provide a base for forming opinions and making assumptions and eventually for creating an investment judgement on a particular stock or share.

Which are the most important? This tends to be a function of fashion in the stock markets. In the early 1970s trade figures and balance of payments statistics were regarded as the most important series of figures. The oil shocks of the mid 1970s led to increasing worries about the Public Sector Borrowing Requirement and the level of price inflation. The establishment of monetarism has led to increased emphasis on money supply figures both in the U.K. and in the U.S. Unemployment figures are used by politicians as debate fodder but as the current level is so high and is the consequence of severe structural deterioration publication of the figures does not tend to affect markets very much. Conversely, at its current lower level inflation will not be regarded as a key figure again until it begins to turn upwards. After the dramatic rise in the value of the dollar during 1983/85 there has been a tendency to examine foreign exchange reserves in the U.K. and West Germany to determine the level of support given by central banks to halt the progress of the dollar.

CHAPTER TWO

THE CAPITAL MARKETS

2.1 Introduction

Capitalism is the system under which investors supply capital for Government, local authorities and companies and are free to choose the projects in which they invest. If the State owns all the capital and makes its own decisions on where to invest there is no element of individual choice and this system is the basis of Communism. In a mixed economy with some State ownership, most markets are free and by and large the price of capital is set by the consensus view of countless individual investors. Their requirements for investing savings will reflect conditions of scarcity or glut of financial commodities in the investing markets and the return on their assets will reflect the degree of risk they attach to the investment.

Individual countries have their own financial structures for the purpose of raising money. For the U.K., however, the 1960s and 1970s saw the economy becoming gradually more integrated into the world economy. One consequence of this, for example, was the development of the euro-dollar market which was hardly in existence at the end of the 1950s. As the U.S. continued to run trade deficits, and overseas holders of U.S. dollars wished to trade their holdings, the eurodollar market began to flourish. The oil crisis of the mid 1970s with the large recycling of oil funds has further expanded the market, and national money markets have become more integrated. U.K. membership of the European Economic Community (EEC) in 1973 also strengthened London as a centre for international finance.

We now set out the nature of the main bodies that raise capital in the U.K. and the forms in which the money or 'finance' can be raised.

2.2 Government borrowing

Governments used to borrow most frequently in the past to finance wars. Nowadays, defence still accounts for a significant proportion of government borrowing but capital projects for hospitals, schools, roads and their like are social necessities and require heavy funding. It is also necessary to borrow for non-capital items such as social security payments which unlike some capital projects cannot be shown to be yielding an immediate economic return. Borrowing is necessary in both cases because modern economic planning rarely assumes a balanced budget and 'deficit funding' can be met only by borrowing in one form or another. In the early 1980s a move to reduce the Public Sector Borrowing Requirement (PSBR) as a proportion of GDP was adopted by the Conservative administration. Note, however, that in a mixed economy it is possible for the Government to raise money by selling assets it owns and this has been another feature of the Thatcher administration (e.g. sale of shares in British Telecom in 1984).

When the Government borrows money it used to offer only fixed terms for interest and repayment. Thus $5\frac{3}{4}\%$ Funding 1987/91 was issued in May 1964 at 97 when interest rates were at the level of 6% with the promise to repay at par in the period 1987 to 1991. After issue, the price of such stocks varies with interest rates generally and now (September 1985) that long-term rates are around $10\frac{1}{2}\%$, the price of $5\frac{3}{4}\%$ Funding 1987/91 has fallen to 85. Government stocks are also known as gilt-edged stocks or gilts and are regarded as risk-free because there is virtually no risk of default by the Government (they can always raise taxes to produce revenue!). Although there is a mathematical relationship between the current price of the stock, the coupon, the redemption value and date and the current level of yields, prices of individual stocks may deviate from arithmetic rules because of investors' subjective considerations and other factors such as tax.

Although the Government continues to borrow using conventional gilt-edged stock, it has broadened the methods of finance to include convertible Government stock, short-term variable rate stock and index-linked stock. In addition short-term funding through the Discount Market by way of Treasury Bills helps to smooth longer-term requirements. The innovation of index-linked stock has been the most significant change and enables investors to measure risky investments in real assets (shares or property) against the Government's risk-free real rate of return. The Government in the U.K. has accepted the market's discipline but in many countries it is required that a minimum percentage of certain insurance and/or pension funds should be invested in government stocks which provides the government with part of its borrowing requirement. In the U.K. environment, however, the free market system means that the Government may be itself competing for funds against businesses and this sometimes produces the 'crowding out' whereby the Government bids up for funds to a level of interest they can sustain but which companies cannot afford. Similarly, the Government's efforts in the savings market with savings schemes, premium bonds and, more importantly, index-linked savings act in direct competition with the institutions (insurance companies, banks, building societies and others) offering their own savings products.

2.3 Company borrowing

Before the middle of the nineteenth century most businesses were either carried on by individuals or by small partnerships. Joint stock companies existed but were regarded as partnerships. Family businesses like the Rothschilds were already strong, and corporate bodies such as the Hudson's Bay Company were incorporated until 1837 solely by Royal Charter or Act of Parliament. Agricultural estates or merchanting businesses could be owned by families and passed down from father to son without undue financial hardships. New industrial enterprises requiring capital could not always be financed from within a family. A partnership or syndicate system was not appropriate because of the need to continue as a going concern over a long period of years in order to obtain good returns on the large investment in heavy capital assets involved. Most partnerships today exist in the service industries (e.g. accountancy and the legal professions) where no large capital assets are owned and the principal asset is goodwill. Until recently most stockbroking firms were partnerships but the need for capital as a consequence of changes in the City has led to incorporation and the introduction of outside shareholders.

The wealth accumulated by enterprises in the nineteenth century found its way to one or two owners who as rich individuals had substantial savings for investment. Their desire to invest was matched broadly by the need for capital in new industries and the principle of limited liability established in the Limited Liability Act of 1855 was the financial key which enabled the industrial revolution to come to fruition. The Act allowed a corporate body to exist whose shareholders had a liability only to the extent of their subscriptions in the company. Before the passing of the Act 'shareholders' could be called upon to pay the company's debts which could be a daunting prospect at a time when many wild schemes were floated, the information given in a prospectus could be minimal and accounting principles were elementary.

Before describing the means of raising finance available to companies one should ask the precise reasons for needing the finance. An industrial company will need 'fixed assets' and 'working capital'. Fixed assets are the plant and machinery that it needs for its manufacture plus any land and buildings that it owns for this purpose. Working capital is needed to finance the company's products up to the point where money is received from a sale; it starts with the stock of raw materials, and then includes the partly made products called work-in-progress, manufactured stocks awaiting sale, and finally the amounts owed by customers for products sold to them but for which payment has not yet been received. A company's capital needs may fluctuate seasonally or with the level of trade. It may need to balance long-term finance against short-term needs. These options will now be explored.

2.4 Loan capital and short-term borrowings

Capital is either raised by the issue of shares or borrowed. The shareholders (or proprietors) own the company, whereas those who lend money generally have no say in the running of the company unless interest or repayments get into arrears. Those granting loans are entitled to receive certain contractual payments of interest and repayment, and in the event of winding up or bankruptcy loans rank ahead of shareholders and must be repaid before shareholders receive anything. In practice loans are often secured against specific assets (which means that they have a right to obtain repayment by selling the specific assets) whereas 'unsecured borrowings' rank with other creditors on a winding-up. The long-term loan capital together with shareholders' capital should meet the company's long-term finance needs. It will also need to borrow short term to iron out fluctuations in its trading receipts or disbursements. This short-term borrowing will normally be from a bank and despite its name is often a permanent form of finance for some companies. Bank borrowings may be truly 'overnight' through City institutions such as other banks or insurance companies to enable them to balance their books. Bridging loans often last more than a few days and are a familiar way of meeting commitments over a short but unknown period as, for example, occurs for individuals in buying a house. Finally, overdrafts or general loans, usually secured against assets pledged to the bank, enable businesses to smooth their capital financing. A summer tourist hotel may need finance to survive the winter months, the borrowings being repaid as summer bookings are made and cash received. If the size of the borrowings becomes large in relation to the company's assets and earnings ability the bank may suggest conversion to more permanent long-term finance. It could be fixed loan capital supplied by insurance companies or pension funds, or equity capital.

The sophistication of banking markets has increased the number of ways in which finance can be raised. Although banks have traditionally sought to secure loans against assets there are forms of lending which place more emphasis on earning capacity. An Australian mining firm may contract to sell ore to Japan and then borrow from a consortium of American banks against the contracts in order to fund the development of the mine. These loans usually restrict the payment of dividends to shareholders while loans are outstanding and constitute a form of finance mid-way between 'short'- and 'long'-term borrowings. Banks in the U.K. have not traditionally provided industry with medium-term finance, although other EEC countries do (e.g. France and Germany), but this has recently changed to some extent. The recent development of new vehicles such as floating rate notes and note issuance facilities has enhanced considerably the options open to larger corporations for the control of liquidity.

2.5 Equity capital

Shareholders provide the 'risk' capital for companies and share in any profits after all obligations are met. The synonymous term 'equity' capital implies that the shareholders have a stake in the equity of the company i.e. a right to participate in its worth. Finance can be raised from new share-holders by, for instance, an offer for sale of new shares. The cost of a full quotation on the Stock Exchange can be prohibitive and a quotation on the Unlisted Securities Market (USM) or the Over the Counter (OTC) market is a cheaper form of capital raising for an emerging company. For a company with existing share capital further cash can be raised by the issue of more shares (usually on a proportionate basis called a 'rights' issue).

2.6 Retained profits

For a company already trading, retaining profits is a common way of providing working capital needed by the company. In effect shareholders forgo dividends otherwise due to them from profits and thus supply the company with capital. The retention of these profits increases the worth of the company and strengthens the security of capital supplied by share-holders and loanholders.

2.7 Industrial leasing

A common way for a company to acquire a computer is to arrange to lease it. A leasing company buys the computer and receives certain investment allowances and then leases to the company. At the end of the lease period the computer can usually be retained by the payment of a much lower regular payment. Another form of 'off balance sheet' finance is hire purchase, which is more common for acquisitions by individuals. In both cases title is retained by the vendor whereas a credit sale indicates immediate transfer of title, subject to a lien.

2.8 Sale and leaseback

This is an arrangement whereby a company with excess capital in the form of property can release that capital in a form to provide finance for its own business. A manufacturing company owning its own factory and needing capital for new plant might approach an insurance company and arrange to sell it the factory with the proviso that the insurance company will lease the factory to the manufacturing company over a long period. The insurance company purchases a real asset; the manufacturing company has long-term security of tenure and can use the cash generated to increase the worth of the business.

2.9 Trade credit

If the interests of a buyer and seller are interdependent they may agree to extend credit. A supplier of asphalt to a layer of roads may give credit until the roads themselves have been paid for. The system is common with suppliers and manufacturers.

2.10 Bills of exchange and factoring

Bills of exchange are a very old form of City finance and are used as a way of obtaining early payment for goods sold with a period of credit. If payment is due in three months, say, the vendor can invoice the buyer and sell the bill to a discount house which will discount the face value of the bill over the unexpired period. The rate of discount will reflect the current level of interest rates and the standing of the 'name' on which the bill is drawn. An overseas government may be considered a first-class name but a small, unknown company might need a banker's guarantee in order to effect the transaction.

   Two other ways of financing against outstanding bills are to obtain credit from an accepting house and to factor trade debtors. Factoring is a method of financing bills by using a factor to settle the account immediately for cash and then the factor receives the face value of the invoices at the end of an agreed period. The factor will charge for this service depending on the level of administrative services which he supplies, whether the factor or the company takes the risk on bad debts and on the level of interest rates prevailing.

2.11 Market value of U.K. securities

Table 2.1 sets out the value of the securities listed on the Stock Exchange in London at 31st December 1984.

Table 2.1

Sector	No. of securities	Market valuation £ million
Public Sector – U.K.	116	114,434
Public Sector – Irish Government	101	5928
Public Sector – Local Authority	225	1686
Public Sector – Public Boards	84	168
Public Sector – Overseas	172	2309
Eurobonds	1126	68,522
Company Securities – U.K. and Ireland	4477	214,936
Company Securities – Overseas	592	678,875

The table shows that the largest single category by value is securities of overseas companies. Most of the companies will be quoted on another stock exchange and the dealings in the securities may be concentrated elsewhere. The two most important sectors in terms of the volume of transactions are U.K. company securities and U.K. public sector debt. Although the number of company securities which are quoted is large, the securities of the largest 100 companies constitute well over one half of the value shown. Most of the value of the company securities is in equity form and the issues of company loans and debentures have been very small during the last decade.

2.12 The London Stock Exchange

The London Stock Exchange is currently undergoing fundamental changes. For many years it has existed using a 'single capacity' system which separates jobbers (the wholesalers) from brokers (the retailers or agents). There has also been a system of fixed price commission terms. It is likely that by the end of 1986 the Market will have changed to dual capacity in which market operators may act as both principal and agent for U.K. stocks and shares.

The move to dual capacity may bring negotiated commissions, although in many situations 'net' pricing may be used. 'Net' pricing would mean that the market maker would quote a price inclusive of all charges apart from statutory levies. For example, the market maker may quote a price of 99–101 under a 'net' price system. He is prepared to purchase stock at 99p and sell at 101p. The buyer knows that the total cost of the shares is 101p (plus, where relevant, stamp duty), and the seller knows that he will actually receive 99p for each share (since there would be no other costs). The 'net' price system is simpler for buyers and sellers than the current method where commission has to be taken into account (see 2.13 below), and where the commission varies according to the size of the deal. Dual capacity is already permitted for U.K. brokers wishing to trade in overseas stocks but they have to do this through a separate trading organization, usually a subsidiary, called an 'international dealer'.

The existing jobbing system in the U.K. is now described, followed by the likely system in the U.K., and then those in overseas markets.

2.13 Present system

The Stock Exchange is an independent association of stockbrokers and stockjobbers operating in a large number of U.K. and Republic of Ireland cities and towns.

The most important feature of the existing structure of the Stock Exchange is the 'single capacity' system of separation between jobbers and brokers. Jobbers fulfil the market-making function of dealing in securities as principals, for their own profit or loss. Brokers are intermediaries, acting as agents bringing together buyers or sellers with the jobbers. With limited exceptions jobbers undertake not to deal with non-members of the Stock Exchange, except for overseas securities.

The jobber who deals in a particular share must be prepared to deal in that share with any broker who approaches him and will compete through his price-making with other jobbers. When a broker approaches a jobber asking for the price of a share he does not indicate whether he wants to buy or sell and the jobber quotes a two-way price – his buying price and his selling price. For example, the jobber may quote a price of 99½–100½ in 5000. The jobber is prepared to buy up to 5000 shares at 99½p per share and sell up to 5000 shares at 100½p per share. The stockbroker's commission would need to be subtracted from the sale price to arrive at the sale proceeds, and commission (and where relevant stamp duty) added to calculate the total purchase consideration. A jobber's profit comes from the margin between the prices at which he buys and sells shares. When jobbers buy shares and there is no other buying interest in the market, they are taking a 'long' position; when they sell shares they have not yet bought, they are taking a 'short' position.

The traditional role of the stockbroker is to act as the agent of his clients for the purchase and sale of securities. In addition many provide investment advice normally backed by research analysis. In the case of individual and trust clients a broker will frequently act as an overall investment adviser producing portfolio valuations and advising not only on individual shares but on investment strategy, taxation and sometimes on alternative investment outside the Stock Exchange. Some brokers also act as corporate finance advisers, assisting client companies in raising further capital and mounting takeover bids. Other services include fund management, performance measurement services, and overseas broking.

Brokers charge a commission on purchase and sale transactions on the basis of a tapering scale of minimum charges set by the Stock Exchange. Corporate finance and investment services may be provided against a specific fee whilst other services are usually provided for no extra fee, remuneration coming in the form of commission on transactions thus generated. Banks, solicitors and accountants may act as a link between individual investors or trustees and a broker. With investment advice from the broker they advise their clients and transact dealings for them through the broker, usually being paid a share of the commission (which may be somewhat higher than if the client deals without the use of an intermediary).

Some stockbrokers act in the U.K. money markets as sterling brokers placing sterling deposits with local authorities and banks. There are also some firms of stockbrokers who are recognized by the Bank of England as money brokers and whose role is to assist the financing of the jobbing system by arranging for institutions to lend stock or money as required for settlement.

There are certain specialized functions in which jobbers act as principal, and brokers can act as either agent or principal. These are dealings in eurobonds, arbitrage dealing (to take advantage of price differentials between stock markets in the same share) and option dealing (to enable clients to pay for the right to take up or dispose of shares, at an agreed price within a stated period). This form of option dealing is not the same as traded options (see 3.5).

The function of the jobbers is to try to create a smooth, orderly market and make buying and selling possible in any given share with reasonable speed. This has become increasingly difficult in recent years as the market has become increasingly institutionalized. At times the market is 'one-way' and prices have become more volatile as jobbers become reluctant to hold or sell large lines of stock in such markets. In recent years the number of jobbing firms has contracted sharply. Jobbing is a risk business which requires very large amounts of capital and some jobbing firms have now raised capital from outside sources. To be healthy, a stock market must provide a vigorous active market, capable of handling reasonable-sized deals, and it must be economical, quick and efficient; the 'efficiency' applying not just to dealing and communicating with the client, but also in the settlement of stock and money. In gilt-edged stocks one can deal in

London in large sums, quickly, cheaply and efficiently; expenses for equity stock are heavier and one cannot always deal in large lines, but even so it is surprising what large numbers of shares one can buy or sell over a relatively short period. For example, in one of the largest companies with a market capitalization of over £500m, one could hope to invest £5m within two or three weeks without moving the price significantly. There are some companies, however, whose shares have restricted marketability because part of their capital is tightly held by, for example, another company or by the family thus withholding a large slice of the equity from the market. There are some small fixed interest issues which are in the hands of only a small number of institutions so that deals are rare and the quotation is nominal; but in most shares there is a steady flow of bargains.

Quotation of prices over the dividend period needs further explanation. If a dividend has been declared, but has not yet been paid, then the price will be defined as either 'cum dividend', in which case the buyer receives the dividend, or 'ex dividend', in which case the buyer does not receive the dividend, which is retained by the seller. For practical reasons the registrars of any stock have to fix a date (known as 'Books closing' date or 'On register' date) before an interest or dividend payment and declare that after that date no changes in ownership can be considered to rank for the interest or dividend, as the payments have to be calculated, lists processed and envelopes prepared so that holders can receive their interest/dividend on the correct date. At a fixed period ahead of the 'on-register' date (i.e. the time it takes for transfers to be lodged) a stock goes 'ex div'.

The process of negotiation between brokers and jobbers is called 'dealing'; when the bargain has been struck the broker has 'dealt' and 'a deal' is synonymous for a bargain. Immediately after dealing the stock broker issues a contract note to the client. This is a simple document, but legally binding, which sets out the details of the deal, giving the name of the client, the number of shares bought or sold, the price, the various expenses – the commission payable (plus VAT), and any duty payable – and finally the total due from the client on a purchase or the net proceeds due to him on a sale.

2.14 Costs in the U.K.

For an investor the costs of buying and selling are important. There are two costs to be considered (apart from the jobber's turn, i.e. the difference between the jobber's buying and selling prices):

1. Broker's commission   Fixed minimum scales apply until late 1986.

2. Transfer Stamp duty	On sales there is no stamp duty. On purchases $\frac{1}{2}\%$ stamp duty applies to purchases of equities and convertible stocks. In most other cases no stamp duty is payable.

2.15 Future U.K. system

By the end of 1986, the system described in section 2.13 for transactions in the U.K. will have seen a dramatic change.

The first move in this process was the commencement of an investigation of the Stock Exchange by the Office of Fair Trading. This was terminated when a deal was struck between the Government and the Stock Exchange. The Stock Exchange agreed, inter alia, to introduce negotiated commissions in place of the minimum fixed scales which had existed for some time. Although the Stock Exchange has operated within a self-regulatory framework for many years it forms only part of the City of London. The Government wished to open up all the City to market forces, domestic and international; to increase competition between institutions; to improve information for investors and their advisers; to provide a high level of self-regulation capable of enforcement of the rules and to give protection to investors. Whilst the Stock Exchange has been constantly in the limelight, the process which the Government started was intended to encompass many other activities taking place in the general field of financial services.

In examining its role the Stock Exchange noted that the number of substantial jobbers had reduced to only 5 by 1976. Pressure was arising from the increasing internationalization of markets and the presence in London of a strong overseas contingent. After further discussion the Stock Exchange also abolished another set of rules – those obliging the separation for the most part of the activities of brokers and jobbers. A deadline of 27th October 1986 has been set for the implementation of changes arising from the abolition of the two rules. The phase 'de-regulation' is often used in relation to what is happening. This is a little misleading. Although two significant rules are being abolished by the Stock Exchange, a number of new measures are being introduced to protect investors. The Stock Exchange has also permitted partial ownership of stockbroking firms in order to create capital for funding principal positions. Full ownership will be allowed from April 1986.

As part of the wider regulatory framework a hierarchy of responsibilities has been established, at the top of which is the Secretary of State for Trade and Industry. He will delegate his authority to a regulatory body which

will have responsibility for most financial services. The Securities and
Investments Board will regulate the securities industry, insurance and
certain other savings activities. There are a number of existing self-
regulatory bodies, such as the Stock Exchange itself, who will have to be
'recognized' by one of the Boards. There is still considerable discussion
and debate taking place on the role and effectiveness of the proposed and
existing self-regulatory bodies.

(a) New groupings

The abolition of single-capacity trading, i.e. the separation of brokers
acting as agents on behalf of clients, and jobbers dealing with the brokers,
has created a new player in the London securities industry – the market-
maker. The main activities of the City fall now into the following groups:

1. Broking/investment advice
2. Principal trading
3. Fund management
4. Market making
5. Corporate finance
6. Underwriting/banking

The introduction of dual capacity means that a broker will in future
continue to act as an agent but, if he wishes, can also act as a principal by
buying and selling stock for his own book. Jobbers are replaced by market-
makers, in effect, but will in future have the ability to deal directly with
clients as principals. Agency brokers will continue to act for commission at
some negotiated rate. Market-makers or brokers acting as principals
will usually buy and sell securities net of commission and thus their
remuneration will be the net profit or loss incurred as a consequence of
trading.

In the gilt market the two types of operator available to institutional
investors will be known as market-makers and broker/dealers (agency
brokers). There will also be inter-dealer brokers who will have no direct
contact with clients and will act to assist liquidity in the market by
dealing between market-makers. The market-maker in gilts will be regulated
by the Bank of England in view of his importance and role in Government
funding and the issue of tap stocks. In return for a number of unique
privileges (and controls) he will make continuous markets in agreed sectors
of the gilt market. Broker/dealers will have no obligation to make markets
and will take a position only if they choose to do so. Apart from their
traditional agency business they will probably fulfil a role in matching

bargains between their clients (known as block trading in the U.S.) and in developing specialized services.

The equity market will also have market-makers and broker/dealers but there is no specialized group of inter-dealer brokers planned although many will act in this capacity and the supervision of the Bank of England is not necessary. At the time of writing the position of market-makers in equities is not entirely clear. In particular, the requirements for continuous market making are not known.

(b) Changes in practice

The impact of the changes on the practice of institutional investors is considerable. First, the changes in gilt trading, apart from the obvious impact on issue and control of tap stocks, are likely to lead immediately to a very different approach by institutions. At present a great deal of institutional gilt trading is related either to switching activity aimed at minimizing the payment of capital gains tax or to the practice of controlling coupon flow by buying and/or selling stock cum or ex dividend. In some cases the two activities are connected. In 1986 the rules relating to CGT on gilts are being changed and also, from 1986 all gilt stocks will be traded clean of accrued interest (at present only shorts are so traded). The bread-and-butter business of many gilt brokers could be reduced substantially unless other compensating activities commence. Even if this were not the case the institutional approach to these deals is almost automatic and the ability to deal directly with market-makers is extremely attractive. The larger institutions will probably turn their gilt manager into a specialized trader dealing with a small number of market-makers. A number of other broker connections will be retained for specialized agency business. The paradox is that at a time when the number of 'primary dealers' in gilts is increasing dramatically the amount of steady business from life companies and pension funds may fall sharply. In the circumstances, it is not surprising that many institutions will expect dealing costs to fall to virtually zero and many will not be prepared to pay for gilt research. The new system for gilts is planned on the lines of the primary bond markets in the U.S.

The new system for equities is modelled on the U.S. Over-The-Counter (OTC) market and the consequences are less predictable. The re-groupings within the City have formed a number of financial conglomerates which, typically, include a broker firm, a merchant bank, a fund management organization and a market-making function. Many of these firms have already announced plans to service the retail end of financial services by dealing in the high street and through the medium of other savings institutions. They and the many smaller broking firms, often in the provinces, will compete for private client business. Whether in the longer run the costs of dealing through these agencies in the high street will prove cheaper than at present is a moot point. The man in the street will hardly be in a position of strength to negotiate commissions. For institutions the position will be different. First, some institutions will wish to use market-makers if transacting business in large capitalization stocks because, as in the case of gilts, they will have decided in advance on a course of action and will be looking for the cheapest mechanism of effecting a bargain. What institutions will be most anxious to keep is their valued relationships currently enjoyed with equity brokers in which ideas for investment, analytical research and market gossip are constantly discussed and exchanged. For many this relationship built up over many years will be more important than the ability to trade a large line of popular stock infrequently. From the point of view of performance cheap lines of stock are clearly important but so are the suggestions for purchase that will produce sound above average growth in the medium term. There will be a ready market for those agency brokers prepared to find the ideas of tomorrow rather than concentrate on trades in the big capitalization issues of today.

More generally, those institutions who retain at present external fund managers may well review this policy in the light of the potential conflicts of interest perceived, whether these be real or illusory, within the con-glomerates. Perhaps, as in the United States, a new breed of independent fund managers will emerge.

(c) Remuneration

The whole development began with a desire to remove fixed minimum commissions. At this stage it is still not clear how all different parties will be remunerated. If most gilt business is in future conducted through market-makers, then agency gilt commission levels will in aggregate reduce drama-tically. It would seem unlikely that broker research on gilts will be paid for by the larger institutions in future since they will deem payment to be incorporated in the margins of the market-makers. Some clients will con-tinue to pay for research indirectly through agency commission. In a world where fees are becoming increasingly important it is probable that some houses will try to charge for gilt research and expect ready money.

Equity research may need more careful discussion concerning payment and no doubt before Autumn 1986 a number of hard bargains will have been driven. Institutions will probably argue for all services (sales, research and dealings) to be paid for within the new (lower) level of agency commission. Some brokers may request a retainer.

The position of the conglomerate in the equity markets may well prove interesting. Some have already indicated that their fund management arms will be free to solicit research from any source, including the research arm of a rival conglomerate. If a new group of independent fund managers springs up this may be accompanied by new independent research houses. If commission levels are driven too low some institutional clients may not be large enough to generate sufficient commission to pay for research. There may be a temptation to cut dealing costs to the bone in order to enhance performance of discretionary funds. In this eventuality fund management houses might be forced to pay fees for research or advice and debit their management accounts or, of course, to increase their fees.

(d) Conflicts of interest

The City institutions have always known potential conflicts of interest. The work of corporate finance departments in merchant banks has always had to be isolated and the phrase 'Chinese Wall' is used to describe the process. Access to confidential, price-sensitive information is tightly controlled not only from outsiders but also within different parts of the merchant bank or stockbroker. Nevertheless, the rapid re-groupings and the formation of financial conglomerates, sometimes including all six of the activities described earlier, has led to renewed concern about the effectiveness of these controls. This led one national paper to lead an article with the banner headline 'Chinese Walls have Chinks'. The concern has caused some conglomerates to house staff in different locations in the City in order to avoid potential embarrassment.

The pressure to perform on many of these securities houses will be intense. Indeed, this is what the Government set out to achieve. Each organization will be attempting to operate profitably and there is justifiable worry that this pressure may lead to unscrupulousness. For example, at present there are two principal gilt jobbers and a very small number of others. By contrast, there will be twenty-eight market-makers in gilts at the end of 1986. This market being regulated by the Bank of England will, hopefully, remain free of impropriety but other, less well-known or less well-controlled, securities markets may provide a *cause célèbre* or two before the decade ends.

The broker can be considered as an example of current and future potential conflicts of interest. He will have to indicate to a client whether he is acting as a broker for the client, as a principal for his own account, as a market-maker, as a broker for some other person, or as a broker for both such client and some other person. Obvious conflicts could arise if a broker has a principal position in securities on which he is giving advice but even where a broker offers an 'execution only' agency service he may experience conflicts of interest and he is bound already by the fiduciary obligations imposed by Common Law on agents. The Stock Exchange has issued a discussion document listing potential areas of conflict for the agency broker, many of which exist already. A broker dealing with his client as a principal has fairly obvious conflicts of interest and the Stock Exchange has decided to prohibit the simultaneous combination of the agency and principal capacity in domestic securities. What is still under debate is the extent of disclosure a broker/dealer should make about the profit made on a principal transaction with a client. Agency commissions will be required to be printed on contract notes as at present and the Stock Exchange has taken the view that if a broker/dealer acts as a principal he should disclose his terms on a 'riskless principal trade' i.e. where as a principal he has fulfilled a client's buy order by buying the stock elsewhere and selling it directly to the client.

A number of potential conflicts of interest arise in the case where discretionary portfolio management and principal trading are combined in one firm. An even deeper conflict could arise if a corporate finance function were also part of the business where, conceivably, investment managers might come under pressure to support unattractive issues. The concept of 'triple capacity', a combination of broking, fund management and market making, raises further possible conflicts because the firm's market-making interest may conflict with its agency duties to corporate clients, investment advisory clients and to funds under its management. Integrated firms of this nature might seek to exploit their 'captive' clients, and some controls may be necessary to overcome this potential problem. 'Compliance Officers' are being appointed within conglomerates as a means of self-supervision.

Whilst potential conflicts of interest can arise, the Stock Exchange and other bodies are doing all they can to provide practical solutions to ensure that the City retains its premier position as a financial centre, where all investors have full confidence in the system.

(e) Technology

For the new Stock Exchange procedures to work efficiently it is necessary for new technology to be introduced. The Stock Exchange has split its new systems into three broad areas – trading support, surveillance and settlement. The settlement system, Talisman, will continue in use but will be replaced gradually over the longer term. The principal information source for brokers, jobbers and clients at present is TOPIC. This is an extensive system based on Viewdata technology and is fed by the EPIC computer system of the Stock Exchange. A new system called SEAQ (Stock Exchange Automated Quotes) is expected to be introduced in time for the changes in late 1986 which will receive quotations and reports on trades from market-makers which will then be fed to EPIC. SEAQ is planned to cover around 1000 securities including all the leading U.K. equities, the main gilt issues and certain international securities. It is not intended at this stage that SEAQ will support the primary gilts market. Longer-term plans are naturally intended to be much wider in their scope. There are, in addition, a larger number of proprietary information systems which are used alongside the official Stock Exchange systems.

Although much of the future dealing will take place with the aid of screens and sophisticated technology some personal presence will still be required on the floor of the Stock Exchange to deal in second-line stocks and more esoteric issues. Markets in over-the-counter (OTC) stocks are made by non Stock Exchange firms and this could be an area of considerable future expansion.

2.16 Overseas markets

Prior to December 1979 U.K. investors could not purchase freely overseas assets at the prevailing exchange rate and needed to pay a premium to obtain currency for investment purposes. After 1979 levels of overseas assets increased substantially in pension and life assurance funds after the Conservative administration removed foreign exchange controls.

No other major market has the same type of dealing system as in London, with single capacity of brokers and jobbers. The U.K. system for the future is likely to be fairly similar to that of the U.S. where dual capacity market makers are a key feature.

The two major markets for investment by U.K. institutional investors are the United States and Japan, although there are smaller holdings in Australia, Hong Kong, Singapore, Canada and Europe. Each market has its own dealing system and its own rules for settlement.

The increasing sophistication in communication and information systems means that the problems of implementation of overseas deals can be easily overcome. The improvement in communication has also led to twenty-four-hour dealing in currencies and certain securities, as different markets trade in different time zones. Thus shares in Hitachi could be traded in Tokyo; then in Hong Kong when Tokyo dealings cease; in the U.K. when London dealings commence; and in New York when it opens at mid-afternoon London time. This constant tuning of prices is particularly noticeable in currency markets and helps to explain their volatility. Investors in overseas markets may be subject to taxation and levies in the overseas country. Most countries levy withholding tax on overseas income which may not be recoverable.

2.17 International exchanges

Table 2.2 gives some guide to the market capitalization of various stock exchanges throughout the world.

Table 2.2

	Market capitalization 31.8.85	
	$bn	*% total*
North America	**1923.8**	**55.0**
USA	1782.9	51.0
Canada	140.9	4.0
Europe	**699.5**	**20.0**
UK	301.5	8.6
Germany	117.8	3.4
France	57.5	1.6
Netherlands	41.7	1.2
Switzerland	63.3	1.8
Far East	**850.2**	**24.3**
Australia	60.0	1.7
Japan	731.2	20.9
Hong Kong	35.6	1.0
Singapore	23.4	0.7
World	**3493.6**	100.0

(*Source:* Capital International SA Geneva)

2.18 Registered and bearer stocks and shares

Nearly all stocks and shares in U.K. companies are 'registered'; that is, ownership is established by being on the company's share or stock register and if a certificate is lost it can normally be replaced because by itself it is not complete evidence of ownership. By contrast holding a 'bearer' stock certificate is complete evidence of ownership, as if holding a pound note. This makes some aspects of transfer between buyer and seller easier, but the certificates have to be held securely – usually in a bank – and are at risk in transit; ownership can be anonymous and interest payments are often made against a 'coupon' detached from the certificate. Bearer certificates are usually beautifully printed, and highly ornate to defy forgery, and although rare in London they are in common use in some other countries. Note that the eurobond market, discussed later, is dominated by bearer issues.

2.19 Settlement

The process of settlement for transactions carried out on the Stock Exchange is set out in Appendix 1, as are the two main international settlement systems – Euroclear and CEDEL.

2.20 Public confidence and regulation

For the Exchange to function efficiently it needs public confidence. The famous motto 'Dictum meum pactum' ('my word is my bond') is no empty boast. The speed and efficiency of the Stock Exchange depends on personal trust and the complete adherence to oral agreements. Orders, negotiations and dealings are all conducted orally, often over the telephone, which ensures speed and efficiency but depends on personal trust. The name and integrity of a member and his firm are paramount.

Nevertheless, in the event of failure or impropriety, clients' rights are protected and a compensation fund covers amounts due to clients. The Stock Exchange has its own rules for the granting of listings of new securities which sets standards stricter than those of the Companies Acts. The Stock Exchange has done a lot to protect shareholders and to help them by insisting on full and proper information, at the time of new issue, when results are announced, or on a significant acquisition or disposal. Occasionally institutions have been forced to take steps to consult with weak or misguided managements although this is very much a last resort because of the heavy management resources required.

Banks and licensed dealers in securities have been permitted to become Stock Exchange members but as these institutions move more into the role of market makers an increasing proportion of business could still fall outside Stock Exchange control. As mentioned in Section 2.15, a further problem for investors is the increase in the potential conflicts of interest since the market makers will often be part of integrated securities houses offering a wide range of services, and the protections of single capacity will not be available. It seems that the likely system of regulation for the securities industry will be self regulation within a legislative framework and it is hoped that this will bring effective control without the need to move towards the more rigid framework in the American system of the Securities and Exchange Commission (SEC).

Any system of regulation needs to be flexible enough to allow change to be implemented swiftly, but sufficiently rigorous to maintain the first class reputation of the London market.

CHAPTER THREE

TYPES OF SECURITY

3.1 The gilt-edged market and fixed interest market

The gilt-edged market provides about three-quarters of Stock Exchange trading measured in terms of value. It comprises predominantly British Government and government guaranteed stocks, but in addition stocks issued by local authorities, public boards and some other quasi-governmental bodies. Some Commonwealth and other foreign governments or quasi-governmental bodies have also issued stock which is dealt on the gilt-edged market. Stocks are denominated in sterling and dealt for cash settlement next day. British Government stocks carry an absolute guarantee in money terms by the U.K. Government. British Government stocks may be short-dated (i.e. with up to five years to redemption), medium-dated (with a life of between five and ten years), long-dated (with over ten years to run), or undated (irredeemable). They may be conventional stocks, or convertible into another gilt, and, in the past, some have carried a variable interest rate. Finally, the Government has also issued a number of index-linked stocks which, although not carrying a fixed coupon, are nevertheless part of the gilt-edged market.

Operations in the market for government stocks by the authorities play an important part both in the execution of monetary policy and in the management of the National Debt. Official operations are conducted by the Government Broker (the senior partner in a firm of stockbrokers – Mullens & Co. – although following the planned changes in the City he will be an employee of the Bank of England) on the instructions of the Bank of England. New issues of government stock are made by the Bank of England on behalf of the Government. Nearly all issues of government stock are made by way of public offers for sale, but are not underwritten. Any surplus stock not subscribed by investors is taken up by the Issue Department of the Bank of England and subsequently sold by the Government Broker in response to bids from gilt-edged jobbers in the stock market. The time this process takes varies according, amongst other things, to market conditions; during this period the stock in question is referred to as a 'tap' stock.

A number of changes have been made in recent years in the types of British Government stock and their methods of issue. In 1973 a convertible stock, offering a short-dated stock with an option to convert at a given date into a longer-dated stock, was first issued. Another new type of instrument – Treasury variable rate stock – was introduced in 1977 and has been issued on three occasions, with six-monthly interest payments based on the average discount rates for Treasury bills over the preceding six months. This particular experiment was not a success and, effectively, has been replaced by the index-linked stocks. In 1977 the Government adapted their issue technique to provide for only part of the subscription money for a new issue to be paid at the time of application, with the balance being payable in instalments timed by reference to the Government's expected financing needs. Partly-paid stocks have since been used frequently. Since March 1979 many issues of stocks to the public have been made by tender. For these the authorities have set a minimum tender price and the stock has been allotted at that price (if the issue is undersubscribed) or at the lowest price at which any tender is successful (if the issue is oversubscribed). A further innovation has been the introduction of 'taplets' which allow the Government Broker to issue small further issues of existing stocks. This method has also been used for issues of new stocks. Through this mechanism he can direct his attention to certain parts of the yield curve or adjust the mix between conventional stocks and index-linked without the need for the disturbance of a full tap stock.

In 1981 the Government issued the first of its Index-Linked Stocks. Initially, only approved pension funds were allowed to hold this stock but since 1982 there has been no limitation on the status of the holder. These have many of the features of conventional stocks but the coupons payable and the redemption values are linked to movements in the Retail Price Index. They offer a yardstick for measuring the rate of real return (in price terms) for a risk-free asset in the U.K.

The main features of U.K. Government or quasi-government quoted borrowings as investments can be summarized as follows:

(a) They are highly marketable when compared with most other securities.

(b) They comprise a wide range of stocks to suit most investors' requirements in terms of life and coupon.

(c) They incur low dealing costs. The position after the introduction of negotiated commissions in the U.K. is likely to enhance this feature of U.K. Government stocks.

(d) They may bear tax or statutory privileges for investors resident in the borrowing country.

(e) They have a high degree of security in monetary terms. This is not always the case, however, for U.K. local authorities or public boards.

One class of local authority borrowing deserves special mention. Local authority negotiable bonds are all quoted on the Stock Exchange and are issued for any maturity between one and five years. Since late 1977 some have been issued at a variable rate for periods of three, four and five years. Broadly the coupon varies at six-monthly intervals and is fixed at a margin above the six-month inter-bank rate. Most issues continue to be at fixed rates. Local authority stock issues are much the same as negotiable bonds, but are usually underwritten when issued on the Stock Exchange and the sums raised by an issue are usually in excess of £10 million. Stock issues are also generally for longer maturities.

A further addition to the range of stocks available in the U.K. fixed interest market are stocks known as 'Bulldogs'. These are loans raised by non-residents, often overseas governments, in sterling denominated bonds at a yield in excess of that obtainable on U.K. Government stock. The bonds trade in the fixed interest market are the responsibility of the issuer and are not in any way guaranteed by the U.K. Government. The London market is very liquid and has access to many potential investors and is thus very attractive to overseas borrowers whose domestic market is limited, or who may wish to diversify the currencies in which their liabilities are expressed.

One other innovation in recent years has been the drop-lock loan. The borrower (often a local authority), at a time of high interest rates borrows money at some margin over LIBOR (London Inter-Bank Offered Rate) from a syndicate of banks. The interest payable varies according to money market conditions. At some predetermined level if rates fall the loan 'locks' into a traditional bond, the capital for which has been provided by institutional lenders on an agreed basis at the beginning of the syndicated loan. The borrower has the advantage of not being committed to a fixed interest loan at rates he believes to be temporarily too high.

3.2 Company securities

Corporate capital comprises a wide variety of forms of security which can be broadly classified into two groups – loan capital and share capital.

3.3 Loan capital

Loan capital represents borrowings other than current liabilities. Should a company be wound up these borrowings are repayable before any distribution of residual assets to shareholders. The principal is a liability of the company, and the interest is a charge against the company's income and a liability until paid. The various types of loan capital can be categorized as follows:

(a) Debentures   The legal definition of a debenture includes any acknowledgement of a loan issued by a company under seal. The commonest form of debenture involves a liability to pay a fixed rate of interest on certain dates and to repay the capital sum on one of a number of specific dates. Most debentures are secured by a floating charge on the assets of a company; the debenture holders thus become entitled in certain circumstances (usually when the company is insolvent) to appoint a receiver. The receiver will sell the assets of the company and pay the proceeds to the debenture holders in preference to all other loan creditors.

(b) Perpetual debentures and irredeemable debentures   These are debentures where the company does not undertake to repay the loan, except on liquidation.

(c) Mortgage debentures   Such debentures are principally secured by a fixed charge upon specified property.

(d) Unsecured loan stocks   The equivalent of debentures except that they are not secured in any way and, on the liquidation of the company, the holders are treated in same way as trade creditors.

(e) Bonds and notes   Usually short-term loans which tend not to be secured.

(f) Guaranteed loan stocks   These loans are secured by an outside guarantor, usually by the parent company of a subsidiary.

(g) Convertible loans   These are normally unsecured and give holders the right to exchange the stock for new ordinary shares at a stated price on stated dates. The rate of interest is normally higher than the dividend yield on the equity but, because of the potential equity participation, not as high as would be necessary for an unconvertible loan stock. Convertible loans are frequently offered in a takeover as they defer dilution of the equity capital until the benefits of the takeover have been established (although earnings per share are generally reported as if conversion had taken place).

(h) Variable interest loans   Occasionally any of the above forms of loans may be issued with a rate of interest which is not fixed, but which varies in accordance with a formula commonly linked to the six-month inter-bank rate. A novel variation of this is a loan for which the coupon rises in steps until it reaches a market level after several years. The borrower eases his cash flow in the early years; the lender is compensated by a higher than average yield to redemption at outset, this yield being calculated by a variation of the usual compound interest formula.

(i) Eurodollar borrowings   The growth of the eurodollar market (see section 3.7) has enabled many U.K. companies to borrow dollar loans through a fairly liquid and well-established market. Interest payments may be fixed or related to current money market rates.

From the investor's point of view the advantage of loan capital, apart from the high yield, is that it tends to be more secure, both as to income and repayment of capital, than shares. The interest is payable whether or not the company has made profits, and loan creditors rank for repayment before shareholders. For the company interest on loan stocks is deductible from profits before taxation and repayment terms are fixed regardless of any depreciation in money values. The company is obliged (failing any renegotiations) to meet payments of interest and the repayment of capital regardless of its trading position. The Companies Act 1948 (now consolidated with other Companies Acts in the Companies Act 1985) allows a company to buy back in its own loan stock.

3.4 Share capital

Share capital is the risk-bearing capital of the company. It represents, together with reserves, the shareholders' participation in the enterprise, whether or not on terms which afford a preference as to the payment of dividend or, in the event of liquidation, as to the return of capital. Interest is paid after corporate taxes and shares are usually irredeemable, although the Companies Act 1985 now permits a company to buy back its own shares for cancellation. It can be divided into two classes – preference capital and ordinary share capital.

Preference shares usually give the right to a fixed dividend out of post-tax profits and, in a liquidation, priority over ordinary shareholders as to repayment of the original capital. They normally have no vote except in relation to varying their rights, or if their dividend is in arrears. There are the following variations of preference share issues:

(a) Cumulative preference shares   These have the right to payment of accumulated arrears of dividends as soon as there are sufficient profits to pay them.
(b) Redeemable preference shares   These are preference shares that the company has undertaken to redeem on a specified date, often with a premium over their nominal value.
(c) Participating preference shares   These normally have the right to a fixed dividend before any payment is made to ordinary shareholders but, in addition, confer a further participation in profits, often related to the dividend payments on the ordinary shares.

(d) Convertible preference shares These shares carry a right of conversion into ordinary shares at specified dates and at specified prices.

Ordinary shares are the true capital of a company and offer neither security of capital nor of dividend, but confer on the shareholders certain proprietorial rights which normally include the right to such dividends as the directors may declare, the right to appoint and dismiss directors and the right to share in the residue of a company's assets on liquidation after all creditors (including loan stock holders and preference shareholders) have been repaid in full:

(a) Ordinary stocks and shares The distinction between stocks and shares is a technical matter of little importance. In the absence of any restriction the owners of ordinary stocks and shares in a company have all the proprietorial rights referred to above, including the right to vote in proportion to their holding.

(b) Non-voting or restricted voting shares A few companies have issued shares with no, or restricted, voting rights. Non-voting shares must now be specifically designated non-voting, although before this policy came into effect they were normally designated 'A' shares. The Stock Exchange is reluctant to grant a listing to new issues of non-voting shares.

(c) Deferred shares These normally confer full rights as to voting and as to return of capital in a liquidation, but their entitlement to a dividend is deferred until a specified date or the company's profits have reached a stated level.

(d) 'B' shares A number of companies have issued shares which entitle holders to fully paid shares in lieu of dividend. These are normally designated 'B' shares.

Shareholders, whether preference or ordinary, are not entitled to any dividend unless recommended by the directors. Dividends can only be paid out of profits whether earned in the current year or brought forward from previous years. Shareholders are entitled to reject or reduce, but not increase, a recommended dividend. Prices of ordinary shares are normally more volatile than prices of fixed interest stocks.

3.5 Other corporate instruments

Other corporate instruments which can be dealt in are:

(a) Warrants A warrant is a contract entered into by a company to issue on certain dates shares at a specified price on application by the holders. The warrants usually originate as an attachment to an issue of loan stock and normally have the effect of reducing the rate of interest on the loan stock which would otherwise have been necessary. Holders of warrants receive no income from them.

(b) Stock options   For many years the Stock Exchange has provided a market in which clients wishing to purchase or sell options on a company's stock or shares within the following three months can be matched with clients prepared in return for a premium (the option money) to surrender or take up the underlying stock or shares to which the option relates. In this, the traditional Options Market, the buyer and the seller of the option remain locked into the option agreement until either the option is exercised or until it expires three months later. As such there is no secondary market in traditional options by which an option holder can sell his interest in that option.

(c) Traded options   In April 1978, the Stock Exchange introduced traded call options on the shares of some leading British companies. In addition to giving the buyer the right to purchase shares at a specified price before a given date, the traded option, as its name implies, can itself be bought and sold on the market in a similar manner to a company security. Because of this, traded call options give great flexibility to the investor, whether a buyer or seller, and open up a wider range of choice in investment decisions. The investor's scope was broadened still further by the introduction of traded put options in May 1981. A put option gives the investor the right to sell shares at a specified price before a given date.

In traded options the minimum unit in which an investor may deal is one 'Contract', and a contract normally represents an option on 1000 shares of the underlying security. A traded option has a limited lifespan which is determined by its 'Expiry Date' which in turn is fixed at three-monthly intervals. The price at which an option contract gives the holder the right to buy the underlying security, if he chooses to do so, is known as the 'Exercise Price'.

Example

		Calls			Puts		
		April	July	October	April	July	October
Grand							
Metropolitan	280	22	30	38	9	14	20
(285)	300	11	20	28	28	30	55
	330	3	8	12	55	55	60

The table shows all the call options of Grand Metropolitan which forms a 'class' and all the put options which form a separate class. The line showing for calls the options exercisable at 300 in July is called the Grand Met. July 300 'Series'. The expiry date (July) is the date on which the option's life comes to an end and 300 is the price at which the option gives the holder the right to buy the underlying security. The unit of trading is the number of shares to which an option contract relates and is normally 1000. The 'premium' is the price of a traded option and the price of the underlying security in this example is 285. Thus the July 300 series enables the purchaser for a premium of 20p per share to purchase the underlying security at a price of 300.

The transition from the traditional type of option to the traded option required the link between the original buyer and seller of the option to be severed, the exercise price of the options to be standardized, and the introduction of a clearing corporation – The London Option Clearing House (LOCH). To increase marketability, option series of three, six and nine months' duration are created, with further series being introduced on expiry of a series, or following a substantial movement in the price of the underlying stock. The introduction of further series following movement in the price of a stock ensures that clients always have available at least one 'in the money' series (i.e. for a call option a series whose exercise price is below the current market price of the stock) and one 'out of the money' series (i.e. for a call option a series whose exercise price is above the current market price of the stock).

The writer of a traded option is required to provide security for the options which he has written. The security may take the form of cash, the underlying stock, or other assets approved by the Council of the Stock Exchange.

Dealing in traded options may only be carried out on the specially designated traded options pitch on the floor of the Stock Exchange. All transactions are by 'open outcry' in the market; no transactions over the telephone are permitted.

The member firms with option business to transact congregate around the pitch and form what is termed the 'crowd'. The crowd comprises Board Dealers, who are jobber firms appointed by the Council to deal in one or more traded options classes (e.g. ICI, BP etc.), Market Makers, who may be jobbers or brokers registered with the Council as Option Dealers, and Public Order Member Brokers executing orders on behalf of clients. In executing an order in a traded option, the public order member broker first checks the price with the board dealer and market makers in the class and then deals with whichever member of the crowd makes the most competitive price. For some classes, the Council employs

Stock Exchange staff as Board Officials instead of appointing Board Dealers. Details of the completed transaction are entered on dealing slips which are sorted and matched by LOCH.

3.6 Other investments

So far, the discussion has concerned itself with investments quoted on a recognized stock exchange. There are, however, many alternatives which are not so quoted. To begin with, most of the varieties described above may be found in similar unquoted forms, e.g. in the United Kingdom there is a substantial body of unquoted Government and quasi-Government debt in the form of Treasury Bills, Tax Reserve Certificates, Local Authority Bills and Loans. National Savings is another form of central Government Debt and includes Certificates, Income Bonds, Deposit Bonds and Premium Bonds. Furthermore, there are in existence some 1,000,000 companies in the U.K. alone, of which only a few thousand have any part of their capital or debt structure quoted. Yet every one must have some capital at least. Obviously, all forms of unquoted debt are less marketable than the comparable quoted forms; in some cases, such as Government debt, the difference is marginal; in others it can be of the greatest importance.

There are, however, some forms of unquoted investment which have no strictly comparable quoted form. These may take the form of statutory controlled bodies such as building societies, trustee savings banks in the United Kingdom, and the savings and loans associations in the United States (the latter may, nevertheless, have part of their capital quoted on a stock exchange). Alternatively, they may take a less rigid form, such as the classes of investment associated with property, either debt, in the form of mortgage with individuals (where statute and case law in most countries tends to protect the borrower rather than the investor) or direct ownership, known in England as freehold, where the ownership is absolute, and leasehold where ownership is limited to a specific period and is subject to some restrictions. Similarly, it is possible to invest in movable objects such as paintings or antique silver or immature wines and spirits. Although in the case of silver it is certainly possible to make some quantitative calculations of worth by weight (not necessarily of much relevance), in most of the others it is not. We shall not concern ourselves in any degree with investments where such calculations have little meaning, nor to any great extent with those where the investor must also provide an entrepreneurial function.

3.7 The eurobond market

(a) The market

The eurobond market is an international market which operates alongside the eurocurrency markets. The eurobond market has been essentially a provider of medium- to long-term fixed-interest capital to governments, public agencies and industrial companies, although in recent years issues of floating-rate notes have become quite important. In 1979 floating-rate notes accounted for almost a quarter of new eurobond issues. The important feature of the market is that issues are sold internationally, usually in a number of countries. The market was originally dominated by issues for U.S. corporations and was encouraged by U.S. capital controls; the issues were all denominated in euro (i.e. external) dollars. Many currencies are now used, however, and a large number of borrowers from around the world have issued eurobonds.

A eurobond is a negotiable debt obligation, nearly always issued in bearer form. Issues with an equity element are generally convertibles or straight debt issues with warrants attached. Most issues are officially listed either in London or on a continental bourse, but most of the dealing takes place over the telephone between market makers, notably U.K. merchant banks and banks from the U.S.A., Europe and Japan, and foreign brokers, away from stock exchange floors. Both jobbers and brokers in the U.K. operate in eurobonds as principals, directly with other market makers. There is no obligation to pass transactions through jobbers.

(b) Euro-clear

The Euro-clear system is a clearance system for internationally traded securities. It is described in detail in Appendix 1.

3.8 Other financial instruments

Changing monetary regulations and increased volatility of both interest rates and currencies, particularly after the oil shocks of the 1970s, have led to the development of other financial instruments which assist international corporations and funds in managing their liquidity or currency exposure, and adjusting their risk profile.

(a) Traded options

In paragraph 3.5 stock options were discussed which allow an investor to buy or sell securities at a fixed price and within a specified future time against the payment of a premium. The risk profile of such dealings is clearly different from trading in the securities themselves but careful trading in options can serve to 'insure' a fund against certain contingencies for a relatively modest payment.

The number of U.K. equities in which it is possible to deal is limited (31 at September 1985) but it is also possible to trade options in the FT-SE Index of 100 shares and in three gilts (Exchequer 10% 1989, Treasury 11¾% 1991 and Treasury 11¾% 2003/07). Currency options (£/$ and $/DM) have also been introduced.

Options markets are more highly developed in the U.S., but the scope of the London and Amsterdam markets has increased substantially. OTC (Over The Counter) options can be effected to meet a client's specific needs on size, exercise price and declaration date but there is virtually no secondary market.

(b) Forward foreign exchange deals

This is the traditional means of arranging currency cover. A bank will quote for settlement in the future in a currency after taking into account the spot (current) rate, the interest rate differentials between the two countries for the period quoted, its own view of the market and its own book position. No cash margin is required because the bargain is complete after initial agreement. A trader wishing to unwind such a position would have to deal again with the same or another bank in a new contract. The forward market in commodities, by contrast, requires margin payments.

(c) Financial futures

In practice, financial futures are akin to forward markets in interest rates and currencies but the market arrangements are such that one can take positions or close them out at very short notice. Financial futures have evolved from the commodity markets whose practice requires the payment of margins to sustain futures positions, in contrast to the inter-bank market where money does not change hands normally until a deal matures. Essentially, a futures contract is an obligation to buy a commodity at a specified price on a specified future date. The market in the futures consists of trading in these rights and obligations.

The contract can be completely divorced from the product and in this respect differs from a forward purchase or sale (paragraph (b) above). If, for example, a user of copper buys copper three months forward, the copper will be delivered in three months' time. If, however, he buys copper three months futures contracts he will normally sell ('close out') those futures contracts in three months' time at around the same price as he buys 'cash copper' (the market in the commodity underlying the contract is called the 'cash market' or 'spot market' in the case of currencies). Futures contracts are standardized, are always dealt on margin and there is a properly regulated market.

The London International Financial Futures Exchange (LIFFE) deals at present in contracts based on the following:

(i)   Three-month Eurodollar. The interest rate on U.S.$1,000,000 on deposit at a London bank for three months.

(ii) Three-month Sterling Deposit   The interest rate on £500,000 on deposit at a designated London bank for three months.

(iii) The price of £50,000 nominal value of a 20-year 12% notional gilt.

(iv) The price of £100,000 nominal value of a 10% notional short gilt.

(v)   The U.S. dollar value of:
      Sterling   £25,000
      Deutsche Marks   DM125,000
      Swiss Francs   SwFr125,000
      Japanese Yen   Y12.5m.

(vi) The price of the FT-SE 100 Index valued at £25 per full index point.

(vii) The price of $100,000 nominal value of a 15-year 8% notional U.S. Treasury Bond.

There is a well-established method of dealing by 'open outcry', used in American stock exchanges, commodity futures markets and financial futures markets. This is closely imitated in the London futures market.

There is a trading floor with a number of recessed octagonal 'pits', one for each type of commodity, one for currencies, one for short-dated interest rate futures and so on.

In an 'open outcry' market dealers shout out their offers or bids in the hearing of all the other dealers. This ensures that the best bid is matched to the best offer. When a transaction has been made it is immediately recorded in writing and reported to the market authorities (the clearing house) who become a party to the bargain. Bargains are published on an electronic scoreboard.

Only the members of the Exchange can deal on the floor and all members have the same rights. However, in America the members fall fairly clearly into three categories – 'commission brokers', 'floor brokers' and 'locals'. 'Commission brokers' are those carrying out business for their own clients, 'floor brokers' are those who carry out business largely for other members and 'locals' operate on their own behalf.

'Locals' can be divided into different groups depending upon the time scale of their operations. At one extreme are what are known as 'scalpers' who are only concerned with minute price movements and whose positions are likely to be open for minutes rather than hours. At the other extreme are the 'position takers' who keep the market in balance over a matter of days. Between them are the 'day traders', operating on a technical basis like the 'scalpers' but on a time scale of hours, who would normally close their positions on the day.

This degree of specialization has been an important feature in ensuring the success of the Chicago futures markets so that the distinction between 'commission brokers' and 'locals' will probably appear in the London market. It is likely that the jobbers will become position takers and that the other shorter-term dealers will be provided by people who are accustomed to operating in other futures markets.

Because every deal must take place on the floor of the exchange, dealing hours are important. This is particularly true for futures in which it is possible to deal overseas: for these contracts it is desirable that there should be some overlap with American and Far Eastern market hours. Thus, for currency and short interest rate futures, the pits will start trading around 8.30 a.m. and finish near 4.00 p.m.

In order to ensure an orderly market at the opening, dealings in different contracts are staggered; the currency contracts open at two-minute intervals and the short sterling interest rate futures market opens at 8.20 a.m.

CHAPTER FOUR

ELEMENTS OF ACCOUNTS FOR INVESTORS

4.1 Accounts

Accounts enable the owners of a business to assess the viability, performance and progress of the business. The business may be carried on in the form of a company, a partnership, or a sole trader. Since most investments by institutions are in limited companies, this section will concentrate on company accounting.

Each year a company prepares a report and accounts. The information which is available will vary from company to company but certain minima are laid down by legislation (Companies Act 1985).

In addition to the legal minima, the Accounting Standards Committee produces Statements of Standard Accounting Practices (SSAPs) which give guidance on the treatment of various aspects in company accounts. Significant departures from the recommended standards have to be set out. The annual report and accounts for a company generally contains at least:

1. a directors' report
2. a profit and loss account
3. a balance sheet
4. a statement of source and application of funds
5. an auditors' report.

The reporting requirements for companies quoted on the Stock Exchange are more rigorous and also involve the production of a half-yearly report.

4.2 Fundamental accounting concepts

When preparing financial information, four standard concepts are used:

(a) *Going Concern Basis*   It is assumed that the company will continue to trade in the same line and scale of business.
(b) *Accruals Basis*   Revenue is matched with the costs which have been incurred in earning the revenue. Revenue and costs are accounted for as earned and incurred, not when received or paid.
(c) *Consistency*   The treatments used in successive accounting periods should be consistent, and if not, the effects of the change should be stated.

(d) *Prudence* Many aspects of accounting require estimation and judgement, and most often a cautious view should be taken. Revenue and profits should not usually be anticipated before the point of sale but provision should be made for all known losses even if they have not already been incurred.

Further fundamentals of accounting are:

(a) *Double entry system* Any transaction, such as the payment of cash for some goods, has two equal and opposite effects on the financial position of the business – in this case, the acquisition of some goods and the reduction in the cash balance. The double entry system merely records both aspects of each transaction.
(b) *Historic cost basis* Accounts are usually prepared on a historic cost basis. Revenues are taken into account when a sale materializes but until then assets are retained in the accounts at their original cost. The effects of inflation on accounts will be discussed later in this chapter.
(c) *The balance sheet* This is a financial snapshot of a business at a single point in time. It shows the assets held by the business, the liabilities and the capital (i.e. the owners' interest) of the business. It does not normally attempt to value the business but is a list of balances drawn from the books of account.
(d) *The profit and loss account* This is a statement of the revenues receivable from sales of the products, and the expenses incurred in making and selling the particular products. This statement is drawn up to cover a specific period and covers all sales which have taken place in the relevant trading period.

4.3 The principles of profit and loss accounts

The principles of profit and loss accounts, balance sheets and statements of source and application of funds can be shown by the example of an imaginary company. The tax rates used are notional. The format of the accounts in this example attempts to show the main principles. The layout requirements of the Companies Act 1985 have been ignored.

An individual decided to form a company and to invest £100,000 in that company. A further £150,000 was borrowed from the bank for a period of five years at 10% interest.

The initial balance sheet would be:

Financed by:		Assets	
Ordinary share capital	£100,000	Cash	£250,000
Loan from bank	£150,000		
	£250,000		£250,000

Year 1

The cash was used partly to purchase machinery (£100,000), and to provide working capital. Business was started in a rented factory (rent £30,000 p.a.). During the first year the goods sold totalled £400,000 but the following expenses had been paid:

	£
Raw materials	300,000
Salaries/wages	50,000
Interest on bank loan	15,000
Rent on factory	30,000
Other expenses	25,000
	£420,000

Although £400,000 of sales had been made, £50,000 of this had not yet been received at the year end. The cash at the bank at the year end was £80,000, and goods which have been completed but not yet sold were valued at a cost price of £100,000. The machinery originally cost £100,000 and has an expected useful life of 10 years. The provision for the wear and tear on the fixed assets is called depreciation, and the method to be used in this case is known as the straight line method of depreciation.

This is calculated as:

$$\frac{\text{Initial cost}}{\text{Useful life of asset}}$$

The depreciation charge is therefore £100,000/10 = £10,000 per annum.

In the absence of inflation, i.e. assuming stable prices of individual assets, and nil interest rates, the money deducted using depreciation charges would be sufficient to replace the asset at the end of its useful life.

The profit and loss account would be:

		£		£
Expenses:	raw materials	300,000	Sales	400,000
	salaries/wages	50,000	Stock in hand	100,000
	interest on loan	15,000		
	rent on factory	30,000		
	other expenses	25,000		
Depreciation		10,000		
Profit before tax		70,000		
		500,000		500,000

The stocks in hand at the end of the period are, in effect, transferred to the next year, usually at the lower of cost or net realizable value, to be treated as a cost in the year of sale.

The profit before tax was subject to tax at 35% and no part of this profit was distributed to shareholders in the form of a dividend. No dividend was paid because of the need to build up the business by retaining as much cash as possible. (Capital allowances on the purchase of assets have been ignored, as have expenses disallowed for tax purposes.) In the real world, the profits disclosed in the accounts would have to be adjusted to arrive at the profit or loss for tax purposes.

Profit before tax	£70,000
Less: Tax at 35%	£24,500
Retained profit	£45,500

The balance sheet as at the end of the first year would be as shown opposite:

Financed by:	£	£		Assets	£	£	£
Ordinary share capital	100,000			Machinery (at cost less depreciation)			90,000
Reserves (retained profit)	45,500			Current assets			
				Stock	100,000		
				Debtors	50,000		
				Cash	80,000		
Ordinary shareholders' funds		145,500				230,000	
				Less:			
				Current liabilities			
				Tax payable		(24,500)	
Term loan from bank		150,000					205,500
		295,500					£295,500

The source and application of funds statement states the places where the new funds have come from and what the funds have been used for. It then analyses how the inflow or outflow of funds is reflected in the elements of working capital, and in the cash balances.

For this company the statement for the first year is:

Sources of funds

Operating profit before taxation	£70,000
Adjustment for items not involving movement of funds:	
Depreciation	£10,000
Funds generated from operations	£80,000

Application of funds

	£
Purchase of machinery	100,000
Increase in working capital (i.e. a decrease)	(20,000)

The analysis of the decrease in working capital of £20,000 would be:

(Decrease) in working capital	(20,000)

Comprising changes in:

			£
Stock	100,000 – 0	=	100,000
Debtors	50,000 – 0	=	50,000
Creditors	0 – 0	=	0
Net liquid funds	80,000 – 250,000	=	(170,000)
			(20,000)

Cash balances have been substantially reduced; there has been a build-up of stocks; and there is money owned to the company (debtors).

Year 2

The company had traded at a profit in the first year and now wishes to expand. Expansion usually requires additional resources and this could be financed by internal or external means. At the end of the first year there were no sums owed to others (e.g. traders supplying raw materials) but by delaying the payment of bills to suppliers and by chasing up payments owing to it the company could obtain additional working capital. External finance could be provided using bank overdrafts, loans, or issues of shares.

It was decided to use a combination of a £100,000 bank overdraft and internal finance to purchase new machinery for £200,000.

The profit and loss account for year 2 would be:

		£		£
Stock at start of year		100,000	Sales	700,000
Expenses:	raw materials	650,000	Stock at year end	300,000
	salaries/wages	100,000		
	interest on loan	15,000		
	interest on overdraft	10,000		
	rent on factory	30,000		
	other expenses	55,000		
Depreciation		30,000		
Profit before tax		10,000		
		1,000,000		1,000,000

Depreciation is again calculated as Cost/Useful life and the new machinery is also depreciating over ten years. The total depreciation for year 2 is therefore:

$$\frac{100,000}{10} + \frac{200,000}{10} = 30,000$$

The profit before tax is £10,000, and after tax at 35% (again ignoring adjustments), the reserves are increased by £6,500 because again no dividend was paid to shareholders.

The balance sheet at the end of year 2 would be:

Financed by:	£	£	Assets	£	£	£
Ordinary			Machinery			
share capital	100,000		(cost less			
			depreciation)			260,000
Reserves			Current assets			
(retained profit)	52,000		Stock	300,000		
			Debtors	60,000		
Ordinary share-			Cash	10,000		
holders' funds		152,000				
					370,000	
Term loan			less:			
from bank			Current liabilities			
		150,000	Creditors	224,500		
			Taxation	3,500		
			Overdraft	100,000		
					(328,000)	
			Net current assets			42,000
		£302,000				£302,000

The cost of machines after depreciation at the end of year 2 is the cost after depreciation at the end of year 1 (£90,000) plus machines purchased (£200,000) less depreciation in year 2 (£30,000).

The source and application of funds statement for year 2 would be:

Sources of funds

Operating profit before taxation	£ 10,000	
Adjustment of items not involving movement of funds:		
Depreciation	£ 30,000	
Funds generated from operations		£ 40,000

Application of funds

Purchase of machinery	£200,000	
Taxation paid	£ 24,500	
	£224,500	
Increase in working capital (i.e. a decrease)		(£184,500)

The analysis of this decrease of £184,500 is:

Change in:			£
Stocks	i.e. 300,000 – 100,000	=	200,000
Debtors	i.e. 60,000 – 50,000	=	10,000
Creditors	i.e. 0 – 224,500	=	(224,500)
Net liquid funds	see below	=	(170,000)
			(184,500)

The figure for net liquid funds takes the change in cash balances and the change in bank overdraft into a single figure:

Cash balance end Year 2 – Cash balance end Year 1 = 10,000 – 80,000

$$= (70,000)$$

Overdraft end Year 1 – Overdraft end Year 2 = 0 – 100,000

$$= (100,000)$$

$$(170,000)$$

The source and application of funds analysis shows that there has been a large increase in stocks and in the amount owed to other companies, accompanied by a substantial decrease in the net liquid funds position. Although the company had managed to increase turnover from £400,000 to £700,000, the company was producing at a faster rate than it could sell the goods, and the excess had resulted in an increase in stocks from £100,000 to £300,000. The cash balances were low and the bills outstanding large, but the bankers did not wish to increase the company's overdraft facilities. They suggested that the company should seek further equity finance because the size of the borrowings in relation to the existing equity was already large.

The capital and retained reserves amounted to £152,000 (see the balance sheet under 'ordinary shareholders' funds') and there were 100,000 £1 shares in issue (net asset value of £1.52 per share). Companies are not usually valued in relation to net assets but by having regard to the profits which they are expected to generate. After an analysis of future profit projections an outside investor agreed to pay £200,000 for the issue of 100,000 new £1 shares (i.e. £2 per share). This had the effect of increasing cash balances by £200,000 on the right-hand side of the balance sheet and increasing the share capital figure by £100,000 (i.e. 100,000 shares at a par value of £1). In order to balance both sides of the balance sheet the left-hand side needs to be increased by the £100,000 premium over par value which was paid. The par value is £1. £2 per share was paid and thus the share premium is $100,000 \times £1$.

The company also decided to sell for £100,000 one of its original machines which was in the balance sheet at a figure of £80,000 (cost £100,000 less 2 years' depreciation of £10,000). As the company is not primarily in business to sell machines the difference between the £100,000 sale price and the balance sheet value of £80,000 is not treated as a normal element of the profit and loss account but as an extraordinary item in the accounts.

The balance sheet after these changes at the beginning of year 3 would be:

	£	£		£	£	£
Financed by:			Assets			
Ordinary share capital	200,000		Machinery			180,000
Share premium account	100,000		(cost less depreciation)			
Reserves*	72,000		Current assets			
			Stocks	300,000		
Ordinary shareholders'			Debtors	60,000		
funds		372,000	Cash	210,000		
					570,000	
Term loan from bank		150,000	Less current liabilities			
			Creditors	224,500		
			Taxation	3,500		
					(228,000)	
			Net current assets			342,000
		£522,000				£522,000

*Including £20,000 extraordinary gain.

Year 3

Year 3 was a profitable trading year for the company, and the profit and loss account below is shown in the vertical or tabular format. The format of the table is different from that for year 2 but the principles are essentially the same.

	£	£	
Sales		1,300,000	
plus stock at year end	100,000		
less stock at start year	300,000		
	200,000		
		1,100,000	
less Expenses: raw materials	700,000		
salaries/wages	110,000		
interest on loan	15,000		
interest on overdraft	10,000		
rent on factory	30,000		
other expenses	70,000		
	935,000		
less Depreciation	20,000		
		915,000	
Profit before tax			145,000
plus extraordinary item			20,000
Profit before tax but after extraordinary item			£165,000

The directors decided to pay a dividend of 10p per share, and after tax at 35%, the retained profit was calculated thus:

	£
Profit before tax after extraordinary item	165,000
less Dividend	20,000
less Tax	57,750
Retained profit	87,250

The balance sheet at the end of year 3 would be:

	£	£	£
Financed by:			
Ordinary share capital	200,000		
Share premium account	100,000		
Reserves	139,250		
Ordinary shareholders' funds	439,250		
Term loan from bank	150,000		
	£589,250		
Assets			
Machinery (cost less depreciation)			160,000
Current assets			
Stocks		100,000	
Debtors		380,000	
Cash		277,000	
		757,000	
Less: Current liabilities			
Creditors		250,000	
Taxation		57,750	
Declared dividend		20,000	
		(327,750)	
Net current assets			429,250
			£589,250

The source and application of funds statement for year 3 can be made up as in previous years.

At the end of year 3 the company (Company A) decided to purchase one of its smaller competitors, Company B, and a purchase price of £100,000 was agreed. The £100,000 would not be paid as cash but, instead, £100,000 of a 12% unsecured loan stock redeemable in the year 2000 would be issued to the existing shareholders of Company B. The purchase price takes into account the profits which it is likely to generate and does not necessarily have any relation to the net asset value of the company as set out in the balance sheet. Company B is now a wholly owned subsidiary of Company A and Company A's balance sheet would have the addition of an investment in a subsidiary at cost of £100,000 on the right-hand side of the balance sheet; and the £100,000 of 12% unsecured loan stock on the left-hand side.

B's balance sheet is unaltered by the change of ownership and is as follows:

	£		£	£
Ordinary share capital	10,000	Machinery		30,000
Reserves	65,000	Current assets		
		Stock	25,000	
		Debtors	5,000	
		Cash	25,000	
		less Current liabilities		
		Creditors	(10,000)	
				45,000
	£75,000			£75,000

It is necessary to prepare consolidated accounts of A & B. In order to do this, most items are simply added together (i.e. the figure for machinery in the consolidated accounts is merely that for company A plus that for company B), but the investment in the subsidiary B of £100,000 shown in A's accounts will not appear in the consolidated accounts, nor will the £10,000 ordinary share capital of B held by A. Reserves are not added. Post-acquisition reserves earned by the subsidiary are added in future years. The net asset value of company B is the ordinary share capital plus the reserves (less any fixed loans which are nil in this case) i.e. £75,000. The price paid was £100,000 and a balancing item of £25,000 will be needed in order to make both sides of the consolidated balance sheet balance.

The consolidated balance sheet would be:

	£	£		£	£
Ordinary			Machinery		190,000
share capital	200,000		Current assets		
Share premium			Stocks	125,000	
account	100,000		Debtors	385,000	
Reserves	139,250		Cash	302,000	
Ordinary			less current		
shareholders' funds		439,250	liabilities		
12% loan stock		100,000	Creditors	(260,000)	
Term loan		150,000	Taxation	(57,750)	
			Declared Dividend	(20,000)	
					474,250
			Balancing item		£25,000
		£689,250			£689,250

The balancing item is called goodwill, and where it does arise it is often eliminated by reducing the amount of the reserves by the corresponding figure. There would be a note in the accounts explaining the reserve reduction if this were done.

A consolidated profit and loss account would also be prepared by adding the figures for most amounts but eliminating intercompany payments such as intergroup sales and any dividends paid by B to A.

Company A

	£
Profit before tax	200,000
Tax	70,000
Profit after tax	130,000
plus Dividend received from B	10,000
	140,000
less Dividend paid	(40,000)
Retained profit in A's accounts	100,000

Company B

Profit before tax		20,000
less Dividend paid to A	(10,000)	
less Tax	(7,000)	
		(17,000)
Retained profit to be added to B's reserves		3,000

Consolidated

Profit before tax	220,000
Tax	(77,000)
Net profit after tax	143,000
less	
Dividend	(40,000)
Retained profit	103,000

4.4 Company accounts

The main principles of accounts have been illustrated in the above example. Actual company accounts are in general much more complex, particularly for larger companies. The information disclosed can extend well beyond the legal minima, particularly where it is necessary to demonstrate to investors, and potential investors, that the business justifies a high share price. In addition, accounts can have a valuable public relations aspect and can explain the company's activities and policies to shareholders, employees, creditors, the financial press and the investing public.

Although a large volume of information is given in accounts there are still problems in their compilation. One of the major ones is the effect of inflation, and this is dealt with later in this chapter. Another difficulty is the treatment of projects which take a number of years. Accounts are generally prepared annually in full form and where a project is not completed it is necessary to ascribe a value to it. In some cases, for example in the building of an aircraft, a considerable amount of money is spent on research and development, often a number of years ahead of the sale of the first aircraft. The research and development expenditure could be written off completely in the year in which it is incurred, but this may be much too conservative a treatment, and the research and development may be regarded as an asset against which future revenues can be earned. Over a number of years, the whole idea will be to sell the finished goods at a price which adequately recovers all the research and development expenditure, together with all other associated costs, but naturally there are many other different treatments that can be adopted. Some of these issues are dealt with in accounting standards. The essence will still be to try to match in any one year the revenues receivable with the costs expended in producing the revenue.

A problem with long-term contracts that take a considerable time to complete (e.g. building, civil contracting and heavy engineering) is the valuation of stock and work in progress at the end of a year. In effect, the contract is valued arbitrarily at a given point in time, and a profit or loss is taken for the work done to date. Where long-term contracts are material the assumptions made can have a very significant effect on the profit figures.

A further problem is the statement of asset values at historical cost less accumulated depreciation. Thus the historic cost balance sheet does not show, or intend to show, the breakup value of any asset, nor the worth of that asset in the generation of future income. Similarly, the valuation figures for stock and work in progress may have no regard to the sale value of the items in the form in which they were at the balance sheet date other than to be at the lower of cost or net realizable value (as for all current assets).

INFLATION ACCOUNTING

4.5 Conventional historic cost (HC) accounts

Conventional historic cost accounts work reasonably well in times of stable prices even though a limited amount of subjective judgement is possible. However, in inflationary times HC accounts can produce an inaccurate assessment of the financial condition of a company. Some of the problems are:

(i) Stock
The cost of replacing stock or new materials after a sale of goods is higher than the cost of the stock or raw materials used to make the goods sold. HC accounts take no account of this difference in costs, nor the increased financing needed to retain the stock at the same level. For example, if some goods cost £100, were sold for £150, but cost £130 to replace, HC accounts would show a profit of £50 (i.e. £150 − £100), notwithstanding the fact that £30 out of the £50 profit would be required to maintain the stock at the same level.

(ii) Borrowing

The cost of repaying any loans falls in real terms during an inflationary period but no credit for this is given in HC accounts.

(iii) Depreciation

The depreciation figure spreads the cost of an asset over its working lifetime. Whilst depreciation is not designed to provide a fund to replace the assets, it would in a time of stable prices enable money to be put aside for this purpose. In inflationary times the depreciation allowance is likely to be well below that which would be needed to replace the assets at the end of their useful life.

(iv) Working capital

As inflation increases the level of working capital usually rises merely to maintain the same level of output. This increased capital is not allowed for in HC accounts.

(v) Comparisons with prior years

Since the real value of monetary amounts has altered over time, comparison with previous years' historical cost account figures is difficult. The profit figures can appear to be rising sharply in monetary terms whereas if correct allowance was made for changing monetary values the actual picture may be very different.

Methods of inflation accounting

Two main systems have been developed to overcome some of the historical cost accounting problems:

4.6 Current purchasing power (CPP) accounts

Accounts are maintained on the historical cost basis and adjusted where relevant for changes in the value of money using a single index (usually the Retail Prices Index).

Some features are:

(i)   Sales and costs are adjusted between the date of each transaction and the accounting date. In practice, approximations would be used to avoid large numbers of calculations. Previous years' figures would be adjusted to provide long-term comparisons.

(ii)   Capital assets are revalued each year, and the depreciation charge would also be revalued each year.

(iii) Opening and closing stocks are revalued as at the year end and thus profits from the appreciation of stock are eliminated.

(iv)   The loss from holding cash in inflationary times is taken into account; as is the profit from borrowing.

(v)   CPP removes the distorting effect of general alterations in monetary values but takes no account of the increases in costs affecting the particular business if these differ from the Retail Prices Index.

(vi)   Differences between CPP profits and HC profits can be substantial, particularly for companies which are heavily borrowed and where the profits on an HC basis are low. The borrowing effect is fairly clear cut but where HC profits are low, CPP profits can be boosted as the assets are revalued in line with inflation.

(vii) The concept behind the use of the RPI adjustment is that of maintenance of a shareholder's general purchasing power which may be taken as the minimum objective of the company's directors. The question of replacing the company's assets to stay in business is a totally separate objective and the company's accounts should (but do not under CPP) give an accurate record of this.

   The advantages of the CPP method are that it is relatively straight-forward and that all companies would have used the same indices so that results would be comparable between companies. The disadvantages of CPP are:

(a)   that a spurious impression of accuracy may be given;

(b)   the general price index is not necessarily relevant to an individual company's assets;
       and

(c)   the inclusion of all monetary gains and losses in earnings could give a misleading impression of the financial health of a company either through concealing that a highly-geared company might be dangerously illiquid or, conversely, through concealing the tactical advantage of a company which holds cash at a time of rapid inflation.

4.7 Current cost accounting

Current cost accounting (CCA) is an alternative method of inflation accounting to the CPP method. The CCA system starts from the HC profit and loss account and makes adjustments to allow for the impact of price changes. The idea is that profits or losses would be assessed taking into account the finance necessary to maintain the same level of business in real terms (i.e. maintenance of operating capacity), and a further adjustment is made to allow for the way in which the business is financed.

There are three main operating adjustments which are made to the historical cost accounts:

(i) The depreciation adjustment – this is an allowance for the effect of price changes on the cost of replacing fixed assets.

(ii) The cost of sales adjustment – this is, in effect, the difference between the cost of replacing the stock and the original cost of the stock sold.

(iii) The monetary working capital adjustment – this is the additional sum required to provide working capital as a result of the effect of inflation on the business.

After these three adjustments have been made the CCA operating profit is obtained. Where there are gains/losses on the disposal of fixed assets there is also an adjustment to take account of the difference between the HC and CCA depreciated values of these assets.

The pre-tax profit on the CCA basis is reached by taking the CCA operating profit, deducting interest paid, adding interest received, and making a fourth adjustment, namely,

(iv) The gearing adjustment – this adds back some of the adjustments made earlier in (i), (ii) and (iii) above; and the level depends on the proportion of the business which is financed by loans rather than equity capital.

The four adjustments are now considered in further detail.

The depreciation adjustment
As mentioned earlier HC depreciation amounts are likely to be inadequate to replace plant at the end of its useful life and an addition to the level of depreciation is necessary under CCA accounts.

The first step is to calculate the replacement cost of the relevant fixed assets. In some cases the figure is known but in most cases the original cost is increased by indices which differ for various types of asset. The CCA depreciation for one year would be the replacement cost figure divided by the useful life of the asset, and thus the CCA depreciation adjustment would be CCA depreciation less HC depreciation.

This method requires alteration in cases where the CCA asset value, less CCA depreciation based on the elapsed life of the machine, is higher than the discounted value of the future amounts recoverable from the use of the machine during its remaining lifetime.

The size of the CCA depreciation adjustment will reflect the age of the assets employed. In periods of inflation the alteration from HC to CCA will be higher for older assets than younger ones, and consequently companies with newer plant are likely to show lower CCA depreciation adjustments.

Cost of sales adjustment (COSA)

In order that revenues are matched with the current cost of replacing stocks which were used during the year, the cost of sales adjustment is the summation of the differences between the replacement cost of the stock, and the actual cost of the stock for each item.

In a sophisticated accounting system, which takes price changes of supplies into account, the cost of sales adjustment could be calculated fairly accurately from existing base stock, or last-in-first-out methods. Usually, however, the adjustment is calculated at the year end, at the time the accounts are prepared, by an approximate method based on 'average' prices. Average replacement prices applying during the year would be obtained from the opening and closing stock prices and on the assumption that purchases and sales of stock, together with price changes, took place evenly over the year the COSA can be obtained. The method is arbitrary and its accuracy reduces as the deviation in purchases, sales and price changes increases from those assumed. The COSA will also depend on the number of indices which are used and the level of subdivision of the data.

An example of the COSA is as follows:

Index numbers for cost of stock: beginning of year, 100; end of year, 120; thus average for year, say, 110.

	Historical Cost £		Current Cost £
Opening stock	350	$350 \times (110/100) =$	385
Add purchases	2,300		2,300
Deduct closing stock	540	$540 \times (110/120) =$	495
Cost of sales	2,110		2,190

Cost of sales adjustment therefore is 80.

The Monetary Working Capital Adjustment (MWCA)

Goods are not always sold for cash nor are goods received paid for immediately. Finance is required for the difference between debtors and creditors (i.e. working capital) and as price rises occur the net figure for debtors less creditors usually rises. This increase in working capital to maintain business at the same level is the MWCA.

An example of the MWCA is as follows:

Index numbers as in above example: beginning of year, 100; end of year, 120; hence average for year, say, 110.

	end 1985 £	end 1984 £
Debtors	3,000	2,500
Creditors	1,700	1,500
Monetary working capital	1,300	1,000

Increase in working capital $= 1,300 - 1,000 = 300$

The end of 1984 working capital adjusted for the increase to 1985 average costs is $\frac{110}{100} \times 1,000 = 1,100$.

The end of 1985 working capital, again adjusted to 1985 average costs, is $\frac{110}{120} \times 1,300 = 1,192$.

The rise in working capital due to the increase in the volume of the business is taken as $1,192 - 1,100 = 92$.

The MWCA is therefore the overall increase in working capital (300) less the volume alteration (92) = 208.

It is not always simple to decide which particular assets/liabilities should be included in the MWCA and which should be treated as net borrowings. Generally, the MWCA would exclude cash and overdrafts, unless to exclude these would be misleading.

Gearing adjustment

The three operating adjustments to arrive at CCA profits provide a measure of the additional finance to maintain the business but because they are deductions from profit imply that they are met from that source. Since a business is usually financed by a mixture of equity and loans, and the loan element will not need to be financed by current costs earnings, a proportion of the operating adjustments can be added back to profits by means of the gearing adjustment.

The gearing proportion is average net borrowings divided by the average net operating assets; and this is multiplied by the three operating adjustments (depreciation adjustment + COSA + MWCA) to obtain the gearing adjustment. The figure for net borrowing is the excess of the liabilities in monetary terms, excluding those already included in the MWCA, but including convertibles, over the current assets (excluding any item subject to the COSA or the MWCA).

Net operating assets are fixed assets, trade investments, stock and monetary working capital, valued for the CCA balance sheet.

The gearing adjustment does assume that the proportions of debt and equity finance used in the past will continue and that any additional finance required will also be in the same proportions.

An example will illustrate the calculation of the gearing adjustment:

		£
Operating adjustments: Depreciation adjustment		100,000
COSA		80,000
MWCA		208,000
Total		388,000

Net operating assets at *Current Values*	£
Fixed assets	800,000
Investments	70,000
Stock	550,000
Monetary working capital	1,300,000
	2,720,000

This figure exceeds the historic cost figure by 320,000.

The net borrowings are:

	£
Long-term loans	400,000
Deferred tax	100,000
Bank overdraft	100,000
Taxation	50,000
	650,000

The gearing proportion is $650,000/2,720,000 = 23 \cdot 9\%$, and hence the gearing adjustment is $388,000 \times 0 \cdot 239 = 92,700$.

Current Cost Balance Sheet

The current cost balance sheet will include a restatement of the fixed assets at replacement cost and, if material, the stocks. This will necessitate an additional reserve – the current cost reserve – which is simply the sum of

(i)   the valuation surplus of the assets over the historical cost amounts, and

(ii) the cumulative totals of the CCA adjustments made to date (i.e. operating adjustments less gearing adjustments).

An example of a CCA balance sheet is shown below (not related to the previous examples).

	£		£	£
Capital and reserves		Fixed assets		
Issued share capital	3,000	Land and buildings	1,780	
Current cost reserve	3,030	*less* depreciation	680	1,100
Retained profit	4,300	Plant and machinery	16,780	
Loan capital	2,000	*less* depreciation	9,350	7,430
Current liabilities (inc. tax)	1,000	Current assets		
		Stock and work in progress	4,000	
		Trade debtors less creditors	800	
				4,800
	13,330			13,330

Current cost reserve	£
Balance 1st January	1,180
Surplus on revaluation	
Land and buildings	200
Plant and machinery	1,330
Stock and work in progress	290
Depreciation adjustments	200
Monetary working capital adjustment	100
Cost of sales adjustment	100
less Gearing adjustment	(370)
Balance 31st December	3,030

4.8 Replacement cost methods

It is possible to account so that specific changes in the price of assets are allowed for. This would apply particularly to stocks and to the depreciation of fixed assets thereby arriving at a closer estimate of the true value of an asset rather than the original cost adjusted by some general index.

There are three main possibilities:

(i) 'Replacement Cost' – the amount required to replace the stocks or capital asset by new goods of similar quality (subject to suitable depreciation in the case of a capital asset).
(ii) 'Current Realizable Value' – the amount which would be obtained if the asset was sold on the open market, and
(iii) 'Economic Value' – the present value of the discounted expected future earnings from the asset.

In a number of circumstances the figures obtained using replacement cost and current purchase price are the same, e.g. assets that consist of Stock Exchange investments or property or plant. In some cases, however, the two values would be very different. For example, if the replacement cost of some plant has gone up so much that it would no longer be economic to continue the particular process with new plant at all. 'Current realizable value' has the advantage that it reflects someone else's assessment of economic value rather than that of just the present holder.

Replacement cost accounting is not itself an alternative to CPP accounting. Replacement cost accounting can be used in conjunction with historic cost accounts, or with CPP methods, in order to show the effect of changes in the 'purchasing power of money'.

4.9 The history of inflation accounting in the U.K.: 1970–85

In the early 1970s, attention was becoming focused on the problems of accounting in inflationary times. The favoured method at that time was the CPP method, and in January 1973 an exposure draft (ED8) was issued for comment. This proposed supplementary CPP accounts for companies listed on the Stock Exchange. Shortly before the end of the consultation period for ED8, the Government announced in July 1973 that they had decided to set up an independent committee of enquiry into inflation accounting. This committee became known as the Sandilands Committee. Whilst this committee was sitting, a provisional statement of standard accounting practice (PSSAP7 'Accounting for Changes in the Purchasing Power of Money') was issued in May 1974. This non-mandatory standard was essentially the same as ED8.

In September 1975, the Sandilands Report was published. This rejected the CPP method advocated by PSSAP7 and recommended CCA. The CCA method suggested by Sandilands was not as detailed as that set out in section 4.7, and ignored the effects of inflation on monetary assets and monetary liabilities. In November 1976 an exposure draft, ED18 'Current Cost Accounting', was issued, based mainly on the Sandilands Committee recommendations. This received much criticism, and in July 1977 the Institute of Chartered Accountants in England and Wales voted against CCA being made compulsory.

November 1977 saw the Accounting Standards Committee publish Interim Recommendations on Inflation Accounting (the Hyde Guidelines). These Guidelines proposed that all quoted companies should show a separate statement showing CCA profit and loss accounts, using depreciation, cost of sales and gearing adjustments. This effectively downgraded CCA accounts to a supplement to the HC accounts, and then only related to the profit and loss position. The Hyde Guidelines proved to be more acceptable to industry than either PSSAP7 or ED18. In April 1979 another exposure draft (ED24 'Current Cost Accounting') was published. ED24 was limited to listed companies with a turnover in excess of £5 million, and proposed a supplementary CCA profit and loss account and a CCA balance sheet.

In March 1980, the first mandatory statement of standard accounting practice relating to inflation accounting (SSAP16 'Current Cost Accounting') was published. SSAP16 did not differ materially from ED24. It covered all listed companies and large non-listed companies, and allowed current cost accounts to be the main accounts if required providing that HC information was given as well. Confusion and controversy dogged SSAP16, and CCA accounts did not really receive widespread use. In March 1984, the Accounting Standards Committee issued a Statement of Intent on SSAP16 and in July 1984, an exposure draft ED35 'Accounting for the Effects of Changing Prices' proposed CCA information just as notes to the accounts for most public companies. Some proposed guidelines on simplifications to the ED35 suggestions were published in November 1984, but the move against inflation accounting was sufficient to see the withdrawal of ED35 in March 1985 followed by the suspension of the mandatory status of SSAP16 in June 1985. Many reasons can be forwarded for the absence of an agreed standard of inflation accounting. Some of these are theoretical, some are practical and others relate to the changing environment in which any accounting system has to operate. The early 1980s have seen much lower levels of inflation than the 1970s, and the outcome may have been very different if it had proved possible to introduce a standard of accounting practice on inflation accounting five years before SSAP16.

4.10 Questions and answers on inflation accounting

1.

Question: What is the essential difference between CCA and CPP?

Answer: Both are intended to show the effect of price changes on a
            company. The difference, however, is that CCA is concerned
            with *specific* changes to individual assets, whereas CCP deals
            with *general* national inflation, as measured by the Retail
            Prices Index (RPI).

            Take, for example, a large oil company such as BP; its
            operations include a tanker fleet, and refineries/chemical
            works. Specific price changes during a year will be varied. The
            replacement cost of stocks might fall as world spot prices
            decline, and the CC of the tanker fleet might also decline as a
            world-wide glut in shipping capacity prevails. Conversely, the
            CC of land, buildings, plant and equipment might rise at
            certain rates, and operating costs, such as wages, might move
            roughly in line with the RPI.

2.

Question: What is misleading about HCA?

Answer: Accounts are intended to provide users with information
            regarding the financial viability of the company, its cash flows,
            gearing, and profitability, together with a mass of other infor-
            mation as required by the Companies Acts (e.g. number of
            employees, geographical distribution of sales etc.).

            In times of price changes HC accounts fail to show (i)
            whether a company's profits are keeping up with inflation; (ii)
            whether its operating capability is being eroded; and (iii) the
            CC of assets employed.

            Consider, for example, two companies, the textiles group
            Courtaulds and the stores group Marks & Spencer (M & S). In
            one particular year, the percentage difference between HC and
            CC pre-tax profit was −218% and −13% respectively. Thus, in
            the case of a (say) £10m HC pre-tax profit reported by
            Courtaulds, the corresponding CC pre-tax figure would be a
            loss of £11.8m. For M & S, the pre-tax profit would be reduced
            from £10m (HC) to £8.7m (CC). These dramatic differences
            can be explained as follows:

(a)   *Courtaulds* is a capital intensive company. It used old (and
            hence fully depreciated) machinery. The HC depreciation

charge is negligible, so the CC depreciation adjustment, which is based on current replacement costs, is massive. Secondly, the Company's debtors require a period of credit, thereby giving rise to a MWCA.

(b)   *Marks & Spencer*, by contrast, is not a capital intensive company. It owns virtually no plant and equipment so the CC depreciation adjustment is small. Being an efficient retailer, it turns the stock around every three weeks (i.e. it takes, on average, only three weeks to buy the goods, put them into stock until required, distribute, display and finally sell them). The COSA is thus very small.

The customers of M & S pay cash at the point of sale. The trade creditors (suppliers) might be paid weeks later. Thus, the MWCA is not a charge but a credit. Furthermore, the company shows its many properties in the HC balance sheet at current valuation. The annual HCA depreciation charge on these properties is thus based on current value, and consequently no CC depreciation charge arises.

3.

Question: Which companies are winners or losers under CCA?

Answer: As illustrated above, the winners are those which are *not* capital intensive. These companies avoid the penalties of rising asset replacement costs. Other winners are those which have net current liabilities. It is disadvantageous to have trade debtors in times of inflation, because debtors effectively depreciate as prices rise.

Other examples of losers are the paper and publishing group Reed International, and Distillers. Both companies have a great deal of plant and equipment and a slow 'stock turn-around'. In the case of Reed, months, even years, may elapse during the cycle of timber felling, pulping, processing and printing, prior to making a sale. The COSA will be great. Similarly, stocks of Famous Grouse and other spirits may be aged by Distillers for years. The percentage difference, between HC and CC pre-tax profits, were – 111% for Reed and −73% for Distillers.

Generally, in inflationary times CC profits of companies are less than HC profits. This is because the effects of price changes are taken into account. CCA is thus regarded as more conservative than HCA.

4.

Question: Are investment managers in favour of CCA?

Answer: In times of low inflation, nobody is interested in CCA. It is argued that with low inflation, say, 5%, the matter is rather academic. The criticisms of CCA are listed as:

(a)   the preparation of CCA is a time-consuming, complex and costly job;

(b)   there are practical difficulties in preparation; for example, choosing appropriate indices and replacement costs. Furthermore, the gearing adjustment is, in theory, highly contentious. In practice, there are three different means of its calculation;

(c)   CCA is generally regarded as being too complex and difficult to understand; and

(d)   the Inland Revenue refuses to base corporation tax computations on CCA.

5.

Question: The future?

Answer: If low inflation prevails, CCA will continue to become more unpopular. In the early 1980s, when SSAP16 was fully operative, companies were required to prepare a full set of CCA, i.e. the CC balance sheet, P & L account, fund statement, and Notes. SSAP16 is no longer mandatory and its withdrawal in any mandatory form follows a period of over two years with inflation close to 5%.

In the mid 1970s, we saw inflation raging at over 20%. Until inflation appears to be heading again in that direction, the relevance of CCA will probably fade further into oblivion. If inflation does increase, there is a real problem in that there is no agreed method for inflation accounting.

CHAPTER FIVE

NEW ISSUES

5.1 Introduction

We have described earlier the two principal forms of company finance –
equity finance and loan finance. The mechanism of raising equity finance is
now considered in more detail.

There is a familiar pattern in the development of most successful
businesses. Frequently a sole proprietor or partnership finds that because
of the relatively high rates of personal taxation or because of the need to
restrict their personal liability, the business has to be converted into a
limited liability company (although, of course, many businesses start life as
companies). As we have seen in previous chapters, the company will use,
during its early years of growth, any source of finance that it can obtain at a
reasonable cost. If the proprietors do not have sufficient capital themselves, or personal assets in the form of securities or houses that would
provide security for an overdraft facility from a bank, they will tap other
sources of finance. Fixed assets, plant, machinery, office equipment and
vehicles can all be leased or purchased with the help of a finance house. The
true gross rates of interest on such loans, however, can often be well in
excess of 30% per annum. Working capital to finance stock and debtors
may be obtained from the bank; or by persuading suppliers to give
extended credit terms; or by factoring invoices rendered for goods
supplied.

Many companies grow to a certain size and then find that the competition in their trade does not allow them to capture a larger share of that
market; their directors may have run out of new ideas and zest or may not
wish to take the risks of new projects. Companies with vigorous, efficient
management, trading in an industry where there is scope for continued
growth, can often obtain outside capital from a merchant bank or from an
institution such as Investors in Industry (which specializes in providing
medium- or long-term finance for small- or medium-sized companies).
This capital, sometimes called 'risk capital' or 'venture capital', is usually
put up on the basis that the body providing it receives a percentage of the
equity capital and often gives financial advice and 'nurses' the company
until it can 'go public'. With these various sources of finance a successful
company can build up its business until it is of a sufficient size to be able to

approach the principal capital market, that is, the Stock Exchange. At this stage it 'goes public', with the aim of raising additional finance or realizing part of the owner's investment in the company by arranging that a portion of its share capital is offered for sale to members of the general public.

5.2 New issue organizations

Two types of body are active in the new issue market – issuing houses and stockbrokers. The main issuing houses are merchant banks and are members of the Issuing Houses Association. Non-banks and licensed dealers in securities also act as issuing houses but often for smaller issues. Stockbrokers are concerned in every issue on the Stock Exchange since it is they alone who can carry out the requirements of the Stock Exchange authorities. The involvement of an issuing house is not obligatory, however, and the sponsoring brokers may sometimes handle the whole issue alone.

New issues can be made by companies seeking a Stock Exchange listing for the first time or by companies which already have a class of listed shares, and may or may not be 'new money issues'. This latter distinction depends on whether the shares in the issue are newly created shares or whether they are shares which are already in existence and are being sold by their holders.

5.3 Methods of issue

There are a number of methods of new issue:

(a) Introduction – A Stock Exchange introduction alone cannot raise new money. It is the simplest method of creating a market in, and obtaining a listing for, existing shares. No shares are offered to the public.

(b) Offer for Subscription – This is made by, or on behalf of, the issuer of its own securities. If the offer is underwritten the underwriters agree to subscribe for shares which are not subscribed by the public.

(c) Offer for Sale – With this method the company sells its shares already in issue en bloc to an issuing house (or stockbroker) at an agreed price. The shares are then resold by the issuing house, which is therefore acting as principal, to the public. The issuing house may sell the shares at the same price or the price may be marginally higher; the differential usually covering the costs of underwriting the issue. In the former case the underwriting fee will be paid separately to the institution.

By first purchasing the shares the issuing house underwrites the issue and it usually will arrange to share the risk that the subsequent sale to the public may be unsuccessful by arranging sub-underwriting with investing institutions such as pension funds and life assurance companies. An example of an offer for sale was the issue of British Telecom in 1984.

(d) Placing – With this method the shares are acquired by the issuing house but instead of being resold to the public are 'placed' with clients of the issuing house. At least 25% of the issue must be made available to the public through the market, i.e. the stockjobber. The Stock Exchange limits the size of placings by companies and a placing is normally permitted by the Quotations Committee of the Stock Exchange only when there is unlikely to be significant demand for the securities or for very small companies. Costs are lower than for a public issue because of the avoidance of underwriting.

(e) Issue by Tender – This is similar to the ordinary offer for sale or offer for subscription except that the shares are not offered to the public at a fixed price. A minimum price only is stated in the prospectus and the public are invited to submit a tender stating a price and the number of shares they would accept at this price. The total issue is usually allocated at the highest price which would clear the issue and maintain an orderly after market.

(f) Rights Issue – With this method a company (already listed on the Stock Exchange) offers its shareholders the right to subscribe cash for further shares in proportion to their existing shareholdings, generally at a discount to the ruling market price. If the shareholders do not wish to take up their rights they can sell them in the market. Typically the issue will be underwritten by the issuing house and sub-underwritten by the institutions. The Companies Acts require that issues of new shares for cash be offered pro rata to existing shareholders unless the prior approval of those shareholders has been obtained at a general meeting. The privilege is known as pre-emptive rights.

(g) Vendor Placing – When one company purchases another or part of another it may offer shares as consideration to the vendor. If these are not required by the vendor they are placed with institutions at a discount to the market price and the vendor receives cash.

The table below shows the amount of new money raised from the various methods of issue in the year to 31st March 1985. The figures for introductions, offer for subscription, offer for sale and placings include the full value of the company even when only part of the shares

were offered for sale. The rights issue amounts are the proceeds of the
actual issue only.

New issues – Year to 31st March 1985

Method	Number of companies	Listing value £m
Introductions	3	38
Introductions (previously on USM)	17	645
Offer for subscription	1	11
Offer for sale (fixed price)	17	8622
Offer for sale (by tender)	5	1272
Placing	2	26
Rights issues	127	2364

The offer for sale for British Telecom (with a listed value of £7,800m)
dominates the issues but, excluding this, the most popular way of raising
money was by a rights issue. There are substantial fluctuations in the
amounts raised by each method of issue each year depending on
companies' demands for funds and the state of the market. Details of issues
on the Unlisted Securities Market (USM) are given in section 5.14.

5.4 Mechanics of a new issue

A company seeking a listing must be represented when dealing with the
Quotations Department of the Stock Exchange by a broking member firm.
Hence when wishing to make a new issue a company or its issuing house/
merchant bank adviser appoints one or more firm(s) as sponsoring
broker(s). The issuing house produces drafts of the prospectus and other
documents through the sponsoring broker for checking by the Quotations
Department which will advise on whether further information is necessary
for disclosure to the public. The sponsoring broker and issuing house
advise on the price of the issue.

The timing of any sizeable issue (over £3 million) is controlled by the
Bank of England through the Government Broker. The sponsoring broker
applies to the Government Broker for an 'impact day' on which the issue
will be announced and the sub-underwriters approached. The Bank's
responsibility in this area is to ensure that the announcements of large
issues do not coincide, and that the total number of new issues open in the
market at any one time is not excessive. Further, the Government Broker
will try to spread the effect of large subscriptions for new money so that, for

example, the subscription to a large rights issue does not coincide with the subscription to a new government loan.

Immediately before the announcement of a new issue the principal underwriting is agreed. On impact day the sponsoring broker or the issuing house will, where relevant, arrange for the issue to be sub-underwritten by institutional investors. Institutions agreeing to participate in an underwriting will be rewarded with a commission out of the proceeds of the issue amounting normally to 1¼ per cent. When the underwriting of an issue is complete, and prior to the subscription for the shares, the sponsoring broker will apply formally to the Quotations Committee for a listing. Once listing has been granted, dealing in the new securities will normally take place in the Stock Exchange on the day after shareholders are sent their provisional allotment of shares.

The Stock Exchange's listing requirements include the arrangements for the issue and the content of the prospectus, for a record of trading covering at least five years, and for a wide spread of shareholders. Initial charges are payable to the Stock Exchange by listed companies when seeking a listing for their securities, the amount being related to the expected market value of the securities. In addition, an annual listing fee is payable related to the nominal value of listed equity.

5.5 Practice overseas

It is useful to compare the position in the United Kingdom with that in Continental Europe where stock exchanges exist in all the financial centres but do not operate on such a sophisticated scale. On the Continent, and especially in Germany and the Benelux countries, the banks provide the main source of buyers to the principal shareholders of companies who wish to realize their investment. One of the principal reasons why the capital market in this country has been able to develop is that the disclosure requirements laid down by the Companies Act and by the Stock Exchange are sufficiently stringent to safeguard investors and to provide them with the necessary information about the economy to be able to make a reliable judgement of its prospects and work. In particular, the requirement that the figures for subsidiaries must be consolidated with those of the holding company ensures that the investor has a meaningful picture of the assets and profits of the group as a whole; there was of course a flourishing capital market before this requirement became law in 1948, but in the intervening period investors have become far more sophisticated and accountancy techniques and attitudes have also developed to a high level.

The EEC has issued three Directives on listings. These apply to all EEC countries and lay down minimum legal requirements and provide a degree

of standardization. In the U.K. these were implemented in the Stock
Exchange (Listing) Regulations 1984, but the overall requirements for
listings in the U.K. are stricter than the Directives and of most other
European Exchanges.

The mechanics of raising fresh capital in the U.S.A. are rather different.
Issues are normally made by offers to the general public and only rarely by
offers to existing shareholders through subscription rights because U.S.
stock exchanges impose no requirement on companies comparable to that
in the U.K. to give their shareholders pre-emptive rights. A syndicate
usually buys the entire issue and takes its remuneration as the difference
between the public offer price and the price it pays the issuing company. It
is entitled to conduct stabilizing transactions in order to maintain the
market price of securities during the offer period.

5.6 Requirement for public issue

'Going Public' implies responsibilities to the public shareholders, and it
also involves a detailed prospectus which requires a thorough study of each
aspect of the company's business. If the issuing house is not already fully
aware of the company's activities it will have a number of meetings with
officials of the company and will visit the company's premises and examine
its operations. At this stage the requirements of the principal shareholders
of the company and the appropriate policy for the company will be made
clear, and any problems of preparing and presenting the company will
come to light. Although the business may have flourished over the years
and achieved a size acceptable for a flotation, many of the aspects of its
organization may need rationalizing or placing on a formal basis – in fact, it
needs a spring cleaning operation:

(a) The capital structure may need simplifying, for it may be unsuitable
    requiring an increase in the authorized and issued share capital; or the
    company may be heavily dependent on short-term loans which need
    funding on a longer-term basis.

(b) The business of the company may depend on unwritten agreements
    that need formalizing; or there may be business transactions between
    the company and partly owned subsidiaries or associated companies
    which need rationalizing. Similarly, management contracts may need
    formalizing.

(c) Any special processes that the company operates may need to be
    protected by the registering of a business name, trademark, or patent.

(d) The assets in the balance sheet may not be in a suitable form for a prospectus. For example, land and buildings may need to be revalued, or the company's factories and premises may be leased at uncommercial rates, possibly from a friendly party.

The issuing house will also advise on the best time to come to the market – it would not be wise to float too close to a budget or a general election and naturally the owners wish to come to the market when prices are high and conditions are favourable for new issues. This is why the new issue market tends to be either very active or very slack. Indeed, there are periods when the market is difficult and when new issues in any form are impossible or alternatively the type and size of new issues may be very restricted. Even when the market is propitious the time needed for the preparation of the issue and the incidence of the company's financial year (for reasonably up-to-date figures are needed, and often also the need to forecast the current year's results) are constricting factors. Finally, the issuing house will organize the mechanics and timetable of the operation, co-ordinating the professional advisers (mainly solicitors, accountants and stockbrokers), each of whom plays an important part in the issue.

The roles of the professional advisers may overlap to some extent; for example, the drafting of the prospectus is sometimes the responsibility of the issuing house but may equally be prepared by the solicitors to the issue. The pricing of an offer for sale is usually decided by the issuing house on the advice of the stockbrokers but it can be decided by either of them.

It is the solicitor's responsibility to examine the Memorandum and Articles of Association of the company and to eliminate any unusual or restrictive clauses. The Memorandum sets out the name of the company, its objects and nature of the business to be conducted. It is usual for the objects to be framed as widely as possible, for a company incorporated under the Companies Acts has no power to do anything not authorized by the objects clause in its Memorandum. The Articles of Association set out the rights of the shareholders and include, in particular, the powers of the directors, rules for the conduct of meetings of shareholders, the form of issued capital and method of transfer of stock and share certificates, borrowing powers, and requirements for the preparation of accounts and payment of dividends.

A company must hold an annual general meeting at least once in each calendar year and within fifteen months of the previous annual general meeting. Extraordinary general meetings are, as the name would suggest, convened for special purposes. There are rules in the Companies Acts, if not in the Articles of Association, for the convening of meetings, the voting majorities necessary for various types of resolutions, and the use of proxy votes. In a private company the Articles of Association must contain, inter alia, a clause restricting the right to transfer the shares and they often contain clauses limiting the choice of directors or restricting severely the borrowing powers of the company.

The solicitor prepares details of all material contracts entered into within the two years preceding the issue which are not in the ordinary course of trading. He scrutinizes and provides details of directors' service contracts and any employee share incentive scheme. He will also prepare the trust deed if there is an issue of debenture stock (a debenture or loan stock has a trustee who represents the holders and guards their interests and the trust deed sets out the security and safeguards which protect the lender), and examines and summarizes the terms for the conversion of a convertible security.

The accountants have two crucial parts to play. They are usually asked to investigate the company by preparing a 'long form' report on the company which is going public. This is a report of anything over 20 pages (but normally much longer) setting out the details of the company's history, its management, activities and premises, together with a breakdown of its turnover and profits and a summary of the balance sheets for the five years preceding the issue. The report is produced after a thorough examination of the company's accounts over the five-year period, after visiting the company's premises and after talking to the company's directors and officials. It is common for this report to be produced by a firm of accountants who are not the auditors of the company's accounts and they are referred to as the reporting accountants.

The 'long form' report is usually produced during the two to three months prior to the prospectus being advertised and provides the information to the other parties involved. The solicitors for instance can extract details of tax clearances that have not been obtained and which have to be covered by indemnities. The stockbroker's new issues department will examine it carefully since it will disclose more information than would normally be available from the published accounts and it would provide much of the background information to enable the issue price to be struck.

The 'long form' report also provides the information for the 'short form' report which is included in the prospectus itself. This consists of the five-year profit record, the statement of net assets at the end of each of the preceding five years, and a history of dividend payments over the five-year period. The report is set out as a letter addressed to the issuing house and the company and it is one of the most important parts of the prospectus since it gives an immediate guide to the company over its recent past. If there is an independent firm of reporting accountants the short form report will usually be addressed to the directors by both the auditors and the reporting accountants.

The brokers to the issue will have three main functions. Details of the company and, in particular, of the prospectus have to be approved by the Quotations Department of the Stock Exchange before they are published. These details are channelled through the brokers who will negotiate with the Quotations Department any difficult problems in the drawing up of the prospectus. Secondly, they will suggest the price at which the issue should be offered to the public. Their close connections with the market, supported by their analyst's reports on the industry and comparable companies, provide them with the information on which the pricing will be based. It is important that the company's debut in the market is successful within the two conflicting aims: the need to realize as high a price as possible for the benefit of the vendors; and the need to find sufficient support to ensure the shares are received enthusiastically by buyers. Finally, the brokers will arrange the sub-underwriting of the issue. In general an issue would be regarded as successful if the share price in early dealing was up to 10% above the issue price; and regarded as unsuccessful if sub-underwriters were called upon to take up part of the issue.

There are two other bodies who are often involved in an issue though not to such an extent. In times of a bull market (that is, when share prices are rising and there is investment optimism) some new issues are so attractive that they are very heavily over-subscribed – up to 100 times in some cases; and in exceptional cases this can happen even in a declining (or 'bear') market. The physical job of handling the applications, cashing the cheques relating to the successful applications, and returning those that are unsuccessful is so enormous that a clearing bank is frequently appointed as a receiving banker to an issue. The size of their staff enables them to concentrate a large number of people on to the job which is completed within the space of two or three days. At the time of the new issue an 'outside' registrar (frequently a corporate body) is often appointed, although they are not involved to any great extent in the issue. Their work starts at this time, for they are responsible for the issue of the first registered certificates and they normally make the dividend and interest payments, etc. As the handling of share transfers is a task which is technical and tedious, it is far more easily carried out by a professional registrar. Companies are required by law and by their Articles to keep a proper register of members and to make it available for inspection at certain times.

5.7 The prospectus

Turning back now to the prospectus itself, this follows a well-established pattern. Although it is effectively an advertisement there are very clear, well-defined rules which have to be followed, rules laid down by the Companies Act 1985 and the Stock Exchange. The Companies Act rules are not extensive but have been considerably enlarged by the Stock Exchange requirements which are revised more frequently. Although the Stock Exchange does not carry out such continuous policing activities as the Securities and Exchange Commission in the U.S.A., its requirements for a prospectus are as financially stringent as those of the SEC. The SEC, however, also requires a disclosure of the commercial structure and method of operation of the company.

An example of a prospectus is printed in full in Appendix 2. Whilst not all follow the same style of presentation, the following structural pattern is common:

(a) Name of company
(b) Details of share capital
(c) Statement of company's borrowings.
(d) Name of issuing house
(e) Details of number and price of shares offered for sale
(f) Details of: Directors
                   Bankers
                   Brokers
                   Solicitors
                   Auditors
                   Reporting accountants
                   Registered office
                   Registrar's and transfer office.
(g) 'Long letter' from the chairman of the company to the issuing house setting out the history and nature of the business, including a detailed background of the directors and often a profit forecast or profit illustration on certain assumptions
(h) Reporting accountant's report
(i) Statutory and general information

Date of incorporation
Details of share capital of company
Details of subsidiaries
Details of Articles of Association, including the voting rights of share-holders and borrowing powers of the company
Details of subscription of shares by the issuing house.

Summary of material contracts entered into within the preceding two years, not in the ordinary course of business

Directors' and family interests in the company following the issue
Particulars of shares to be issued under an executive share incentive scheme
Extract from any trust deed constituting a debenture or loan stock.

Details of expenses of issue and underwriting commission given
Details of any pending litigation or material claims
Whether a close company or not
Amount required to be raised to cover preliminary and issue expenses and to provide working capital
Statement by the directors that following the issue the company will have sufficient working capital.

(j) Consent and documents

Each independent reporting adviser must make a statement that he has given, and not withdrawn, his consent to the issue of his report.

Details of these consents and the full reports from each adviser, the company's accounts, and the Memorandum and Articles of Association must be made available for public inspection for fourteen days following the publication of the advertisement.

(k) Form of application

A form setting out the minimum number of shares to be applied for by the subscriber stating when the application lists will open and close, and the multiples in which applications should be made.

5.8 Allotment letters

If, following the offer for sale, there is an excess of applications, they are either subjected to a ballot or reduced in appropriate proportions to the amount of shares being offered to the public. The basis of allotment is then published and dealings will commence three or four days after allotment. If the number of applications falls short of the number offered for sale, the underwriters will be called upon to take up pro rata the number of shares not applied for by the public.

It is usual with offers for sale for the new shares to be issued initially in 'Allotment Letter' form. This means that the applicant is issued with a letter stating his allotment of stock, which can be partly paid or fully paid depending on whether part subscription or full subscription is demanded on application.

Allotment letters are dealt in as cash stocks, usually for a period of five to six weeks. They can be renounced on the signature of the original allottee and after that subsequent holders do not have to sign, so that the letters are effectively bearer stocks until the eventual owner's name is inserted in order that he can become registered. Renounced letters can be split into similar letters for smaller amounts. Allotment letters are also used for 'rights' issues but in this instance the holder is issued with a provisional allotment letter 'nil paid' which becomes a partly paid or fully paid allotment letter when he accepts the stock; in other respects they are the same as other allotment letters.

5.9 Underwriting and sub-underwriting

When an issue is made using an offer for sale it is usual for the issuing house to purchase all the issue which is to be offered to the public. The issue is therefore underwritten by the issuing house and the vendor is then certain of receiving the price which he expects for the entire shareholding which is offered for sale. The risk that the public will not purchase all the shares is transferred to the issuing house but they would not wish to retain all this risk. Hence sub-underwriting of the issue is arranged by the sponsoring broker with institutions which agree to take up a certain amount of stock if the public do not fully subscribe for the stock, in exchange for a commission. The sub-underwriting commission depends on the time for which the institution is at risk but is commonly $1\frac{1}{4}\%$ + VAT. For example, if 10 million shares are being issued at £1.50 each, there might be 100 sub-underwriters each underwriting 100,000 shares for $1\frac{1}{4}\%$ of £150,000 (i.e. £1,875). If 20% of the issue was not subscribed by the public, the sub-underwriters would each have to subscribe for 20% of 100,000 shares at £1.50 (i.e. £30,000), but would receive the sub-underwriting commission (£1,875 in this case) irrespective of whether the issue was fully subscribed or not.

A similar demand for underwriting and sub-underwriting results at the time of a rights issue from an issuing company's wish to obtain the full amount of the desired finance, despite the possibility of an adverse movement in the share price eliminating the discount during the rights issue. The larger the initial discount the less the risk of the rights issue failing. Beyond a certain point the risk will become so small that for practical purposes it can be ignored. In recent years a small number of companies have taken advantage of this to avoid the cost of underwriting by making rights issues at a 'deep discount' to the existing share price. A rights issue which is underwritten may be issued at about $12\frac{1}{2}\%$ to 15% discount to the market price, i.e. if the share price was 200p, the rights issue may be at 170p to 175p. A 'deep discount' rights issue may be at say 50% or more discount i.e. at 100p in this case. For example, on 7th March 1985 Barclays Bank shares were priced at 583p, but a 'one for one' rights issue was announced at 150p. A rights issue at this price has the effect of making the post rights share price much smaller – in this case about 366p. It has not been clear in all cases, however, whether the use of deep discounting has been the result of a deliberate choice or because of difficulties in obtaining underwriting on acceptable terms.

Provided they intend to take up all their rights, shareholders should in principle be indifferent to the size of the discount on a rights issue. Different sets of terms will lead to different share prices after the issue and to different numbers of shares in circulation. This should not affect shareholders other than psychologically since the value of the company will be the same in each case, as will the fraction of the company which each shareholder owns. Shareholders who are unable or unwilling to take up their rights are faced with an inevitable dilution of their interest in assets and earnings. The extent of this dilution does not depend upon the amount of the discount. If the discount is large the market value of the nil paid rights is also high, and the shareholders can in principle sell enough of them to enable them to take up the same proportion of the allotment as if the shares had been offered at a lower discount. In doing so they will, however, incur selling costs and a potential capital gains tax liability.

5.10 Reverse takeovers

At one time it was possible to achieve a public quotation by the unorthodox method of a 'reverse takeover'. Suppose Company A, a highly successful private company which wants to obtain a listing and to extend its business, thinks of taking over Company B, which is a somewhat ailing company with a fair business or assets and a quotation. Then it used to be better for Company B to take over Company A for shares, which were after all listed shares, on terms which gave Company A's shareholders a large share of the equity and which left Company A's management running the business; by this means Company A acquired Company B and achieved a listing. However, the Stock Exchange has clamped down on this method and on the use of 'shell companies' which was the description given to a company if it had a listing, perhaps cash, and no business. Nowadays reverse takeovers involve the automatic suspension of the quotation and the procedures for re-listing are identical to those for a completely new company.

5.11 Timing of rights issues

The timing of rights issues is determined primarily by movements in share prices, both in general and in those of the particular company concerned.

Companies prefer to seek additional outside equity when their share prices seem to be relatively high, and the cost of new equity consequently appears to be low, and to avoid them when prices are low except in cases of overriding need, for example, to reduce gearing. The result is that rights issues tend to come in cycles. Great attention is paid by companies and their advisers to careful timing with respect to market conditions and in some cases shareholders are left rather in the dark about the purposes for which the issue is being made.

It is sometimes argued that this phenomenon may be partly caused by a misconceived idea of the real cost of equity capital and by an implicit distinction in the minds of company management between the interests of the company and those of its shareholders. Strictly speaking, the cost of equity capital is not determined simply by the current dividend yield and share price, but also by anticipated future dividend payments. When share prices are high in relation to current dividend yields this may reflect an expectation on the shareholders' part of future earnings growth.

In practice, however, companies may not see it in this way. Current dividend commitments are known while future increases are discretionary and problematical. It is therefore understandable that managements should wish to raise new equity at a time when the associated dividend commitment is low and, conversely, that they should avoid raising permanent capital when the immediate cost is high. Moreover, if they are unwilling to contemplate cutting their dividend at the time of a rights issue the immediate effect on their cash flow will be greater the lower the price at which the issue is made.

A further factor is that when share prices are low management and long-term shareholders may believe their company to be undervalued in terms of what they regard as realistic asset values. A rights issue in such circumstances would compel those shareholders who cannot take up their rights to cede part of their interest in the company on what they would regard as unfavourable terms.

For these reasons, many companies feel compelled to raise long-term funds in advance of known requirements when conditions seem favourable, for fear that when the funds are needed conditions will have deteriorated.

5.12 Vendor placings

If a company wishes to raise additional finance by means of the issue of shares then such shares must be offered pro rata to existing shareholders (i.e. a rights issue) unless the shareholders agree as set out in sections 89 to 95 of the Companies Act 1985.

If a company wishes to take over another company or acquire assets it can issue shares to the vendors who can sell them if they so wish. If the vendors require cash the shares can be placed with institutions to provide the cash sum required. This avoids prolonged selling of the shares which may depress the price. The shares are effectively issued by the company and then placed with institutions to raise the required cash. For example, in February 1985 Rowntree Mackintosh plc decided that they wished to acquire a U.S. company called the Original Cookie Company for U.S.$ 36 million. U.S.$31 million of the purchase price was financed by the allotment of 8 million Rowntree Mackintosh shares to institutional investors at 353¼p per share (compared with a market price on the date of the announcement of 365p). This method of financing a purchase is far less cumbersome than a rights issue. It is convenient for institutions which can receive large amounts of equity at a slight discount to the prevailing market price but small investors may feel that vendor placings leave them with a diluted interest in the company, without the opportunity to participate in a rights issue or in the vendor placing at a discount.

5.13 Share placings

The main reason for predominance of rights issues as a way of raising additional equity is that it is a requirement of the Stock Exchange listing agreement that any substantial issue of new shares must be made in this way except in exceptional circumstances. Small issues can, however, be made by way of a 'placing' with clients of the issuing house or sponsoring broker and with the jobbers.

It has been suggested that this limitation should be relaxed in order to facilitate the raising of equity capital by smaller listed companies. Such companies, it has been argued, are sometimes inhibited from making rights issues because by comparison with larger companies their shares are held to a greater extent by private shareholders who may not have the means to take up their rights. In these circumstances a placing would give the company greater security of being able to place shares in firm hands, and of avoiding the risk of a rights issue being left with the underwriters creating a subsequent weak market in the shares. A further factor is that rights issues are more expensive than placings for small amounts. It is estimated, for example, that, ignoring the discount, a rights issue to raise £1 million would normally cost 4 to 4½ per cent of the proceeds including underwriting fees whereas a placing for the same amount would probably cost between 2¾ per cent and 3¼ per cent.

5.14 The Unlisted Securities Market

During the 1970s there was a marked fall in the number of companies seeking a full Stock Exchange listing. This in part reflected the general economic climate, with low profitability, and the attractions of bank finance as a means of financing expansion. It also was because of the disclosure conditions imposed on listed companies by the Stock Exchange and the costs of obtaining a listing. Some companies believed that the initial costs and the continuing burdens of regulation on listed companies outweighed the potential benefits from a listing. The Stock Exchange did permit occasional deals in unlisted securities under Rule 163 and, after increased publicity was given to this Rule in 1977, several companies issued securities specifically with a view to their being traded on this market. This raised regulatory problems. Whilst it was clearly desirable for the Stock Exchange to aim to satisfy the needs of small and developing companies there were obvious problems in continuing to deal with the needs of these companies in an unregulated environment, with no disclosure requirements, and using a rule mechanism designed for occasional deals.

With a view to placing this type of trading on a sounder footing the Stock Exchange set up, in November 1980, the Unlisted Securities Market (USM). Companies whose shares were likely to be frequently traded would have to obtain a USM listing (or a full listing), and Rule 163(2) (now called Rule 535(2)) is now used for genuinely occasional transactions.

The USM is much closer in form to the listed market than the previous market under Rule 163(2). The listing requirements for the USM are less onerous than for the main market and the major differences are as follows:

(i)   Only 10% of the shares of the company need to be sold for a USM issue, compared with 25% for a full listing.

(ii)   Companies need only have a three-year trading record for the USM, compared with five years for a full listing. In addition, it is possible for companies with no trading record but with a fully developed product or project to come to the USM.

(iii)   Much less advertising is required for a USM listing with a consequent cost reduction.

(iv)   A USM company must send a circular to shareholders for transactions exceeding 25% of its size, whereas a listed company has to report transactions exceeding 15%.

The total costs of a USM issue are substantially less than a full listing. Full listings via placings can cost between £50,000 and £200,000 whilst full listings via an offer for sale will for most companies cost between £250,000 and £600,000.

In general, USM companies are younger and the management has less of a track record. The Stock Exchange warns that USM companies have not been subjected to the more rigorous examination and degree of regulation as those whose shares are traded on the main Exchange. The term 'unlisted' for this secondary market is, in some senses, rather misleading. USM shares are traded in the same way as those with a full listing, and the latest trading prices are also published in *The Financial Times* and in the Stock Exchange 'Official List'.

The USM has had considerable success in attracting companies that were not prepared to apply for a full listing. At the end of March 1985, there were 282 companies traded on the USM with a total capitalization of £3,334 million. (In comparison, there are 2887 companies with listed status.) A larger number of companies than the 282 above have come to the USM but some have obtained full listings, have been acquired or have been suspended from USM listing. Approximately 23% of companies coming to the USM had their shares introduced, 64% used the placing method, 10% had an offer for sale and 3% have used a tender offer.

The interest in USM securities can be out of proportion to the amount of stock available since USM companies are often small and offer only a low percentage of their equity to the public. Valuation of a share will be difficult in many situations, particularly where products are novel and untried. In many cases a USM share will offer the prospect of substantial potential returns, coupled with a higher level of risk than with many listed companies. In these circumstances, it is not surprising that large price fluctuations can occur in USM shares and price volatility can be expected to be much greater than for large company listed shares.

The development of the USM does not appear to have hampered companies from obtaining a full listing. In the late 1960s and early 1970s about fifty companies obtained a listing each year, but in the second half of the 1970s the annual figure was well below this. By contrast, in the year to 31st March 1984, 136 companies obtained a listing and 149 companies did so in the year to 31st March 1985. New companies admitted to the USM in these two years were 106 and 89 respectively, so entrance to the USM was not as popular as to listed status in these years.

The Stock Exchange does also permit a continuous market in the shares of certain mineral exploration companies which do not have a full listing or USM status. This is done using Rule 535(3) (previously Rule 163(3)).

5.15 High-risk finance

In this section we are concerned more particularly with considerations which arise with the financing of a project involving an unusually high degree of risk, by which we mean projects with a positive expectation of substantial gain associated with a relatively high chance of failure. The extent to which an economy is prepared to encourage projects of this sort is often argued to be directly related to its rate of growth. It is also sometimes suggested that the U.K. financial system has particular difficulty in coping with high-risk projects and that this alleged inefficiency is likely to have particularly serious implications over the next decade or so because of the need to assimilate and develop the new technologies which are now becoming available. It is possible that an increasing share of industry's requirements for external finance will be associated with high-risk projects. To put this in context, however, it has to be pointed out that the most substantial part of all investments, including high-risk investment, is financed out of retentions by existing companies and that the willingness of companies, and individuals, to take risks is conditioned by a wide range of factors of which the availability of finance is only one.

In practice, there is no single feature which distinguishes 'high risk' from other forms of investment. There is a spectrum of risk affecting all investment. This makes it extremely difficult, if not impossible, to generalize very meaningfully either about what determines whether or not a company undertakes high-risk projects or about their financing. There are a large number of factors affecting risk of which the nature and state of development of the technology involved are only two. Other related considerations include, for example, the length of time before projects come to fruition, the extent to which they involve the penetration of new markets, the amount of preliminary market research and the demands placed on existing management capability or experience.

The size of the project in relation to that of the company involved is important in a number of ways. An established large firm with a proven track record is likely to have sufficient access to the capital markets on the strength of its balance sheet at most times to finance reasonable propositions, even if it is unable to do so out of retentions. Large companies are also more likely to have the experience and resources to take advantage of the various techniques for reducing risk including, for example, market and other research.

Small companies have particular difficulties in undertaking high-risk projects. By definition any given project is more likely to be large in relation to the size of the firm, and the resources which can be devoted to it in terms of finance and management more limited. A small firm may, however, be unwilling to enter into a joint venture because of reluctance on the part of the proprietors to surrender control or cede part of the equity. It may be possible to get round this by some form of royalty arrangement. This is a method often preferred, for example, by the National Research Development Corporation (NRDC) and is also used in the Department of Trade's Market Entry Guarantee Scheme (MEGS). But such solutions do not help where the constraint is one of managerial resources. The best course for a small company with a big idea is often to get itself taken over by a larger firm.

As mentioned earlier the main source of finance for investment is retained profits. As most high-risk investment is undertaken by established companies it follows that most of this is also financed out of profits. Where retentions are insufficient, the companies concerned can go to the capital markets in the normal way to augment their resources. Only in exceptional circumstances would the funds so raised be earmarked for particular projects.

New ventures are unable to raise risk finance through a full Stock Exchange listing because of a requirement that companies seeking a listing should be able to demonstrate a record of success covering at least five years. The requirement for a wide spread of shareholders may also be a barrier. Issuing houses can, however, raise capital for a new venture from their institutional and private clients on the basis of a Companies Act prospectus, and the Stock Exchange does in certain circumstances allow shares in such companies to be dealt in under Rule 535 or on the Unlisted Securities Market (USM).

Assistance with the financing of high-risk investment has also been available in the past from the public sector through, for example, interest relief grants via the National Enterprise Board and the regional development agencies or, where the product or process involved is of a technological kind, from the NRDC.

The development of provision of venture capital has accelerated in the 1980s and a number of funds have been established which enable institutions and individuals to invest in new companies at an early stage of development.

The government introduced generous tax incentives in 1981 for individuals investing in the Business Start-up Scheme and subsequently the Business Expansion Scheme (BES). Whilst some institutions such as pension funds and insurance companies do get involved in venture capital, the tax reliefs for the private investor through the BES mean that private investors are more likely to finance new ventures than institutions. Private investors can also often take higher levels of risk than institutions particularly since BES investors effectively have a substantial slice of their investments paid for by tax relief.

(a) Venture capital

The term 'venture capital' is often used to describe investments in non-quoted stocks. It is a term equally often used to describe investments in very young companies or start-up situations and implies a high risk reward ratio for such an investment.

The wider definition of non-quoted stocks will range from green field start-up situations through investments in companies in various stages of development to larger Management Buy Outs and Institutional Syndications. The final category sometimes includes investments arranged only a short time before a Stock Exchange quotation is obtained.

Set out below are the prime reasons for investing institutions contemplating investments in non-quoted, often small, companies:

(i) A potentially higher return than is available from other traditional areas of institutional investment. This arises from the following factors:

   (A) the potentially high growth rate of some small, dynamic companies

   (B) the 'Quotation Kicker' which gives the valuation of any stock a once and for all uplift at the time of listing (mature non-quoted companies are normally valued on a 25–50% discount to their expected market value if quoted)

   (C) the terms that can be negotiated for unquoted risk money in small companies can in certain circumstances generate a good running yield.

(ii) A higher profile amongst small- and medium-sized companies which could bring positive spin-offs to an investing institution's main business and, indeed, help cement a business relationship.

(iii) A possible political defence to Government criticism of institutional use of funds.

It is reckoned for the reasons outlined above that a non-quoted investment portfolio can generate between 20% and 25% per annum return to a long-term investor (before management expenses). It is reasonable to anticipate returns on individual investments of between 25% and 50%. Indeed, some will achieve much more than this, while others will be total failures. These figures are, of necessity, estimates since past performance cannot be strictly correlated to the future. In any event, non-quoted institutional investment in the U.K. has a relatively short history with much of the pool remaining as on-going investments. Figures for the U.S.A. indicate that these figures may be conservative. U.S. venture capitalists claim returns from portfolios as high as 39% p.a.

It should be noted at this stage that if, for example, 5% of a fund is invested in non-quoted investments which achieve an annual return of 22.5%, this would add 0.5% to an overall return on total funds of 13%.

Department of Trade and Industry valuation regulations for insurance companies will require many of the likely investments to be written down below cost and many of them written down to zero even when their prospects remain good.

It must be emphasized from the outset that non-qoted investments require a long-term view to be taken since only in very rare circumstances can they be traded. Investment realization, an important factor in the review of any such investment, tends to come from flotations, acquisitions by other companies, or redemptions. The majority of holdings will remain unquoted for a considerable time and therefore, dividend/interest income must not be overlooked and hopes must not be set too high for an eventual divestment.

(b) Types of non-quoted investment

Non-quoted investments can be divided into the following broad categories:

(i)	Green Field Start-ups	Totally new ventures albeit with management with some experience in the area of operations.
(ii)	Early Stage Developments	Very young companies that might have developed a product and be seeking to bring it to market. Indeed, at this stage the company might have a balance sheet deficit arising out of development costs and justified in a valuation by way of the cost of entering the market.
(iii)	Early Stage Tranche Financing	This could include either of the two categories above but be funded in stages, giving the investing institutions the ability to monitor the progress of the company and limit the down-side risk.
(iv)	Development Finance	More mature companies. The finance required is clearly less than

the value of the company before refinancing. There is an ongoing business which may be looking to finance a particular project.

(v)   Management Buy-outs (MBOs)   Again more mature companies where their holding companies are looking to divest. These should have a good all-round management with at least reasonable prospects for the future. The terms of the deal to the investor are often less attractive than the other categories but the risks involved should also be reduced.

(vi)   Late Stage Syndications   Like the larger MBOs these tend to be organized by large development capital investors, merchant banks or stockbrokers. These are usually mature companies which need finance for expansion to carry them through to a market quote in a relatively short period of time.

(c) Investor protection

When investing in usually small, non-quoted, companies the institutional investor cannot rely on the protections of the Stock Exchange. In addition, the management may be used to running the business for its own ultimate benefit as shareholders. The institutional investor, therefore, needs to build into the investment agreements certain protections and rights to information. The shares used often have more complex rights than those found in quoted companies, for example, giving priority of dividend payment and capital repayment before other shares, providing for a minimum dividend and a set formula for participating in profits. The possibility of the ultimate sale of the company is provided for by way of conversion rights and redemptions to simplify the final structure. A package of ordinary shares, preference shares and loan stock can be appropriate in certain circumstances.

It is equally important for the investor to show an interest in the management, their problems and their successes and to have an empathy with their situation. Where necessary, it is important to be able to call on the skills of consultants, advisers and contacts to help with their problems and help them expand into new markets and ultimately achieve the investment return requirements.

(d) Investment using specialist funds
Some institutions use specialist funds for higher-risk investment. The principal reasons are:

(i)   To invest in non-quoted investments without committing the necessary resources in-house.
(ii)   To obtain a portfolio spread of risk and potential rewards.
(iii)   To gain access to a flow of deals which might not be available to the institution in the normal course of business.
(iv)   Where possible to have the opportunity of investing alongside the investee fund, where the opportunity looks particularly good, thereby increasing the potential return for the institution.
(v)   To benefit from the experience and abilities of the investment managers where they are able to contribute positively to the success of the companies in which they invest.

Investment through funds can be expected to reduce the potential overall return by about 4% to 6% per annum due to the costs of management. However, when making comparisons with direct management of unquoted investments by an institution, it is important that allowance is also made for the internal investment management costs of the institution. For example, a fund of £50 million in unquoted assets directly managed by the institution, may require between four and six managers and analysts, plus back-up staff and facilities. This reflects the normally high rejection rate of proposals; the need for individually negotiated terms; the necessary checking of references; the drafting and completing of legal documentation and, ultimately, the monitoring and 'after care' of investments made.

5.16 Over the counter (OTC) markets

There has been an OTC market in existence since the early 1970s. A firm called MJH Nightingale (now called Granville) commenced to operate a matched buyer/seller market. Granville do not take a position in the shares, and the system permits sellers to avoid disposals of shares to undesirable holders. This allows mature private businesses to obtain a public quote whilst retaining control over their business.

The second type of OTC market is the one which has mushroomed over the last three or four years. The market is made by about a dozen licensed dealers in securities (e.g. Harvard Securities, Hill Woolgar, Prior Harwin), and has grown from about 20 stocks to around 150 stocks in three years. This is due partly to the publicity given to the USM and the wish of many companies to include some sort of public quote in their corporate plans, and to the Business Expansion Scheme (BES), which gives tax advantages to investors at the time of a share issue (subject to certain conditions) providing that the share does not have a full listing or USM quotation.

The OTC provides capital to mature companies as well as those requiring venture capital for speculative ventures. The licensed dealers operate as market makers and charge no commission to their clients. They make their money from the difference in buying and selling prices, and from the 'long' or 'short' positions which they may take in the shares.

The OTC market makers have expanded the shares in which they deal over the last couple of years to include a number of shares which are listed on the Stock Exchange. This is an area which may expand substantially and one licensed dealer has set up a high street share shop.

A company may be attracted to the OTC by the lower costs and the lower level of 'red tape' involved in obtaining a quote by this method compared with a full or USM listing. The costs involved are still substantial. A company raising say £½ million by selling 25% of its equity could expect to pay about £60,000 in expenses with a placing and £80,000 with an offer for sale using the OTC market. Less red tape for companies also means less protection for investors. Protection for investors is by means of the Companies Act 1985 for the content of a prospectus and from the legislation covering the conduct of licensed dealers (Prevention of Fraud (Investments) Act 1958 and subsequent regulations). Trade organizations such as the Association of Stock and Share Dealers, the National Association of Security Dealers and Investment Managers, and the British Institute of Dealers in Securities may provide some further protection to investors.

The OTC market in the U.K. is much less developed than that in the U.S. However an OTC automated price information system called MMAPIS (Market Makers Automated Price Information Service) has now been launched, and this could be the first step towards the U.K. equivalent of the highly successful U.S. automated system called NASDAQ. Much will depend on the attitude of the Securities and Investment Board to these bodies in the future and the extent to which they will be permitted to establish a self-regulatory authority.

CHAPTER SIX

PORTFOLIO THEORY AND PLANNING

6.1 Elementary principles

There is a useful acronym which very succinctly summarizes the considerations necessary in assessing investments and constructing portfolios. It is SYSTEM T:

Security
Yield
Spread
Term
Exchange risk
Marketability
Tax

This book is primarily directed at fund managers of insurance companies and pension funds, by whom some of the expressions above will already have been assimilated during analysis of the liabilities of those institutions. The acronym, although simple, does encompass at a stroke the ideas essential to an understanding of institutional investment and can be readily adapted to other investors.

(a) Security

This useful word avoids the necessity of using the word 'risk'. Each investor will have his own idea of risk. To some it will be the possibility of the investment losing value in monetary or real terms. To others it will be the chance that the return on investments will be less than some specified amount necessary to meet liabilities. Each will impose constraints on the portfolio in order to feel a sense of security. A widow on a fixed pension will not wish to invest a relatively small amount of savings in volatile equities. She will probably want security of capital in monetary terms. The trustees of a pension fund will be able to accept investments whose capital values fluctuate because of the size of the portfolio but will be keen to preserve the capital in *real* terms. A millionaire investing money in an uncertain business venture may not be too dismayed by the prospect of total loss of a marginal part of his portfolio if there is the chance of high total return. His concept of risk is very different from the widow's. Each investor will define the level of security he requires (albeit subconsciously) and his portfolio or investment will reflect his choice.

Apart from using the word 'security' to introduce one aspect of 'risk', the type of investment can also be classified by security. Thus a British government stock is regarded in the U.K. as risk free in monetary terms and a British government index-linked stock is risk free in real terms (allowing for subtleties in the calculation of the yield). An investment in equities is riskier and this is reflected by the higher expected yield, whether measured in monetary or real terms. Using the earlier examples, the widow will want total security of capital and would not choose to deposit her only capital with a 'fringe' institution. The millionaire can afford to be more cavalier in his choice of 'savings' medium.

(b) Yield

By 'yield' is meant the overall return from capital and income combined expected by the investor from his investment. This may be certain, as in the case of a money market deposit, or unknown but estimated, as in the case of a property investment. In theory, returns will range upwards from those on risk-free government stock to those on high-risk venture capital investments. The expected return from a high-risk venture will be well in excess of that on three-month Treasury bills but the probability of failure is obviously higher. The yield required may be set by the nature of the liabilities from which a break-even return is calculated. A portfolio must then be constructed from available assets to produce an expected return of appropriate size. Alternatively, the investor may be relatively indifferent to yield and accept the rate on a single investment set by the market.

(c) Spread

Spread is a concept well known to insurance companies and pension funds who determine their liabilities by using tables constructed by reference to many observations on deaths. In constructing asset portfolios along the same lines institutions and investors avoid 'putting all their eggs in one basket'. The widow may be perfectly content to invest all her savings in a building society if this meets her need for security and yield. A pension fund which has to invest in real assets in order to obtain real returns will need to obtain a spread of such investments in order to diversify the risk.

(d) Term

This reflects the need for determining the dates at which cash flow is required. Thus a life company whose sole liabilities were non-profit endowment policies all maturing in ten years' time would require investments which offered security of payment ten years hence to the value of the maturing policies. Such an investment would be mostly in ten-year gilts. An investor with a longer time-span can be more sanguine, particularly if the dates are spread. Personal financial planning in this way can be seen in school fees arrangements or mortgage liabilities.

(e) Exchange risk

Many assets have prices which fluctuate in accordance with prevailing interest rates, investors' preferences and so on. For a U.K.-based investor who holds assets overseas there is an additional element of risk, namely, the fluctuation of the asset's value in sterling terms caused by movements in the exchange rate between sterling and the local currency. If the investor's liabilities are expressed in sterling this is, of course, a real risk. Each investor should be able to define the extent to which he can diversify into overseas currencies. Thus a life company may feel it can invest its free reserves overseas without fear of being 'unmatched'. The reason for investment overseas in these circumstances will be to obtain a higher expected return than in the U.K. because of different economies, potential weakness of sterling and so on. An investor can still invest in other countries, but remove the exchange risk by 'hedging' the currency.

(f) Marketability

This refers to the ease of converting assets into ready cash. A Treasury Bill which can be discounted at the Bank of England is highly liquid because it can be converted into cash virtually instantaneously. A property, however, may be turned into cash after a matter of months. Portfolio construction requires a knowledge of the needs and cash flow of the investor. A pension fund with strong cash flow is unlikely to need many marketable assets whereas a savings institution such as a building society needs a good proportion of its portfolio in assets readily realizable. Government stocks are the commonest of the marketable assets but, nevertheless, the investor may face a loss on the face value of his investment.

(g) Tax

Regrettably, the subject of tax in investment affairs tends to exercise the mind more than other considerations on too many occasions. Investors will determine the expected return on their investment by reference to their rates of income and capital gains tax. Usually it will be the marginal rate of tax that matters and not their average rate of tax. Tax planning is an important feature of portfolio construction.

108 INSTITUTIONAL INVESTMENT

6.2 Other factors

Apart from the items covered by SYSTEM T there may well be other factors affecting portfolio construction by investors. Some of these have already been mentioned.

(a) Immunization

The actuarial theory of immunization is well known to life companies, and the relationship between actuary and investment manager is particularly important. The extent to which the theory may diverge from practice will depend on the maturity of the fund, nature of the business, size of assets and so on. Further comments are made in 6.4.

(b) Index-linking

Some liabilities such as pensions are expressed in real terms (in relation to price or earnings). For such funds index-linked investments may be important. Note, however, that although index-linked gilts offer real returns relative to prices it is axiomatic amongst the investment public that equities offer real returns because companies' earnings and profits are expected to grow in real terms. An equity yielding 5% whose dividends are expected to increase in line with price inflation has an expected real yield of 5%. Similar considerations hold for property.

(c) Performance

The construction of certain portfolios may be heavily influenced by the behaviour of competitors. In certain circumstances this may lead to a compromise on investment principles for the sake of, say, continued new business.

Unit linked funds within insurance companies are examples of funds where competitive forces may lead fund managers towards certain common standards of behaviour.

(d) Practical constraints

Similarly, personal or corporate prejudice may lead to portfolios heavily biased to or away from certain areas. Portfolio managers are usually aware of these constraints and manage the assets accordingly. Severe bias acting against the interest of a saver in an institutional fund cannot, of course, be tolerated at the expense of sound investment judgment. As a corollary, if all other investment factors and principles are satisfied, the investment manager should choose investments which do most to further the objects of his own business.

6.3 Institutional portfolio structures

At this point it is appropriate to formulate some rules for investment management of institutions such as life companies and pension funds.

(a) The liabilities of the fund, as far as they can be specified, must be met as and when they arise.
(b) The first objective must be met with as much surplus (or as little cost) as possible.
(c) The range of the possible in (b) above will be limited by the priority of (a) above. In other words the risk involved in maximizing the return must not be so great as to imperil the fulfilment of liabilities within the bounds of any significant likelihood.

6.4 Matching

An investment manager will not merely follow these 'rules' – he will wish to demonstrate to those for whom he acts that he is, indeed, doing his best for them. He will therefore account at regular intervals for his management. He will wish to show at these intervals that the funds at his disposal are accumulating at the rate required to meet the liabilities, and that his management has left an ample margin either to provide a profit or a reduction in costs for his savers.

The normal practice is to have such an accounting once a year. Investments take time to behave in accordance with expectations and more frequent accounting is a hindrance to policy development. This is not to say that the management of a fund should not itself consider all its investments more frequently – they obviously should – but only that a manager cannot have reasonable freedom to manage if he must justify himself more often. Unit trusts approved by the Department of Trade and Industry must publish their valuations at much more frequent intervals – a serious obstacle to longer-term investment policy, although not in any way an obstacle to a very active one.

Obviously, where a manager's funds cover no more than the liabilities, at his expected rate of return, there is little scope for risk-taking. He will, in such a case, endeavour as far as he can to invest in securities producing returns equal to and coincident with the liabilities. This practice is known as 'matching'. 'Matching' has been described in the fullest detail by Haynes and Kirton in a paper which sets out the effects and implications for a life office. In fact their illustrations work out equally well for any other long-term fund, the worst problem being that in certain funds the length and size of the liabilities will be such that pure matching is unattainable. This topic was developed by Redington in his paper on the mathematical theory behind the different situations where the assets and liabilities would not necessarily be matched, but yet the fund would at all times meet the liabilities as they fell due, despite changes in interest rates (on, however, the fundamental assumption that the interest rates applicable to all durations of investment changed by the same amount).

In summary the problem is that liabilities (Li in i years' time) in terms of incidence and amount will tend to fall in without any precise uniformity, so that the 'length' of the liabilities is in fact calculated from the value of 'n' such that

$$v^n \Sigma L_i = \Sigma v^i L_i$$

summing over the Li liabilities. It will be evident that a change in the rate of interest will cause a change in the value of the liabilities and in 'n'. However, if the assets match these liabilities exactly no change will make any difference. If the 'spread' is different a change in interest rates will cause a divergence between assets and liabilities. Simply, this is what investment management is all about – the fund must aim to move away from a matched position so as to make profits; it is evident that unless matching is done with precision (and this is patently impossible) there must be either a reserve of profits built up to carry losses or an external guarantor in the last resort (e.g. possibly a company supporting its own pension fund). Furthermore, in those funds with long liabilities or liabilities tied to the cost of living, say, or otherwise subject to prolonged growth, matching may never be possible at all. The only hope of investment success is in effect to stay ahead of the game! In other words, the manager must have regard to the extent he has diverged from the matched position or, at least, from a position immune to deterioration arising from interest rate changes (see Redington) since the greater the divergence the greater the risk. Beyond that he must simply try to find the investments giving the highest rate of return!

It is worth noting here that a considerable difficulty of any form of 'immunization' of a fund against interest rate fluctuations is that the pattern of interest rate change is rarely consistent throughout a portfolio of fixed interest stocks. Thus even if the liabilities of a fund are valued on varying interest rates, it will be impossible to make such continuous (and perhaps inconsistent) adjustments as would be necessary to achieve something resembling true immunization. This is not to suggest that the theory is of little value – on the contrary, it describes the ideal risk-free distribution of investments against these liabilities.

It must be noted that from the liabilities aspect also, care must be taken to provide for 'optional' liabilities against the assets (e.g. guaranteed surrender values in a life fund). It should be assumed that options will always be exercised against a fund, and investment policy adjusted accordingly.

6.5 Performance constraints

A manager will, therefore, expect to begin each accounting period with the portfolio of investments best suited in his opinion, in terms of diversification, in terms of individual risk and in relation to the liabilities. He will then manoeuvre these investments, together with such extra monies as may come to hand (or the converse), to end the period with what he then considers his ideal portfolio, which may even be entirely cash! The test of his management is the increment of the fund, both in terms of capital and income, over the period. It must first be compared with that required by the original savers to fulfil their requirements. The excess is the profit the manager has achieved: in these terms, his position is similar to the manager of any other business.

Unfortunately for simple comparison, the last paragraph is the counsel of perfection. First, he may be restricted by the intentions, expressed or implied, of his savers. If his fund has a reputation for secure and cautious investments, it is to be assumed that savers contributing will presume that the policy is continuing, and there is in consequence an implied contract to this effect. For example, life insurance companies are looked upon as models for security and there is every justification for their maintaining such a policy; indeed they publish in their balance sheets a form of analysis of their funds, which must be taken to be accepted by the policyholders. An investment manager will not therefore move far or quickly from the established position of his fund without at least the tacit consent of those interested or their representatives. (This is not, of course, to say that he might not do so under any circumstances – the need to fulfil the liabilities is paramount and a massive revision because of an urgent threat to this aim is wholly justifiable). Secondly, the investment manager may be constrained by the size of his funds and the supply of investment opportunities from adopting the ideal portfolio at any time. To the extent that at the end of a given interval the portfolio is not ideal the profit achieved in that interval must be diminished. Thirdly, in a continuing fund, an active and unhampered investment policy must either lead to fairly extreme profit fluctuations or substantial reserves must be built up to smooth their apparent effect. It is traditional in British industry to endeavour to smooth profit movements from year to year, and again, it can be accepted as an implied condition on the part of savers unless it has been made clear to them at the outset that the converse will hold. Fourthly, the investment manager is always conscious of a flow of opportunities, and the incidence of his purchases and sales of securities upon that flow, his 'timing', must be consistent with all that has gone before.

It is always said that the objective is to buy at the bottom of the market; the only comment needed is that by definition the bottom of the market occurs when the sellers are no longer prepared to sell and therefore it is not possible to buy! An old Stock Exchange saying goes 'they don't ring a bell when the market turns up'. Timing therefore really means understanding other investors, and judging in advance a change in their decision-making.

A partial solution to the problem of timing is to spread out purchases or sales over a period of time, usually employing fixed money sums (a practice known as 'pound-averaging') in each account. This method has the merit that one buys more stock when prices are low and less when prices are high. It has, however, the serious demerit that it ignores changes in the prices of other stocks and since all decisions are relative, it may mean that better alternatives are being missed.

Size is the fifth aspect of the problem for the institutional investor. From the point of view of investment management, the larger the individual holding, the more time can be spent on making decisions regarding it and the more profitable it should therefore be. On the other hand, it is impossible to be certain about any one decision, and therefore some diversification of holdings is also important. In general, therefore, one does not want so small a holding that its management takes an inordinate time in relation to its value, nor so large a holding that one wrong decision imperils the entire profitability of the portfolio.

The restrictions imposed by size have just been mentioned. They operate not merely to hamper activity but also to restrict choice. Any investment contemplated or chosen must be managed in the sense that a continuing study of it is demanded in order that the development of adverse situations can be foreseen. Therefore, unless the rewards are enough to justify the attention, the investment is unsuitable. Small investments must therefore be significantly more profitable than large ones if they are to be selected; equally the larger the fund to be managed the greater the weight that must be given to this factor.

From what has already been said about the ability of a fund to take risks, a student will realize that even if the chances of profit or loss from an investment are equal, the prospects of profit and loss will not necessarily be of equal importance to a given fund; and psychologically a manager may be less willing to accept a loss particularly if his Board, or Trustees, react unfavourably to 'red' figures!

Finally, the investment manager must be conscious of the competition for the funds he is handling. His success-rating (i.e. his profit achievement) is vital both in securing new funds and retaining the contributions of his existing savers. The motivation of savers is not always clear-cut: security, profit, fulfilment of objectives, even fashion, will all matter. The policy a manager adopts must have regard to his rivals; a failure to modify his methods can have fairly severe consequences. This, of course, applies a great deal less to life offices and pension funds than it does to, say, unit trusts – but it still applies, as anyone contemplating a history of the last two decades can easily see. Life offices certainly in the last few years have been forced to demonstrate investment performance to a greater and greater degree, simply in order to maintain their new business levels.

6.6 Objectives

So far, investment policy and practice has been discussed in terms of principle. For the manager to achieve his goals within the principles, the policy must be set out in an objective form in order that it may be implemented by the investment organization. In its simplest terms this means a set of current rules (or basic assumptions) must be prepared, and kept up to date, in order that investment decisions may be made with efficiency. These rules will usually contain at least the following specifications:

(a) The rates of tax on income and on capital which will be employed in decisions. These will normally be the 'marginal' rates for the fund, and will therefore perhaps be different from that applicable to decisions affecting the entire portfolio at any moment.
(b) The trend of interest rates to be anticipated in decisions. This will not merely affect decisions in gilt-edged stocks, but such matters as the liquidity of the fund.
(c) A summary of prospective economic conditions, e.g. world trade, U.K. consumption, capital investment and, of course, industrial profits.
(d) The approximate proportions of the funds that may be invested in different broad categories, e.g. in British Government securities, in non-sterling equities, in securities not quoted on any Stock Exchange, etc.
(e) The approximate length and trend of the fund's liabilities.

6.7 Portfolio structures

An outline of the way in which the nature of their liabilities, taxation and statutory or informal restrictions affects the principal classes of investor is now given.

6.8 Banks

(a) Liabilities

In general, bank liabilities are short term, the great bulk of their assets being derived from deposits, most of which are repayable at call or at fairly short notice. They also make loans with a longer average maturity and for a variety of purposes.

(b) Taxation

All income and capital profits from investments are taxed as if they were part of the trading profits. They, therefore, bear corporation tax at the applicable rate. In 1981 a 'windfall tax' was levied.

(c) Assets

The banks' principal liabilities are their deposits in sterling and foreign currencies. A bank's operations are supported by its long-term capital resources.

A bank's choice of assets is constrained by solvency and liquidity considerations and by the need to comply with official credit control requirements and other guidelines. The banks keep the total risk exposure of their assets low by holdings securities with a negligible default risk.

Banks require liquidity for three reasons: to be sure that they can repay deposits as they are withdrawn; to honour existing overdraft commitments; and to satisfy demand for new loans. Assets are structured so that liquid funds are constantly being replenished from loan maturities and repayments, and as a further safeguard they hold a substantial part of their assets in highly liquid investments.

The official regulatory requirements under the Banking Act 1979 impinge on the structure of banks' assets in two ways. First, the Bank of England monitors the composition of each UK registered bank to ensure that the maturity and risk structure does not endanger the bank's liquidity or solvency. Secondly, each bank is required to hold adequate liquidity (in various forms) appropriate to the circumstances of the bank. The Bank of England does not now regulate by across-the-board ratios for liquidity or capital adequacy, but uses relevant ratios for guidance. Nevertheless, this flexible type of regulation will still effectively mean that banks will hold certain proportions of their assets in readily realizable form.

Subject to the regulatory requirements and the need to conduct its affairs 'prudently' (as required by the Banking Act 1979), the management will naturally try to place its assets in the form to achieve the most profitable result for its shareholders. The distribution of the sterling assets of banks in June 1985 can be seen from Table 6.1.

Table 6.1   Distribution of banks' sterling assets – June 1985

	%
Advances	52.9
Market loans (including loans to discount houses, bank CDs)	31.1
Bills (including Treasury and Commercial)	3.1
Gilts	3.1
Other investments	3.1
Notes/coins	0.9
Deposit at Bank of England	0.3
Net loans to central government	−1.4
Miscellaneous assets (items in collection, leased assets etc.)	6.9
	100.0

The banks included in this section are the London clearing banks, Scottish clearing banks, Northern Ireland banks, accepting houses, other British banks, overseas banks (American, Japanese etc.) and consortium banks. The Banking Department of the Bank of England and the discount houses have their own particular asset requirements. The former holds most of its assets in Government securities; the discount houses' principal assets are Treasury, local authority and commercial bills.

6.9 Trustee savings banks

(a) Liabilities and assets

The trustee savings banks (TSBs) have been unincorporated societies providing banking services to the personal sector. The Trustee Savings Bank Act 1976 relaxed government control over the TSBs and removed the most restrictive statutory limitations on their activities. The 1976 Act permitted the TSBs to lend to their customers and they now offer a range of credit facilities and grant mortgages. They have expanded their services in recent years, and now have over six million customers, a large range of unit trusts, insurance and instalment credit activities.

(b) Taxation

The trustee savings banks are liable to corporation tax.

(c) Regulation

The TSBs operate principally under the Trustee Savings Bank Acts of 1969 and 1976. The 1976 Act provides for the laying down of liquidity requirements by the Treasury and also specifies the classes of assets in which the bank may invest. The Banking Act 1979 did not include TSBs within the usual regulatory mechanism for banks, but its exclusion was only designed as a temporary measure. This was because the TSBs were moving from a position of total Treasury regulation to one where they would be free to operate as private sector banks. Many functions have now been centralized and amalgamated. An Act was necessary in 1985 to clarify the ownership of the assets of TSBs, prior to a Stock Exchange floatation of the TSB Group plc.

6.10 Finance houses

(a) Assets and liabilities
Finance houses are primarily involved in the provision of medium-term instalment credit facilities to both industry and consumers. Historically, finance houses have had a close association with hire-purchase. Business has now diversified and apart from other credit facilities some finance houses also offer facilities of a banking kind such as the maintenance of current and deposit accounts and the issue of cheques. The main items among their assets are loans and advances to U.K. residents on direct credit agreements; but they also have significant amounts of other forms of lending as well as holdings of real assets for leasing and of cash and liquid assets, and other investments.

(b) Taxation
No special tax treatment applies to finance houses and they pay corporation tax.

6.11 Building societies

(a) Assets and liabilities
Building societies are mutual organizations which borrow personal savings and lend most of them to individuals buying their own homes. Their most important characteristic is that they borrow short and lend long. Shares and deposits form the major part of building societies' liabilities and reserves and except for a small proportion of shares which are for a fixed term of a year or more, they can be withdrawn at relatively short notice. Reserves represent the excess of assets (at book values) over liabilities and provide a solvency margin for societies to cover the risk of loss on mortgages or on investments.

About 80% of societies' assets are held as mortgage advances. Although these are long-term loans, they are secured against what has in recent years been an opportunity asset, and the risk of loss is low. A proportion of building societies' assets is held in liquid investments to provide working capital and to cover any short-term excess of withdrawals and lending over deposits. These investments are made in cash and short-term bank deposits, short-term public sector debt, and in British Government and local authority securities mostly with a residual maturity of less than five years. The financial assets in which building societies are allowed to invest their liquid funds are laid down by the Chief Registrar of Friendly Societies. The societies are now able to raise money in the wholesale markets by the issue of yearling bonds. In October 1985 the first index-linked unquoted bond was issued by the Halifax Building Society.

A minimum reserve ratio (general reserves as a percentage of total assets) is required for trustee status and for the membership of the Building Societies Association. At the end of 1984, the average reserve ratio for all societies was approximately 4% of total assets. The percentage of total assets represented by cash and investments is known as the liquidity ratio. Trustee Status and membership of the BSA require a minimum liquidity ratio of 7½%. In practice, however, societies work on much higher ratios, and at the end of June 1985 the average liquidity ratio for all societies stood at 16½%. The Registrar of Friendly Societies has indicated that existing levels of reserves and liquidity may be inadequate if societies expand the range and type of service which they provide (see (c) below).

(b) Taxation

Building societies pay a composite rate of income tax on behalf of their investors, which represents the average marginal liability to basic rate tax of their investors. As many investors are not liable to tax the composite rate is substantially lower than the basic rate. For example in 1985/86 it was 25.25% compared with a basic rate of 30%. (The same system applies to most bank deposits for individuals.) Building societies have paid a special rate of Corporation Tax (40%) on their surpluses for periods to 31st March 1985, but now pay at normal corporation tax rates.

(c) Legislation

Legislation of building societies is consolidated by the Building Societies Act 1962 which contains detailed provisions relating to the management of building societies and gives responsibility for their prudential supervision to the Chief Registrar of Friendly Societies. A substantial liberalization of the services which can be offered by building societies is expected by 1987, but this will require further legislation.

6.12 Unit trusts

(a) Assets and liabilities

Unit Trusts are open-ended funds in which individuals invest in order to obtain a share of a much larger and more diversified portfolio than they could hold by themselves. The constitution of a unit trust is in the form of a trust deed to which the parties are a trustee, and a manager (a limited company) who must be independent of each other. The trustee is responsible for the safe custody and income of the trust and for the supervision of the terms of the trust deed. The management company is responsible for investment and administration and for making a market in the units. The managers derive their income from five principal sources:

(i)   by a preliminary charge included in the price of units,
(ii)   by a periodic charge out of the assets,
(iii) in certain cases by retaining a rounding-up adjustment made in the pricing of units,
(iv)   by repurchasing units and reselling them,
(v)   by retaining repurchased units in the expectation of a rise in the value of the underlying assets with a view to cancelling such units when a satisfactory level of appreciation is attained.

Unit trust portfolios consist very largely of ordinary shares although there is a wide variety of trusts suiting investors' desires for particular sectors of the market e.g. high income, gilts, technology. The investment policy of unit trusts is thus limited to a certain extent by legislation and by the stated objective of the fund (income, capital growth, general, overseas or investment in various specialized sectors). Authorized unit trusts may only invest in shares, debentures and government securities. Over recent years, particularly after the abolition of exchange controls, the proportion of assets invested in U.K. company securities has declined and there has been an increase in holdings of overseas company securities and short-term assets. Unlike investment trusts (see 6.13), unit trusts normally have an inflow of funds to be invested, but there is a tendency for this to be cyclical and related to the strength of the stock market.

(b) Taxation

An *authorized* unit trust is subject to corporation tax and not income and capital gains tax. Income from shareholders in U.K. companies is 'franked' and is exempt from corporation tax in the hands of the unit trust but other income, such as that earned on investments in gilt-edged stocks or bank deposits, is 'unfranked', so is liable to corporation tax. Since the Finance Bill 1980, however, income tax – instead of corporation tax – treatment is applied to the income of authorized unit trusts investing only in U.K. interest-bearing securities and having only individual shareholders. Since 1980 unit trusts have been exempt from tax on their chargeable capital gains.

Exempt unit trusts were mostly set up before 1980 exclusively for investment by pension funds, charities and other U.K. residents which are exempt from tax. The tax treatment of an exempt unit trust is now the same as an ordinary authorized unit trust, and the main difference is in the level of charges, which are usually lower for an exempt unit trust. Funds located offshore in tax havens are a specialist sector not controlled by U.K. authorities.

(c) Legislation

In order to be able legitimately to promote sales of its units to the public a unit trust must be authorized by the Department of Trade under the Prevention of Fraud (Investments) Act 1958. The provisions of authorized trust deeds limit investment in any one company to not more than 10% of any one class of capital, and limit the value of the trust's holding in any one company to 5% (or occasionally 7½%) of the value of the trust fund. No more than 5% of a unit trust's fund may be invested in unlisted securities. For many years the DoT set limits to management charges but from December 1979 unit trust managers have been free to fix charges at any level.

The 1958 Act prohibits unauthorized unit trusts from distributing, without special permission, circulars containing an invitation to subscribe for units. One of the major groups of unauthorized unit trusts is that of property unit trusts.

6.13 Investment trust companies

(a) Assets and liabilities

Investment trust companies are joint stock companies incorporated with limited liability under the Companies Act 1985. They are closed-ended funds formed for the collective investment in shares and other securities of monies subscribed as share and loan capital by their members and loan stockholders. Investment Trust Companies (ITCs) are not trusts in the legal sense and most ITCs are listed on the Stock Exchange. Responsibility for running them lies with their boards of directors, but most now have a relationship with a manager – or individual, partnership, investment management company or the investment management department of a merchant bank – who deals with administration and investment management. ITCs benefit from gearing by being able to issue fixed-interest capital in the form of debenture, loan and preference stocks when market conditions are favourable. The investor in an ITC does not buy the underlying assets (as in a unit trust), but shares in the company that owns them. Personal shareholders obtain professional portfolio management and a spread of risk which might not be possible on their own investments. Institutional shareholders get the benefit of buying an interest in a ready-made equity portfolio. In recent years there have been several cases of institutions acquiring ITC portfolios by taking over the ITC itself.

As ITCs are closed-ended funds the market price of their shares is subject to supply and demand in the usual way so that there is normally a difference between the market value of the ordinary shares of an ITC and the value of its underlying assets. This difference is known as the discount. The general experience of ITCs since the early 1970s has been a substantial discount on their shares. Recent frustration with the level of discount which represents partially a position of over-supply of trusts and in some cases is a reflection on the underlying asset performance has led to ITCs either being taken over or 'unitized' i.e. the company is liquidated and the underlying assets redistributed to shareholders in holdings of an appropriate unit trust.

The investment policy of an ITC, as with a unit trust, depends on its general objectives. Most are general funds (and it is mainly these that have been unitized), but some concentrate on particular geographical areas or industries. Some seek to maximize long-term capital growth; some aim for high income; some have a capital structure whereby one class of ordinary shareholder is entitled to all the income and the other all the capital appreciation. The major class of assets is ordinary shares, with some loan stock, preference shares and British government securities. A substantial proportion of assets is held in overseas shares, but a much lower proportion than the permitted maximum of 15% is held in unlisted company securities.

(b) Taxation
As companies, ITCs are subject to corporation tax on unfranked income less management expenses and interest. Following the Finance Bill 1980 ITCs are no longer liable to tax on their capital gains.

(c) Legislation
ITCs are subject to the requirement of the Companies Acts 1985. To obtain a Stock Exchange listing ITCs must limit investment in any one company to 10% of its investments and investments in unlisted shares to 15%.

6.14 Insurance companies

(a) Assets and liabilities

The essential characteristics of insurance companies' business is the spreading of risks, be it over time, among policyholders (whether individuals or organizations), or both. The activities of insurance companies are generally divided into two main categories: 'long term' and 'general', the latter comprising classes such as fire, accident, motor and marine insurance. Composite offices, which transact both categories, are required to keep their long-term funds separate from other funds.

General insurance business involves incurring liabilities to meet claims from policyholders for losses which occur within a specified period, usually 12 months, from the date of issue of the policy. In a typical general insurance company, about two thirds of the assets held represent provisions to meet estimated liabilities to policyholders, whilst the remaining one-third represents shareholders' funds (or 'free reserves') to meet statutory and prudential requirements for a solvency margin.

Long-term business is mainly concerned with life assurance, but also includes permanent health insurance and capital redemption business. Life assurance is principally divided between industrial business (also known as 'home service') and ordinary business, the distinguishing feature of industrial business being that the premiums are collected at regular intervals at the home of the policyholder by agents employed by the life office. Ordinary business is further subdivided into individual business and group pensions business. Life assurance policies may be 'with profits' or 'without profits', the former demanding higher premiums but entitling the policyholder to a share of the profits of the office. Under 'unit-linked policies' the benefits are calculated in whole or in part by reference to the value of, or the income from, specified assets, or to the movement in a share price or other index. 'Pension managed funds' are the equivalent of unit-linked contracts for the trustees of occupational pension schemes. These unitized funds are limited in the investments they may make. The permitted links are published by the Department of Trade and Industry (DTI).

Long-term business involves the accumulation of funds over many years while general business assets are held against liabilities that are mainly short term. A company's policy in investing its funds must have regard to the nature, mix and term of the relevant liabilities. The different emphasis on long-term investments by life and pension funds and on short-term investments by general funds is reflected in Table 6.2 which shows the distribution of investments by type held in life and general funds at the end of 1983.

Table 6.2   Distribution of insurance company investments at 31st December 1983

	Short-term assets/cash %	Index-linked gilts %	Conventional gilts %	U.K. company securities %	Overseas securities %	Loans %	Property %	Other %
General funds	11.8	0.8	30.4	28.2	14.0	2.9	10.5	1.4
Long-term funds	2.9	1.5	25.6	33.0	9.3	4.1	18.1	5.5

Notes
1. Figures exclude agents' balances.
2. Figures from Financial Statistics (CSO).

The table shows that cash and short-term assets accounted for 11.8% of the total assets of general funds compared with 2.9% for long-term funds. Insurance companies held about 25% to 30% of both their long-term and general funds in British Government securities, but a higher proportion of the long-term funds were actually in long-dated gilts. Long-term funds also held a higher proportion of their assets in property (18.1%) than did the general funds (10.5%). Both types of fund held about 42% of their assets in company securities.

The nature of the liabilities thus puts some constraint on the investment by the insurance companies of their annual inflows. Further constraints are imposed by legislation. In demonstrating solvency to the DTI some types of asset are totally or partially inadmissible and hence a company's freedom to invest in such assets will depend upon the extent to which its admissible assets exceed the sum of its liabilities together with the required solvency margin.

The DTI allows for valuation according to the type of assets. The value may be either the market value (as is the case of most ordinary shares); a value calculated by reference to a formula as in the case of certain fixed-interest stocks); or nil (as in the case of certain risk-related venture capital investments). Limits are also imposed on the proportions of assets allowed in any one security.

(b) Taxation

For non-life insurance business profits are taxable under the normal corporation tax rules, but life business has been subject to special taxation provisions.

A life assurance fund has been taxed on its investment income rather than on its trading profit and specific provisions has been made for relief in respect of management expenses, provided that the total tax payable is not less than would apply if the fund was taxed on a trading profits basis, on profits allocated to shareholders. There was a ceiling of tax of 37½% on unfranked income of the life fund, but this was removed in March 1986 when the corporation tax system was simplified. Realized capital gains are chargeable at a ceiling rate of 30%. Since March 1982 some element of indexing of book values has been allowed in calculating realized capital gains.

Exemption from tax is given on the income and capital gains resulting from funds held in respect of Inland Revenue-approved pensions business. An annuity fund is taxed on a profits basis, the profits being computed after allowing annuities paid to be deducted from investment income. In a life company, therefore, total investment income has to be apportioned between the life assurance, general annuity and pensions business funds before the tax calculations can be made.

(c) Legislation

Supervision of insurance companies with the aim of protection of policy-holders from the possibility of insolvency of companies is administered primarily through a number of acts, the first of which was the Life Assurance Companies Act 1870. Certain statutory duties have been imposed on the actuary of the company as regards life business. The law has been strengthened in recent years and most of the legislative requirements now result from the Insurance Companies Act 1982, and its extensive associated regulations. The regulations cover many aspects of an insurance company's operations, including advertising, Department of Trade returns, valuation and admissibility of assets and actuarial valuations. Policyholders are protected by the Policyholders Protection Act 1975.

6.15 Pension funds

(a) Assets and liabilities

Pension funds are financial institutions for the accrual of funds to meet future pension liabilities normally established in respect of a particular organization for its employees. The majority of occupational pension schemes are funded in advance. Funds are built up from contributions paid by employers, and usually also by employees, together with income arising from investment of the assets, out of which ultimately pensions and other benefits are paid. Funded occupational pension schemes can be divided into two types; those where the funds are directly invested in various markets (self-administered schemes); and those where the funds are invested by, and the actuarial risk borne by, a life assurance office (insured schemes). The fund management of self-administered schemes is often wholly or partly sub-contracted to life assurance offices, or other fund management specialists such as clearing banks, merchant banks, investment and unit trust managements and stockbrokers. The assets of insured schemes and self-administered funds managed by insurance companies are included in their long-term funds.

The liabilities of pension funds are to the current and prospective pensioners and other beneficiaries. Each year the funds invest their surplus cash flow, that is the income from contributions *plus* interest and dividends on existing assets *less* pension payments and any administration costs borne by the funds.

It is broadly accepted that pension liabilities should in some way be divorced from the overall liabilities of the employer concerned, so that pension rights are secure even if the employer should go out of business. The investment performance of the fund does of course benefit the firm as

Table 6.3 Distribution of pension fund investments at 31st December 1983

	Short-term assets %	Conventional and index-linked gilts %	U.K. company and overseas securities %	Property %	Other %
Private sector	3.4	20.6	59.6	11.1	5.3
Local authorities	2.7	22.8	64.2	7.7	2.6
Other public sector	3.6	19.1	55.0	17.0	5.3
Total	3.3	20.5	59.4	12.3	4.5

Note
1. Figures from Financial Statistics (CSO).

well as the members, in that the firm is commonly the major contributor to the fund and normally in practice meets the balance of any costs required to provide the benefits promised. In a situation of stable money prices and incomes pension funds would eventually mature in the sense that each year income would equal outgo and there would be no surplus for investment. Most funds are far from this position, and inflation or growth in GDP that is shared by employees would tend to defer that maturity position.

Table 6.3 gives the percentage breakdown of the assets of non-insurance self-administered funds as between types of investment for the three main categories of funds separately and for all funds combined, at end 1983. Taking into account the subdivision between UK and overseas securities not shown in Table 6.3, overall pension funds have about 45% of their assets in UK company securities, 15% in overseas securities, 20% in government securities, 12% in property, with the balance being widely spread between cash, loans, mortgages, local government securities and non-property unit trusts.

(b) Taxation

Pension funds approved by the Inland Revenue are gross funds, i.e. they pay no tax on either the interest earned on their investments, or on any capital gains they make. This applies only to bona fide U.K. pension funds. Even these may be charged to withholding tax on overseas dividends and to corporation tax on any trading activities. Certain transactions, such as foreign currency hedging, may also be taxable. In addition, they pay Value Added Tax in certain circumstances.

(c) Legislation

Funded pension schemes are normally set up as trust funds under a trust deed and as such those appointed to run the schemes are subject to the general law of trusteeship and the specific terms of the instrument under which a particular fund is established. Supervision by the Inland Revenue is mainly limited to ensuring that tax exemptions are restricted to bona fide pension schemes and that benefits paid are not excessive. The supervision of pension funds to ensure that they comply with existing legislation on the provision of occupational schemes is carried out by the Occupational Pensions Board set up under the Social Security Act 1973.

6.16 Friendly societies

Friendly societies provide benefits and have liabilities that are similar to life insurance companies rather than pension funds, but their tax treatment and legislative position are both similar to those of pension funds. Their liabilities are usually shorter in term and less vulnerable to inflationary variations than those of pension funds.

6.17 Individuals

The private individual's investment policy, if it exists at all, is variable in every possible way. His liabilities are difficult to determine and there are few restrictions on where and how he may invest.

His tax rates are usually known, however, and investment policy may be tax planning in another form. There are various systems of taxation avoidance, which are constantly being changed, and which may be worth while only for the very wealthy. In general the private individual, in so far as he operates directly in the market, rather than via the media discussed above, is operating in a marginal fashion in that for most individuals the priority of further investment in his spending allocation will be low and most people use the institutions already listed as a means of saving according to preference.

6.18 Trustee investments

Where a fund is managed under a trust, and there are no specific instructions for its investment in the deeds that govern the trust, the trustees must invest the monies in accordance with the Trustee Acts of which the currently effective enactment is the Trustee Investments Act 1961. Although for full details of these regulations the Act itself, and in particular the First Schedule, must be consulted, it may be helpful to summarize the main conditions which apply. These are as follows:

If a trustee does not obtain advice from somebody with 'ability in and practical experience of financial matters' he may only invest in British Savings Bonds, the National Savings Bank and similar classes of security. As he is required to have regard to the need for diversification and to the suitability of the investments for the purposes of the trust, in the majority of cases a trustee must take such advice (incidentally, the Act does not say how one determines whether an adviser has 'ability in financial matters'!).

Assuming advice is taken, the trustee may then, subject to various alternatives and restrictions, split the fund into two parts of equal value, one to be known as the 'narrower-range' part and one as the 'wider-range' part.

The narrower-range fund may be invested in any of a long list of fixed interest securities, including those of the British Government, of U.K. local authorities and public boards, of any Commonwealth government or local authority or the quoted U.K. registered debt of a U.K. company (provided that the company's issued and paid-up share capital exceeds £1m, and that it has paid a dividend on all its capital entitled to share in profits in each of the five years preceding the calendar year in which the investment is made). Note that Government and local authority debt need not be quoted. Other investments permitted include deposits (but not shares) in a recognized building society and mortgages of property.

The wider-range fund may be invested in any securities of a U.K. registered company (subject to restrictions set out below), in the shares of any building society, and in the units of a unit trust authorized under the Department of Trade regulations (or in 'narrower-range' securities).

It must be emphasized that the foregoing is by no means a full record of the Act's provision; it is merely intended to give a general idea of its implications. There are, in particular, certain provisions to take account of special investment powers that certain trusts may contain, and the reader is referred to the Act itself on this and similar matters.

The definition of the companies in whose debt or share capital trustees may invest is of particular importance. The exact requirements of this part are as follows:

(i)   The company must be incorporated in the United Kingdom.

(ii) The total issued and paid-up share capital (*not* ordinary share capital, necessarily) must exceed £1m.

(iii) The company must, in each of the five calendar years immediately preceding the calendar years in which the investment is made, have paid a dividend on all the shares issued by the company, excluding any shares issued after the dividend was declared and any shares which by the terms of their issue did not rank for the dividend in that year. This clause must be watched carefully – a dividend is sometimes omitted in a calendar year after a merger or reorganization.

(iv) For the purposes of (iii) a company formed either to take over the business of another company or companies or to acquire the securites of, or control, another company or companies shall be deemed to have paid a dividend in any year in which such a dividend has been paid by all the other companies.

(v)   Any share purchased must be fully paid up at the date of purchase.

Finally, it is to be remembered that where a U.K. investor controls a fund receiving statutory privileges in an overseas country, the onus of obeying the investment rules, if any, of that country falls upon him. In recent years there has been some increase in the number of such funds, and it is of great importance to be aware of legislative changes in time to take remedial action. Although certain countries have recently set out to make themselves attractive to overseas investors, by fiscal relaxations or absence of restrictions on capital, such legislation can be abrogated fairly readily, and discretion should therefore restrain the investor from the more unusual portfolio selections.

6.19 Further consideration of risk

In the next section we refer to a definition of risk used in *Modern Portfolio Theory*. Before doing so it is worth considering more traditional concepts of risk.

Some examples of risk have already been mentioned.

(a) Risk of default
An example of risk is in a fixed interest loan where the company makes a loss and defaults on interest or capital.

(b) Dividend risk
There is a risk of dividends not being paid but also for ordinary shares there is risk of dividends being less than expected. Thus the company does not have to lose money for the investment to be a failure; there is a wide range of possibilities and if the returns from the investment fall below the level at which expectations have been set then it will be a failure.

(c) Market movement
Interest rates may change and if, in particular, rates rise then forced realization of fixed interest assets may lead to capital loss. This is a risk. Similarly, equity prices may fall and losses will be incurred if sales are forced.

(d) Inflationary risks
There is a risk that assets may depreciate in real terms even if nominal values are maintained. If liabilities are expressed in real terms there is a risk of 'loss'.

(e) Currency risk
This has already been mentioned in paragraph 6.1(e).

By analysing the various risks, examples of which have just been given, an investor will be able to construct a probability distribution of possible outcomes expressed as financial returns. The expected value derived from the distribution is a fair indication of what the investor is looking for in any particular period of time. He could regard the whole present value of his investment as the discounted sum of the expected values for all the periods comprising the investment's life. Clearly, the expected yield on an investment at a given price would then be the rate of interest at which the whole present value equalled the price. This concept is rough and ready but does indicate a maximization method for investments. It also gives an interpretation of rule 6.3(c). Although a manager may try to maximize the expected yield on his investments he must remember the underlying distribution of risk. If the variances are too high rule 6.3(c) is being broken.

(f) Threshold returns

Another argument is that risk should be defined as the probability of achieving less than some specified threshold level of return which must be achieved and *which will be different for each investor* and that the probability should be measured over a period of time which is also different for different investors. This, in effect, is reflected in construction of portfolios for the investors reviewed in sections 6.8 to 6.17. For example, the trustees of a pension fund will have been advised by the actuary to the fund of the minimum real rate of return assumed in his funding projections and failure to achieve this would mean a reduction in benefits or an increase in contributions. Thus, over a very long period, the Trustees will wish to ensure that the fund achieves this minimum real rate. Their investment strategy will need to define, albeit implicitly, the probability of not achieving this real rate of return.

(g) Comparative returns

In today's competitive savings markets the returns on funds are subject to public scrutiny either because a unit price is available in the press or because a proprietary fund performance measurement service is being used. In either case those responsible for directing the investment managers may express the target return on the funds in performance-related terms. They may wish to see a fund ranked above the upper quartile in a list of comparable investment funds. This encourages the sale of the product by marketing the performance of the fund. In order to achieve this relative performance, however, the fund managers will relate risk to the probability of falling below the upper quartile. There are paradoxes in this approach not the least of which is the implied accusation that the fund ranked first has, by definition, adopted a 'risky' investment strategy in the colloquial sense.

(h) Risk and return

Finally, conventional analysis attributes levels of riskiness to different types of investment and these levels are defined by the relative returns. Thus the return on gilt-edged stock may reasonably be regarded as risk-free i.e. the probability of not receiving the income when due and the capital on redemption is zero. (Note, however, that the *yield* is not guaranteed because future levels of interest rates at which coupons are reinvested are unknown.) Given the certainty of return on this stock it can be argued that an industrial loan stock should yield slightly more to allow for the lesser standing of the borrower – a premium of £1–£2 p.a. will probably suffice. An unquoted loan stock will yield even more to allow for lack of marketability. Preference shares will require a premium but the demand for franked income as distinct from the unfranked income on gilts and corporate bonds often means that the gross yields are only slightly above gilts. Unquoted preference shares may yield up to 4 or 5% p.a. more than gilts. The return on equities is difficult to compare in money terms because of the reverse yield gap. Until the 1950s equities yielded more than gilts, reflecting the extra risk involved. Equities subsequently became very fashionable as a hedge against inflation and yielded less than gilts. The argument was that the initial running yields would be enhanced by the value of dividends and market values increasing in line with inflation. One would expect that equities should yield 3 or 4% more than gilts to reflect their risks. Because of the prospective increase in dividends during a period of inflation the demand for equities, i.e. a real asset, has pushed their yields *below* those of gilts. The difference is the reverse yield gap.

It is possible to remove the inflationary expectations by using *real* returns. The real return on Government securities can be estimated by reference to the yield available on risk-free index-linked Government stock, say 3.5% per annum. The real return on equities is equal to the current yield on the market *if* the market as a whole increases future dividends in line with price inflation. At present (September 1985) the All-Share index yields 4.7% and thus the reward for the risk of equities over the risk-free Government stock is 1.2%.

6.20 Overview of modern portfolio theory

(a) The fundamentals of MPT

The effective and efficient investment of institutional portfolios is a difficult and complex task. Investment managers will differ on the distribution of assets to be followed, the way in which new money should be invested, the choice of securities etc. This difference, and indeed disagreement, merely produces the market place as we know it. However, on one thing all investment managers will agree – namely that the whole investment process is uncertain rather than certain – the manager implicitly deals with possibilities. Nobody can say with absolute assurance what will happen in the markets next week, next year or in five years' time. Commentators and analysts can postulate what influences may arise and investigate the probable impact on financial markets of these influences, but there is no certainty.

Everybody knows that this uncertainty has prevailed in the past and we can be certain that it will prevail in the future. Modern Portfolio Theory (MPT) is based upon this principle of 'certain uncertainty'.

The 'father' of MPT is Harry Markowitz who published an academic paper in 1952. This is a tremendously important paper in the formulation of MPT since it accepted the principle of 'certain uncertainty' and showed how it could be used in investment management.

(b) Diversification

It is a widely accepted belief that institutional portfolios should be diversified. The desire for diversification has to be tempered with the need to obtain a particular rate of return. The desire for this rate of return, subject to the maintenance of a diversified portfolio, leads to considerable amounts of confusion which have not as yet been methodically addressed by the actuarial profession. Thus, institutional portfolios are constructed with often many different classes of assets and usually with very large numbers of securities contained in them. Generally, there is no attempt to quantify the level of diversification required, or the level of diversification obtained. Investment managers generally do not question whether they are so over-diversified that the chances of excess return are minimal.

The pioneering work of Markowitz established a methodology using elementary statistical techniques, familiar to actuaries, as an aid in management of actual portfolios. The theory, as presented, shows how an investor or investing institution can minimize variance, often a measure of uncertainty and 'risk', at different levels of expected return, subject to various constraints. These constraints consist of zero, one or more linear equalities or inequalities, and may or may not be required to be non-negative. For example, borrowing may not be allowed; maximum positions may be imposed on individual securities or groups of securities; constraints may be placed on current income. For input, the analysis requires estimates of the means, variances, and co-variances of the securities eligible to be included in the portfolio as well as the constraints to be satisfied. The solution to the problem of portfolio construction is simply one of quadratic programming subject to linear constraints.

The analysis does not assume that all investors hold the same beliefs.

Nor does it assume that everyone else, or anyone else for that matter, uses a similar analysis. It ignores the liabilities of the investments completely. It simply takes the beliefs of the investor or investment team as given to it and traces out the mean-variance efficient set. No assumption is made that the market as a whole will be one of the portfolios produced in this efficient set analysis. These assumptions are in contrast to those used in, for example, the Capital Asset Pricing Model (see section 6.21(e)).

As has been indicated earlier, the inputs to the analysis include estimates of the investors' expected returns, variance of returns and either co-variance or correlation of returns between each pair of securities. For example, an analysis that allows 1000 securities as possible candidates for portfolio selection requires 1000 expected returns, 1000 variances of return, and 499,500 correlations or co-variances! When viewed in this light, there are a number of major practical difficulties:

(i)   First, the human mind is not easily able to think in terms of variances and co-variances. There are biological difficulties in actually getting the data for the analysis. An investment team tracking 1000 securities may reasonably be expected to summarize the analysis in terms of 1000 expected returns; few would be able to summarize 1000 variances and it is clearly impracticable and unreasonable for them to produce the required number of carefully considered correlation co-efficients.

(ii) Second, even assuming that this information was available (say, from past observations) the computational requirements to get a solution to the portfolio selection problem are inordinately lengthy and would require a large amount of computational power.

However, it should be noted that if the number of securities is small (say 20) then the solutions can fairly easily be obtained. For example, if an appropriately chosen index can be assumed to represent world equity markets, then it is a fairly simple exercise to obtain an international asset allocation model.

It is self evident that some kind of model of co-variance for the practical application of portfolio selection for large portfolios is necessary. It is solely for this requirement that the various portfolio models have been applied in an attempt to quantify that which is too often unquantified.

(c) The investment specialist and MPT

For the professional engaged in investing institutional monies, MPT has been around for so long that the adjective 'modern' is almost a misnomer. Perhaps two business generations of investment managers and investment analysts have grown up with MPT discussions in the background, and some main ideas from the MPT armoury have been absorbed as part of their business education. Equally, although MPT is a developing collection of ideas and disciplines, the passage of time has meant that for many investment professionals it has lost the sense of the shock of new ideas which surrounded the early developments.

In the U.K., many of the broad ideas of MPT are accepted widely – for example the trade-off of risk and return, the idea that the major investment markets are efficient (to some degree), or the choice between active and passive management. For most investors these broad ideas are apparently enough. Few institutions appear to depend on the formal application of MPT methods for share selection or portfolio construction.

The market in U.K. gilt-edged securities is one in which many different groups have developed investment models and quotation techniques which can be regarded as being within a broad description of MPT. For example the widely used measure of 'volatility' of stocks and gilt-edged portfolios, measuring the price movements consequent on yield changes, is very similar to the use of MPT to control the variability of a portfolio according to one's perceptions of changing yield levels and patterns. The development of such systems has reflected the liquidity and low dealing costs in the gilt-edged market.

For other classes of investment such as equities or property, the higher level of transaction cost, the greater difficulty of dealing at fine prices in large volumes, and the effect of capital gains tax have for most large investment institutions dictated that investment managers adopt a long-term horizon for the greater part of their investment. Effectively, the bulk of the securities are held on a passive basis, selected according to long-term preferences or criteria, while a small portion of a size which can be dealt in is invested and maintained on a short-to-medium-term horizon, on a basis of active management.

Such an approach predates MPT and mainly reflects the constraints of marketability and management time. The MPT approach has focused attention on identifying whether a management team has, for example, an ability to beat the averages by 'stock-picking' or dealing activity, and the degree to which this can be used effectively.

Similarly, the idea of diversification and spread of risk in portfolios is a very old one. What MPT has added is a disciplined approach to measuring how much spread is necessary or desirable. In practice, very few investment managers make formal calculations of the efficiency of their portfolios.

A very important reason for this is the question of what constitutes risk. A great deal of MPT development work has treated 'risk' as synonymous with short-term variability in price. When the earlier MPT work was developed in the U.S.A., the economic and investment situation was one of stable taxes, stable politics, relatively stable interest rates and stable foreign exchange parities. In that context it was sensible to use the overall stock market movement for comparison with individual share price movements.

For some twenty years now British investors have been living in a climate of frequent changes in taxes, interest rates, exchange rates, inflation, dividend restrictions, stop-go cycles and so on. In the 1980s U.S. fund managers also have had to cope with substantial swings in interest rates, exchange rates and deregulation etc. A statistical history of price movements ahead of major changes may not be an adequate guide to the movements on or after such a change. An investment manager who has gained his experience in such conditions is likely to be more interested in the susceptibility of a security or of a portfolio to variations in (for example) interest rates or exchange rates than to simple short-term variations in price. At the same time the growth of communications and the tendency for institutions to take a more international view have lessened the independence of world markets. Thus if high-technology stocks fall in the U.S.A. they are more likely to do so also in Japan and Europe. A change in the world oil price will affect oil shares in several countries, and a Third World debt crisis will affect major banks in several financial centres.

The construction of portfolios in such conditions can be handcrafted by an experienced investment professional team without MPT. However, MPT methods have developed to react to these conditions, with more work done on describing cross-correlations between market prices of securities and categorizing in specific areas such as 'interest sensitive'.

Where MPT is virtually mandatory is in the rapidly expanding field of financial futures and options contracts, with the need to value such instruments formally in a way which allows for the statistical variability of prices over a specific term.

A further point is that the portfolio performance measurement services developed in the U.K. have tended to give prominence to simple league tables and ranking of investment performance without allowing for variations in the 'risk levels' of the investment strategies followed. The professionals in the various investment measurement groups, such as consulting actuaries, may seek to appraise individual fund performance in some greater detail, but the major published analysis is a simple league table plus brief comments. Partly this is because MPT ideas have not been carried over widely to lay customers such as pension fund trustees, so that such concepts as trading off risk and return do not follow through at the level of client decision-making on the retention or appointment of investment managers. Those fund managers whose business depends on such tables tend to be forced into shorter-term horizons when making investment decisions. They may also find that, in commercial terms, a risky strategy for them is simply one which involves departing markedly from the main stream of competing fund managers. Accordingly, the development of performance measurement services, often by professionals most able to apply MPT methods, tends to be inimical to some of the basic MPT ideas.

One MPT concept which pension fund trustees and other directors can grasp readily is that of active and passive strategies. The use of passive funds designed to perform in line with stock market indices is not as common in the U.K. as in the U.S.A., but has established a toehold.

6.21 The mathematics of modern portfolio theory

Modern portfolio theory is the process of determining the properties of portfolios of assets given the properties of the individual's assets, delineating the characteristics of portfolios that make them preferable to others and, finally, showing how the composition of the preferred portfolios can be determined.

In order to reach a solution to a portfolio problem two aspects are explored.

First, it is necessary to define the choices available to an investor – called the 'opportunity set' and secondly it is necessary to know the investor's tastes or preferences – shown by reference to 'indifference or utility curves'. By aggregating across all investors and all capital markets, and assuming equilibrium conditions, it is possible to construct mathematical models. It is the *uncertainty* of future returns which necessitates the complexity of these models which are then used to assist in the choice of assets. Several assumptions are made to reduce the considerable mathematical complexity required.

MPT assumes that returns on assets have a normal statistical distribution over short periods of up to three months. For longer periods of observation it is assumed that the portfolio's continuously compounded rate of return is normally distributed i.e. the actual return is distributed log-normally. The mean of the distribution is regarded as the expected rate of return and the standard deviation (and sometimes variance) is adopted as a measure of risk.

The average return and variance of an individual asset are calculated by assigning different probabilities to different outcomes. If two assets have the same variance most investors would prefer the asset with the higher expected return. Similarly, if two assets have the same expected return most investors would choose the one with the lower variance because the

investor is more certain of obtaining the expected return and will have
fewer poor outcomes to contend with. In other words, the investor is 'risk
averse'. Having defined the basic assumptions some of the more common
terms are now explained.

(a) Variance of large portfolios
The variance of returns on a portfolio is given by

$$\sigma_p^2 = \frac{1}{n} \sum_{i=1}^{n} \left[\frac{\sigma_i^2}{n} \right]$$

where σ_p^2 is the variance of the portfolio.
    n is the number of assets which are assumed to be independent
        i.e. there is no correlation between them.
    σ_i^2 is the variance of the i th asset.

The equation says that if the securities of a fund are equally weighted by
market value, the variance of returns of the portfolio is the average of the
individual variances divided by n. Clearly, as n becomes larger, the variance
of the return on the portfolio of assets approaches zero. In other words the
risk of a portfolio decreases as the number of assets increase. It is another
way of suggesting 'don't put all your eggs in one basket'.

(b) Efficient portfolios
In order to construct portfolios the theory develops the idea of an efficient
portfolio by reference to risk and expected return. Risk-return space can
be illustrated as shown in Figure 6.1:

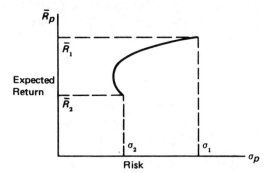

Figure 6.1

where $\bar{R}$ is the expected return on a portfolio and σ is the standard
deviation of returns. If the risk and return of individual assets are marked

with a cross then the mathematics of the theory defines a boundary for the
assets as shown in Figure 6.2:

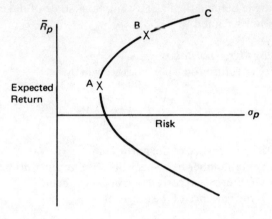

Figure 6.2

Point A is the portfolio with minimum variance and point B is the
portfolio (usually a single security) that offers the highest expected return
of all portfolios. The line AB is called the efficient frontier because any
portfolio selected below it will have a lower expected return for the same
level of risk. If short sales are permitted (i.e. selling assets one does not
own) the line can be extended from point B to point C and the efficient set
of portfolios in the upper half of the hyperbola has no upper limit.

(c) Risk-free securities
The theory postulates a risk-free rate of return, *I*, attached to a risk-free
asset, generally assumed to be short-term Government Treasury bills. By
combining this risk-free asset with the risky portfolio a straight line is
drawn in risk-return space as shown in Figure 6.3:

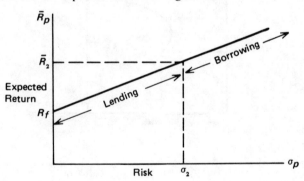

Figure 6.3

If all the combination portfolio is in the risk-free asset the risk is zero and the expected return I. If all the combination portfolio is in the risky portfolio the risk is σ_2 (the standard deviation of that risky portfolio) and the expected return R_2. By borrowing at the risk-free rate and investing further in the risky portfolio the expected return can be increased (as well as the associated risk).

By combining the concept of the efficient frontier and this straight line in risk-return space the graph is constructed as shown in Figure 6.4.

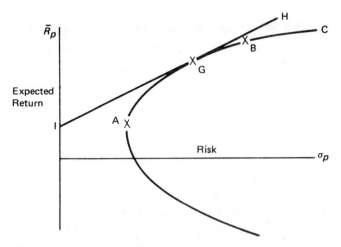

Figure 6.4

Point G is the risky portfolio offering the highest attainable reward per unit of risk. The line IG is the combination of the risk-free asset and portfolios that offer the highest expected return per unit of risk. Every 'efficient' investor invests in portfolio G with a proportion of the risk-free assets from some negative figure (if they borrow funds to invest in portfolio G) to 100%.

The optimization process for constructing portfolios consists of finding the portfolio with the greatest ratio of excess return per unit of risk. In other words:

$$\frac{\bar{R}_p - I}{\sigma_p} \text{ is to be maximized}$$

subject to $\sum_{i=1}^{n} x_i = 1$ where I is the risk-free rate and x_i is the i-th security in the portfolio.

(d) the market and diagonal models
The *market model* is:

$$R_i = a_i + \beta_i R_m$$

where R_i is the rate of return per period per cent for stock i, R_m is a random variable representing the rate of return on the market index.

a_i is the component of return on security i that is independent of the market's performance and is also a random variable.

β_i is a constant that measures the expected change in R_i given a change in R_m.

The constant β_i implies that if the market produces a return, positive or negative, of 5%, say, then stock i will produce a return, positive or negative, of $(a_i + 5 \times \beta_i)\%$.

a_i is independent of the return on the market and may be split into two components α_i, its expected value and ϵ_i, the random element of a_i.

Thus $a_i = \alpha_i + \epsilon_i$ where the expected value of ϵ_i is zero.

The basic equation of MPT is then:

$$R_i = \alpha_i + B_i R_m + \epsilon_i$$

The model if developed produces a mean return of:

$$\bar{R}_i = \alpha_i + \beta_i \bar{R}_m$$

and the variance of a security's return is:

$$\sigma_i^2 = \beta_i^2 \sigma_m^2 + \sigma_{(ei)}^2$$

A stock's risk is the sum of the market risk $(\beta_i^2 \sigma_m^2)$ and residual risk $(\sigma_{(ei)}^2)$. By assuming that securities are related only through their common response to the market, i.e. $(\sigma_{eij} = 0)$, the portfolio optimization process is simplified and the *diagonal model* produced.

$$\sigma_{ij} = \beta_i \beta_j \sigma_m^2$$

The simplicity of the diagonal model is that all necessary co-variances can be estimated from the β_is of the market model.

Betas are estimated by regression techniques using historical data. *Residual risk* (non-market risk) can be diversified away by making the number of stocks sufficiently large.

(e) The capital asset pricing model

By aggregating the actions of *all* investors equilibrium models are constructed which show the measure of risk for any asset and the relationship between expected return and risk. The assumptions are:

(i) All assets are perfectly divisible and marketable and there are no transaction costs.

(ii) There are no taxes.

(iii) All investors can borrow or lend an unlimited amount at the risk-free rate and there are no restrictions on short sales of any asset.

(iv) All investors have identical subjective estimates of the means, variances and co-variances of return among all assets.

(v) The total quantity of all assets is known.

(vi) All investors make portfolio decisions based on their expectations of mean and variance of return which maximize their expected utility of 'terminal wealth'.

The *capital market* line is:

$$R_e = R_f + \frac{\bar{R}_m - R_f}{\sigma_m} \sigma_e$$

where R_e is expected return on an efficient portfolio.

σ_e is its standard deviation.

R_f is the risk-free rate of return.

R_m is the expected return on a risky portfolio.

and σ_m is its standard deviation.

All strategies other than those employing the market portfolio and borrowing or lending lie below the capital market line because the market is efficient. The rate of interest on a risk-free asset is the reward for waiting or the price of time. The slope of the line can be regarded as the reward per risk borne.

(f) The efficient markets hypothesis

The basic tenet of the efficient markets hypothesis is that security prices reflect fully all available known information. This is very stringent and the hypothesis has been subdivided into three categories:

(i) *Weak form* tests have looked at whether information contained in historical prices is fully reflected in current stock prices.

(ii) *Semi strong* tests are tests of whether publicly available information is fully reflected in current stock prices.

(iii)   *Strong form* tests examine whether all information, public or
         private, is fully reflected in security prices and whether any type of
         investor can make an excess profit.

6.22 Modelling

(a) Equity models

Modern portfolio theory uses mathematical techniques to construct portfolios of assets, usually equities. The approach is often criticized because of
the bold assumptions underlying it. Many fund managers do use such
methods, however, and the theory has introduced, in the United States at
least, the concept of 'indexed funds'. This is a portfolio which contains all
the constituents of a published index in the appropriate proportions to
ensure that investment performance is virtually the same. Indexing cuts
costs and removes the danger of underperformance but also rules out the
possibility of outperformance.

In looking at individual shares the simplest model for valuing shares is to
equate the value to the present value of the company's future earnings or to
future streams of dividends.

The Weaver and Hall valuation model for ordinary shares is basically
designed to discover those shares which are relatively cheap or dear. The
method assigns weights to different attributes of shares and uses multiple
regression analysis to obtain 'best' estimates of the regression coefficients
for each factor and then applies these coefficients to each share to determine the appropriate yield. Comparison of the actual yield with the calculated yield provides a measure of the relative cheapness of each share.
Other valuation models for ordinary shares have been designed, each of
which has inevitable limitations. The use of any systematic procedure is
bound to have a major impact on the character of the organization that uses
it. Because of the organizational side effects the value of formal models is
liable to depend as much on the care with which they are implemented as on
their precise formulation.

(b) Gilt models

As with equity models the analysis of the gilt market may be a simple
process or one requiring computer analysis. The gilt market comprises a
number of stocks with differing characteristics – maturity date, coupon, tax
status, size of issue, type of holder etc. The market in the stocks has many
participants with differing liability structures, tax positions and other
constraints, statutory or otherwise. The objective of the fund manager is to
hold a portfolio which optimizes it in some sense. Policy moves are made in
the light of an anticipated change in the level of interest rates. Anomaly

switches are made between stocks on a temporary basis. When investing new money the manager will aim to optimize his return accordingly.

The main objective of a gilt model is to assist in making these decisions – primarily by identifying cheap or dear stocks (or areas of the market) and suggesting anomaly switches:

(i) Simple techniques – The simplest techniques use historical data to identify turning points in ratios of prices or yield differences in order to identify anomalies between pairs of stocks.

(ii) Yield curve analysis – Simple two-dimensional yield curve analysis fits a curve to the redemption yields of stocks plotting yield against term to redemption. The model is little used now but some years ago gave a reasonable model of the market despite systematically overestimating yields on lower coupon stocks and underestimating those on higher coupon stocks. The position of an individual stock relative to the curve, probably after allowing for the history of the average deviation of the gross redemption yield from the yield curve value, gives an indication of relative cheapness or dearness.

(iii) Three-dimensional models – More sophisticated analysis has expanded the model in paragraph (ii) above from two dimensions (yield as a function of life) to three dimensions (yield as a function of life and coupon).

The models developed in this way recognize that yield varies with coupon for a given term to redemption because of the income and capital gains preferences of investors. Gross investors are largely indifferent between income and capital gains whilst net investors (those taxed more highly on income than capital gains) prefer capital gains rather than income. Net investors tend to bid up the prices on low coupon stocks. A number of such models are in use but, as with models used in the equity market, their use requires care and an understanding of their limitations.

6.23 Technical analysis

What is known as fundamental analysis underlines the philosophy of this book. The fundamentalist tends to look forward. Technical analysts tend to look backwards and the word 'technical' implies a study of the market itself and not of those external factors which are reflected in the market. The factors which technical analysts tend to monitor are the level of share prices and the volume of transactions or, indeed, any statistical information produced by the market.

The technical analyst will seek out signals suggesting a particular course of action. The reliance upon past data means that technical analysis, as with MPT, is open to criticism from fundamentalists because of the lack of subjective judgement and all that implies.

In the U.K. the word 'chartist' is often used to describe a technical analyst. Much of the process requires an understanding of the nature of supply and demand. Price rises are attributed to demand being stronger than supply and vice versa for price falls. The volume of activity in a share is a measure of the strength of the move and whether it is likely to be sustained or transitory. Chartists talk of 'consolidation phases' and 'resistance levels'.

Some chartists use 'bar charts' which plot each day's price range as a vertical bar, along with the corresponding volume. Others use 'line charts' which simply connect points representing daily closing prices.

The commonest chart is probably the 'point' and 'figure' chart which uses x and o to monitor price movements. As long as the price is moving upwards movements are plotted in a single column using x each time a unit of price changes. When the share price reverses a new column is used and as long as the price falls unit price changes are marked with o. The patterns thus produced show many identifiable formations e.g. 'head and shoulders', 'double top', 'fulcrum'.

Another approach is to construct 'moving averages' to assess long-term trends. When a share price crosses its own 30- or 100-day moving average, for instance, a signal is said to have been given.

Often, rather than use an absolute share price, the chart may represent a relative figure e.g. the share price divided by an industry price index.

The rate of change of a stock price or market index over some recent period is termed 'momentum'.

The 'Dow Theory' requires that a pattern in the Dow Jones Industrial Average be 'confirmed by a required movement in the Dow Jones Transportation Average before action be taken'.

A further indication of market movement is to compute a cumulative index of the difference between the number of shares rising and the number falling each day and comparing it with the market index.

In the U.K. fundamentalists far outweigh technical analysts, as they also do exponents of MPT. In each case, however, the fund manager may regard the techniques as sufficiently interesting to note their relevance after making his fundamental analysis and before making his final judgement.

CHAPTER SEVEN

INVESTMENT IN INFLATIONARY CONDITIONS

7.1 Introduction

Attention is usually focused on the potential returns from investments in monetary terms, rather than the real rate of return after allowances for the erosion in the purchasing power of money. It may be argued that this is because the rate of inflation is a further variable in the calculations and it is already difficult enough to forecast potential investment returns without this additional variable. Nevertheless, if an investor places money in an investment instead of using the money to consume goods now, he will presumably wish to earn an overall return on his investment which will enable him not only to purchase the same goods as he could buy now at a later date but also some additional return to compensate him for the risks which he is making in this investment, and a reward for giving someone else the use of money in the intervening period. Hence, inflation should be taken into account in investment decisions, particularly since it is now possible to purchase government securities whose return is denominated in retail price index terms (index-linked gilts), and the risk and return of an investment should be evaluated against this alternative.

7.2 Real rate of return

It is possible to define a real rate of return in a number of ways, but it is usual to express it relative to retail price rises (as measured by the Retail Prices Index in the U.K.), and to use monetary values adjusted to the start of the period. A simple example will illustrate this concept. If RPI was I_1 at the start of the year and I_2 at the end, and if the initial monetary investment of X at the start of the year had increased in monetary value to Y at the year end (and no income had been paid to the investor), the real rate of return, r, over the year would be:

$$X(1+r) = \frac{YI_1}{I_2}$$

$$r = \frac{YI_1}{XI_2} - 1$$

7.3 Real returns in practice

Whilst the principle that an investor should receive a return at least sufficient to offset the erosion of inflation on his money may seem reasonable, it is worth bearing some points clearly in mind:

(a) Investments whose returns are easily assessed in monetary terms appear to have greater attractions to investors than those which are variable or uncertain in monetary terms. For example, conventional gilts would be preferred to index-linked gilts (all other things being equal). This does not mean, however, that assets where returns cannot be easily calculated, e.g. equities, will not be purchased by investors.

(b) The tax system in the U.K. is still linked to the monetary as opposed to the real return, although some efforts have been made to improve this situation in recent years.

(c) Many examples can be given where investors have received returns which are totally inadequate to offset the effects of inflation, but this does not appear to have dulled the investors' appetite for such assets (e.g. conventional gilts over most of the period since the Second World War, building society deposits during the 1970s).

7.4 The effect of inflation on various asset categories

Over the twenty years to the end of 1984 U.K. price inflation has averaged over 9% per annum and about 12% per annum over the last ten years. Although inflation has been reduced to about 5% per annum for 1983, 1984 and part of 1985, it may be optimistic to suggest that inflation is under control, and investors will continue to be forced to pay particular attention to the possible effects of inflation in the formulation of investment strategy. Table 7.1 gives details of price inflation over periods to the end of 1984 together with nominal and real returns for various U.K. asset classes and various overseas equity markets for a U.K. gross investor (i.e. no allowance is made for income and capital gains tax).

Some interesting conclusions can be made from these figures:

(a) The real return on conventional long-dated gilts has been negative for all the longer combined periods shown, but is positive for the five- and ten-year periods to the end of 1984.

(b) The real return on a short-term asset such as Treasury Bills has been close to zero (i.e. the monetary return was near to that needed to offset the erosion in purchasing power of the money invested over most periods).

(c) The long-term overall real rate of return (i.e. capital growth plus gross

Table 7.1 *Overall (capital + income) returns in monetary terms to a gross investor investing in various asset categories for periods ending on 31st December 1984*

Period in years	Equities %	Return on long gilts %	Treasury bills %	Price inflation %
5	26.9	18.3	12.6	8.4
10	29.6	18.1	11.6	11.9
15	14.2	11.5	10.4	11.5
20	13.2	9.0	9.5	9.6
25	11.6	7.4	8.5	8.3
30	12.6	6.0	7.8	7.3
35	13.3	5.5	6.9	6.8

Table 7.1 can be rewritten in terms of real rates of return (measured relative to retail prices).

Table 7.2

Period in years	Equities %	Real return on long gilts %	Treasury bills %
5	17.1	9.1	3.8
10	15.8	5.5	−0.3
15	2.4	0.0	−1.0
20	3.3	−0.5	−0.1
25	3.0	−0.8	0.2
30	4.9	−1.2	0.4
35	6.1	−1.5	0.2

Note Returns have been derived from indices compiled by de Zoete & Bevan and published in the de Zoete Equity – Gilt Study in January 1985.

income received) on U.K. shares has been approximately 5%–6% per annum, although this rate has not been achieved for some intermediate periods. It should be borne in mind that the longest periods include the rerating of equities from having an income yield more than conventional gilts in the earlier years to the current position of an income yield less than gilts (i.e. a reverse yield gap). The real returns for the five- and ten-year periods are very high by historic standards.

(d) The major classes of investment for U.K. life offices and pension funds will now be examined to ascertain their suitability for an investment portfolio designed to offset the effects of inflation. As described earlier in Chapter 6, investors need to take many factors into account when making up a portfolio of assets such as the need for diversification to reduce risk, and the pattern of liabilities, but attention in this analysis is concentrated on the inflationary factors.

7.5 Index-linked gilts

At present, these government guaranteed stocks have an overall rate of return from capital appreciation and gross income combined of between 3% and 5% above the rate of increase in retail prices if held to maturity. Investors needing to reinvest the income received prior to maturity do not know the reinvestment rates which will prevail in future years, but because the income element of this stock is relatively small, alternative assumptions for the reinvestment rates in the future do not have a major effect on the overall real rate of return, particularly for the short- and medium-dated stocks and for net funds. A real rate of return over prices is only guaranteed if the stock is held to maturity but there is still a much higher chance of earning a real rate of return on these stocks than with other types of investment. The high degree of certainty of the return in real terms for index-linked gilts should mean that other asset categories offer the expectation of a greater real rate of return but with additional risk. The historic returns set out in Table 7.2 show, however, that if the index-linked gilt had been available in the past with the same real returns as those available now, it would have produced a higher real rate of return than U.K. long-dated gilts and Treasury Bills in all periods considered over ten years in duration.

Investors, such as pensions funds, needing to secure an overall rate of return to at least match salary inflation, may still find this asset attractive because if past trends continue, salaries will rise at about 2% more than retail prices, and the index-linked gilt will offer a rate of return at least sufficient to keep pace with salary rises.

An investment in index-linked gilts enables pension fund investors to ensure a real return for at least part of the fund in excess of the likely rise in liabilities caused by salary inflation. The remainder can be invested with greater attention to the expected return and less to diversification than can a portfolio without such a holding.

Index-linked gilts have the advantage that the bulk of the return is deferred well into the future and the current income is low relative to conventional gilts. Since many institutional funds at the present time usually have greater contribution income than benefit outgo, the lack of immediate income is advantageous because most of the return is effectively reinvested within the stock.

Index-linked gilts may be used to lock in favourable returns from other asset categories. If, for example, an investment was made in U.K. shares on 1st January 1980, it could have earned a real rate of return of about 17% per annum by the end of 1984. If the equities were then sold and index-linked gilts maturing in say 2016 were purchased on a real rate of return of 3% per annum, the total real return from the investment from 1980 to 2016 is likely to be approximately 4¾% per annum. This figure of 4¾% per annum may be compared with the figures for long-term real returns on equities set out in Table 7.2.

7.6 Conventional gilts

These government guaranteed assets have the income and the redemption proceeds fixed in monetary terms. Their ability to provide a real rate of return requires the receipt of sufficient income to offset the decline in real value of the coupons received and the redemption proceeds. The current income is higher than on many other asset types but this can cause a particular problem for those requiring the income to be reinvested as the overall return on the investment in real terms depends critically not only on the level of inflation but upon the future rates at which the income can be reinvested. Unlike index-linked gilts where much of the return is con-centrated in the year of maturity, most of the return for a conventional gilt is in the immediate years following purchase. Under the current tax system the whole of the income from a conventional gilt is taxable even though some of this may be needed to offset the effects of the decline in money values. This factor needs to be taken into account for net funds.

A surprising comparison is often made between the redemption yield on a conventional gilt and the current rate of inflation. It is often argued that, if the redemption yield on gilts is, say, 11% and inflation is currently 5%, then the gilts offer a real return of 6%. This simplistic comparison ignores not only the problem of the rate of reinvestment of income in future years but also of the levels of inflation in future years.

Although gilts may be a useful short-term investment for many insti-tutions when interest rates are expected to fall, and a longer-term asset for those with money-related liabilities, the retention of large proportions in, say, a pension fund portfolio may be hard to justify except on diversi-fication arguments. The long-term case for investment in conventional gilts for most investors should be on the grounds that these assets offer a better rate of return (including a risk premium) than index-linked gilts but there must be a break-even point for future inflation rates where indexed gilts are more attractive. It is, however, comparatively rare to see the argument that indexed rather than conventional gilts should be purchased if the expected long-term rate of inflation is higher than $x\%$. The historical returns on conventional gilts in Table 7.2 illustrate the poor historic record for achieving real rates of return, except for short periods, even for investors whose returns are not diminished by the effects of taxation.

The picture is much bleaker for net investors.

7.7 Equities

Returns on equities depend on many factors and neither dividends nor future capital values are known in advance. Thus, estimates of potential real rates of return on equities may be subject to higher levels of error than certain other asset categories. An investor needs to choose particular stocks in which to invest but in this section the real returns on equities as an asset class are discussed and any profits (or losses) due to individual stock selection are ignored.

From Table 7.2, it can be seen that the real rate of return on equities from income and capital appreciation over long periods has been about 5%–6% per annum. The consensus view for the risk-free real rate of borrowing would be of the order of 3% per annum, and this would imply that the risk premium for equities should be about 2%–3% above the risk-free rate. The prospective real yields available on government-guaranteed index-linked gilts until maturity have been between 2% and just over 5% since the stocks were first issued in 1981, but have been close to the 3% level for long-dated stocks for most of this period. Against this background, a 2%–3% per annum premium for the risk of purchasing equities compared with index-linked gilts would suggest that a 5%–6% overall real return on U.K. equities in general may be a reasonable goal for the future.

A prospective real rate of return for U.K. equities of 5% to 6% derived above needs to be examined against the economic background to see if this rate of real return is consistent with likely growth rates for the U.K. economy. This analysis requires the use of several assumptions, such as the proportion of Gross National Product that will be allocated to equity shareholders in future years, and examines equities in total without taking into account the different growth rates of various sectors of the economy. In the long term, the real returns on U.K. shares must have regard to the real rate earned by 'U.K. Limited' on its capital employed. Similar arguments can be used for individual components of U.K. industry and commerce. The real returns on U.K. shares over the five- and ten-year periods to the end of 1984 have substantially exceeded the real return earned by 'U.K. Limited' on its capital employed.

Although U.K. shares may be expected to earn long-term returns more than sufficient to offset the effects of price inflation, inflation is only one of the many determinants of share prices, and even over periods of some years there may be no clear link between share prices and inflation. Recent indications are that the higher the level of price inflation, the lower the likely level of real return.

An analysis can also be made on dividends of shares, rather than on the overall return including capital appreciation on shares as well. Some have argued that dividends which are based on company profits would be reasonably constant in real terms, rising or falling with the level of trade, with the share of 'value added' deemed to be provided by capital and with the share of the return on capital taken by ordinary shareholders. This assumption of constancy is, however, only justified in rather broad terms in the U.K. and real dividends appear to have long periods of either growth or decline. A real yield on shares of about 3% per annum can be justified on historic data for the very long term.

7.8 Overseas equities

The long-term real rate of return from investment in overseas shares would not be expected to be less than that from U.K. shares. Some reasons for this are:

(a) Apart from arguments of portfolio diversification (see (d) below), there would be little point in investing overseas if the overall return did not exceed that in the U.K., as there are some additional risks in overseas investment compared with investment in the U.K.
(b) It is possible to invest in industries overseas which are not widely available in the U.K., and some of these would be in high growth markets.
(c) It is possible to invest in countries which are likely to display higher levels of economic growth than the U.K., and, hopefully, this will be translated into corresponding rises in equity prices in that country.
(d) The real rates of return on the overseas equity portfolio to a sterling investor may be very volatile due particularly to currency fluctuations. Over longer periods differences between inflation levels in the U.K. and overseas are usually reflected in corresponding exchange rate alterations. By choosing stock markets whose movements are not highly correlated with those of the U.K. it is possible to reduce the volatility in real terms of the total equity portfolio by including an element of overseas shares. For particular overseas stock markets there is some evidence to suggest that higher longer-term overall real rates of return (i.e. real returns to a sterling investor) are accompanied by higher volatilities of real return in individual years.

(e) The connection between share prices and inflation which is believed to exist in the U.K. over reasonable timespans does not necessarily translate into overseas markets, and in the U.S. there appears to be no clear evidence for the view that common stocks act as a hedge against U.S. inflation.

7.9 Property

Property has some similar characteristics to index-linked gilts in that there is usually a low immediate income, a regular increase in income by means of rent reviews and more stability in capital values than with equities.

Investors in property should receive a higher overall real rate of return than is available on index-linked gilts to take into account the lower level of security, the costs of management and refurbishment. Investors can ascertain the rate of growth needed (in RPI terms) for rental values at each rent review in order that the overall real return on a property is higher than on index-linked gilts. In recent years many investors will have found that they need rental growth well in excess of the Retail Prices Index to justify the price paid for certain property. Property rents are an input to industry's costs (in contrast to equity profits which may share in economic growth) which may suggest that rentals will in the long term move more in line with prices than with wages. Industry's future demand for property may also be lower than in the past, there may be the possibility of adverse legislation and rent freezes, refurbishment may be needed, and all these factors may make optimistic assumptions for rental growth difficult to justify.

Property is a major component of institutional portfolios but it is necessary to ensure that the price paid does not require too optimistic rates for rental growth, and that an adequate margin over the index-linked gilt return is obtained.

Overseas property holdings have become fashionable in the early 1980s, but for U.S. property the fundamental arguments which are used to justify property investment in the U.K. (i.e. tight property controls, secure tenants, long leases etc.) are usually absent. In essence, property returns in certain parts of the U.S. may be mainly dependent on economic growth, and if this is so there may be better ways of participating in such growth than with U.S. property.

7.10 The overall portfolio

The assessment of potential real rates of return and their associated levels of risk on various asset categories enables investors to ascertain the likely overall real rate of return in the longer item on their total portfolios. As a minimum, the overall potential real return should never be less than that available on index-linked gilts, and the level above this will depend on the extent that there is a wish to guarantee particular levels of real return, and the level of risk that is taken.

The prospective real rates of return for a gross investor in Autumn 1985 may be summarized from sections 7.5 to 7.9 as:

	Prospective Real Return *% p.a.*
Index-linked Gilts	3
U.K. Property	3½–4
U.K. Equities	5
Overseas Equities	at least 5
Conventional Gilts	?

For gross investors (i.e. pension funds), the prospective real returns from a balanced portfolio investing in the above areas may be expected to be in the 3½% to 5% range, and somewhat lower levels than this for institutional funds which are subject to tax.

CHAPTER EIGHT

PRACTICAL PORTFOLIO MANAGEMENT

8.1 Introduction

In the latter part of this chapter an account is given of how investment performance is measured. Work on this has intensified recently and investing institutions have a much greater awareness of the need for monitoring their own performance. Some of the techniques described later lead logically to an understanding of how fund management works in practice. Analysis of a fund's activities will show whether the correct sectors were chosen for investment (e.g. gilts, property, equities) and how good stock selection was within those sectors; it will also show how propitious the timing was for new money or switches. These three factors, namely, sector weighting, stock selection and timing, are sometimes the responsibility of different groups of people.

8.2 The investment committee

Most institutional funds are governed either by a board of directors or a group of trustees. One or two committee members may have investment experience and it is often the case that an investment committee is formed to which detailed advice will be given either by external advisers (e.g. stockbroker or merchant bank) or, if the institution is large enough, by executive investment managers. The committee will recommend policy from time to time for approval of the full board or trustees and this policy will form the basis for investing new money and managing existing funds.

The policy formulated at monthly or quarterly intervals should not restrict the detailed activities of the investment managers of the fund but should restate or endorse the following items.

(a) Rates of income or capital gains tax to be used in assessing or comparing investments.
(b) A definition of standard rates of interest to be used for the same purposes.
(c) Broad trends expected in the main economic indicators – GDP growth, consumption, inflation, capital investment etc. For a fund investing overseas such a summary will be required for all areas.

(d) A basic statement of the relative attractions of the principal sectors (gilts, property, cash etc.) and the target weightings in each.

It follows from (d) above that the responsibility for performance arising from sector weightings lies with the investment committee of the fund. It may be that they have acted on information and recommendations from their investment advisers but they must also accept responsibility for the appointment of the advisers!

8.3 Implementation of policy

Once a broad policy has been prepared and agreed by the board of directors or trustees it is the responsibility of the investment managers of the fund to implement the action required. For smaller institutions and many pension funds it is not economical to have an internal investment department and it is usual to retain an external investment manager for a fee. There has been a steady growth in the availability of such services from stockbrokers, merchant banks and others commensurate with the increase in the number of investing institutions in the U.K. over the last decade. Annual costs should be targeted at between 1/8% and 1/2% of the funds under management according to the types of sectors managed. Following traditions established in the United States it is possible to arrange contracts such that superior investment performance leads to increased fees, but fees not related to performance are much more common. An independent stock exchange investment department is difficult to justify if the fund size is less than £50 million.

The larger the funds under the control of a particular investment institution become, the more cost effective and competitive it should be because of certain fixed costs which become proportionately cheaper under economies of scale.

It should be remembered that even if it becomes cost effective for an institution to develop its own investment management for stock exchange activity it may not simultaneously be appropriate for it to have its own property team. Even for the larger institutions there is still a role for the specialist external manager of the property portfolio, the overseas portfolio and other specialist sectors. It is perfectly feasible for a committee to agree a policy of investing in a sector which they and the executive investment management find attractive but for a specialist adviser to be invited to handle the transactions.

'In-house' stock exchange investment department

An institutional investment department comprises two distinct functions. The first is responsible for the maintenance of existing portfolios and processes information enabling it to make recommendations or act in accordance with agreed policy. It is, in essence, a research, portfolio management and dealing function. The other principal function is accounting, which ensures that records are kept in an appropriate form, that payments to stockbrokers and others are duly made, and that all payments due to be received e.g. by way of dividends, are made and accounted for.

(a) Research and dealing

The management of a portfolio is largely the assimilation of information and the processing of opinions followed by firm recommendations or actions. The degree to which primary research material is sought will depend upon the size of the institution. Many fund managers will be satisfied with establishing good relationships with several specialist advisers on whom they may rely for in-depth studies of certain topics. Many stockbrokers seek to establish strengths in particular areas in order to attract a clientele. The range of facilities available to investment managers these days is diverse and, as benefits the times, much of it is available in the form of proprietary software through an appropriate computer terminal.

Much information is available from stockbrokers. Written comment encompasses economic notes, notes on different equity sectors worldwide, and detailed company studies worldwide. Some brokers publish strategy documents aimed at assisting the smaller investment departments to develop ideas for submission to an investment committee. This written comment is supported by up-to-the-minute information on the telephone and personal contact. Direct contact with companies themselves is also essential on occasions.

Further written information is available from company reports and accounts, Extel and other proprietary services. These documents form part of the library of written information available to an investment department. This library may be enhanced by newspapers, trade journals and other publications providing a range of comment. Such a library will these days include information on microfilm or microfiche. The diversity of opinion will ensure that staff are still required to develop their critical faculties to a high degree.

A mass of statistical data has blossomed over the past decade as the City has found good uses for the computer. Stockbrokers have developed sophisticated programs enabling them to analyse market data e.g. gilt switches, in a way that twenty years ago was unthinkable. Nor has this mass of data led to uniformity of ideas. Basic assumptions still have to be made for any analysis and the diversity of views guarantees, by and large, a willing buyer of stock for a willing seller of stock. Proprietary services such as Datastream give access to all aspects of records and have been refined to the state of giving the information graphically. For investment managers dealing actively prices are important as are recent results. Services such as TOPIC, the Stock Exchange Viewdata service, can be invaluable. The information flow is enhanced by the 'closed user groups' operated on certain of these services by stockbrokers, foreign exchange dealers and other market operators.

The final data required for active fund management are details of the fund itself. The cash position of a fund must be known regularly and if surplus balances accrue they will be placed on the money market for a short period. For a stationary or declining fund access to data showing how quickly investment should be realized is just as important.

All information received from the sources outlined above is sifted, used, discarded or filed. The objective is to enable fund managers to have sufficient information at their disposal to administer the funds under their control properly and to invest new money wisely. An important aspect of this process is the monitoring of the effectiveness of information from each source. In particular, is it accurate and is it necessary? It is sometimes necessary to indulge in some pruning in order to ensure that staff may see the wood from the trees.

(b) Administration and accounting section

A number of tasks are carried out by this section which may be part of the investment department or may be part of the institution's centralized accounts area. The main duties of this section are as follows:

(i)   Prepare, based on expected inflows or outflows of cash, a calendar of cash surpluses or deficits for the fund managers' guidance. On a day-by-day basis cash positions will be advised to the manager and whoever deals with the placing or calling of money market deposits.

(ii)   Effect the necessary settlement of contracts, stock market or property. This will involve liaison with dealing staff to verify the bargain, with banks and with stockbrokers. The recording of these transactions will probably be computerized through one of several proprietary systems available. Some institutions, e.g. small unit trusts, may hand this part of the operation entirely to an outside agency.

(iii)   Verify income received, particularly changes arising from dealing where a contractual obligation may exist to pay or receive a split dividend or coupon.

(iv)   Ensure the prompt signing and sealing of documents associated with transactions or income e.g. transfer deeds. Also ensure that title relating to completed transactions is correct and that all documents are held in safe custody. This section may be responsible for the completion and despatch of proxy forms associated with bid documents etc.

(v)   Value the assets of the fund as required. As in (ii) above this may be achieved by proprietary systems such as Datastream or Extel. Prices for certain stocks, e.g. unquoted securities, will be supplied through the dealing section as prescribed by the Department of Trade.

(vi)   Conduct negotiations associated with tax. Approved pension funds must obtain tax refunds on dividends as quickly as possible. Life Companies will require records of contingent and actual liability to Capital Gains Tax.

(vii)   A number of minor but important statistical services will need to be carried out from time to time. Reports on business done and the financial situation of funds will be required for investment committees of boards of directors or trustees. The investment management will need to examine the commission paid to stock-brokers and relate the sum to the services provided to the fund. It is also necessary to budget for investment expenses. Performance is the final product and is covered later in this chapter.

(c) Departmental structure

An example of an organization chart is given in Figure 8.1. It is by no means a perfect solution but does illustrate the various functions.

Most institutions will not be able to justify a separate research section. The areas of speciality shown, e.g. U.K. equities, will probably be controlled by a fund manager with some assistants who between them will research and deal in all relevant stocks or shares. The cost effectiveness of stockbrokers' research departments means that most institutions will rely upon them for detailed research material. The department's job is one of conducting its own general economic research followed by 'secondary research' in specific industries or shares which involve finding a stockbroker or other adviser specializing in that area and maintaining close contact with him. Some institutions will follow their own 'systems' of share selections which may require input of share data from advisers.

Another helpful diagram, Figure 8.2, is one showing the decision routes in the department.

As already indicated the investment administration and accounting

Figure 8.1

function may fall within the office's accounts function or may be completely delegated to an outside agency.

Property investment requires expertise and detailed knowledge quite distinct from stockmarket practice and may be delegated to a separate department of surveyors or an appointed specialist outside the organization. Its policy will be subject to the overall direction of investment management as shown in the structure. For small pension funds it may be more practical to purchase units in a property trust.

8.4 Investment performance – the construction and use of indices

Share and bond indices provide a useful barometer of the level of a sector of the bond or equity market, or of the overall market.

Indices can give an indication of short-term changes in market prices. Each day some prices may increase whilst others may fall, and an index enables the magnitude of the net effect to be ascertained.

Indices can be used to identify long-term trends in prices or other factors such as yields and price/earnings ratios. This gives an investor some guidance on the level of the market compared with previous years and may help to identify times when prices are abnormally high or low.

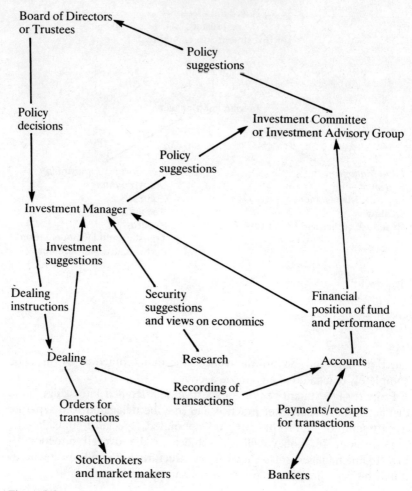

Figure 8.2

Indices can also be used in the measurement of the performance of portfolios and this is discussed further below.

(a) Construction – geometric method
The ratios of share price movements since the base date are multiplied and the appropriate geometric mean calculated.

$$\text{Index} = \sqrt[i]{\frac{P_t^1}{P_o^1} \times \frac{P_t^2}{P_o^2} \times \ldots \ldots \frac{P_t^i}{P_o^i}}$$

Where P_o^1 is the price of share 1 at time o and P_t^1 is the price of share 1 at time t. There are i shares in the index.

A geometric index is easy to calculate and is simple to adjust for technical changes such as scrip or rights issues, or a change in constituent companies. It gives equal weight to each share and a fair indication of short-term price movements. It does, however, have disadvantages. If one share falls substantially in price it has a disproportionate effect on the index and if the price falls to zero, so does the index. If an investor put an equal sum of money into each share making up the index, the index would not move in line with the portfolio value. This can be seen from an example of an index which consists of two shares. At the start share 1 is valued at 100p and share 2 at 100p. Share 1 falls to 50p and share 2 rises to 200p. The investor who puts £100 into each share, sees his £200 investment rise in value to £250 (i.e. a rise of 25%), but the index is unchanged in value.

$$\sqrt{\frac{50}{100} \times \frac{200}{100}} = 1 \text{ i.e. } 0\% \text{ rise}$$

In general in times of rising prices the geometric index will lag a portfolio consisting of the underlying shares, and consequently a geometric index is unsuitable for portfolio performance purposes.

(b) Construction – arithmetic method
This is based on an arithmetic mean of the price ratios. With just a few constituents the index value can be largely influenced by the rise in price of a single share since the base date, and the relative performance depends on the base date. Arithmetic means are generally confined to large numbers of shares.

An arithmetic mean is usually used in a form where it is weighted and where individual shares are given different levels of importance. In general, the weights are usually the market capitalizations of the shares either fixed at a date or altered as the market capitalizations alter.

If the fixed-weight index is chosen, it will be determined as

$$\frac{\sum No\, Po\, \dfrac{Pt}{Po}}{\sum No\, Po}$$

Where Po = price at time o, and Pt is the price at time t

No = number of shares at time o, and Nt is the number of shares at time t.

A current weighted index would be calculated as

$$\frac{\sum \; Nt\, Pt \; \dfrac{Pt}{Po}}{\sum Nt Pt}$$

A disadvantage of a fixed weighted index is that the weights become out of date over time, but the current weighted index does not alter like a meaningful portfolio. In designing a weighted arithmetic index the rules for dealing with changes such as rights issues and weights are a major consideration. An arithmetic index is more difficult and time consuming to calculate but this disadvantage has been largely removed by computerization.

8.5 U.K. share indices in general use

(a) Financial Times industrial ordinary index
This Index is based on 30 leading stocks and is a geometric index. It has been published since 1935 and its main purpose is to provide a quick guide to the market's movements. Other indices should be used to ascertain market changes over periods longer than one year. The index depends on the actual shares making up the index and also the way in which shares are added or deleted. Changes to the index are kept to a minimum. This has led to a bias towards 'mature' companies and at times to distortions caused by the performances of single shares (e.g. Rolls-Royce, John Brown, Turner & Newall) which exacerbates its geometric basis defect as a long-term measure.

(b) The FT-Actuaries share indices
These indices have been produced since 1962 on the main sectors of the market and certain subgroups. The indices are published daily in *The Financial Times*.

The Industrial Group Index consists of 483 shares, and this is split into Capital Goods, Consumer Group and Other Group. Each of these three sectors is further subdivided, e.g. Other Group consists of Chemicals, Office Equipment, Shipping and Transport and Miscellaneous. The Industrial Group plus the Oils make up the 500 Companies Index commonly known as the '500 Share Index'. When the Financial Group, Investment Trusts, Mining Finance and Overseas Traders are added to the 500 Share Index, the well-known All Share Index is obtained (750 shares).

As well as the index value, the estimated earnings yield, gross dividend yield, ex-dividend adjustment and P/E ratio are shown for each sector, except certain financial sectors where such information is inappropriate or unavailable.

The indices are a compromise between a fixed weight and a current weight index. The formula has fixed weight between changes but changes are similar to that which would be expected from a current weight index. At each change in the index constituents, the weights (i.e. the market capitalization of the shares) are altered, but continuity is preserved by 'selling' the portfolio immediately prior to the change and reinvesting the proceeds with nil expenses and using the same share prices in the shares immediately after the change. This means that if the weight given to one company is increased (because of a rights issue) then a small part of each other company is 'sold' to buy the new shares.

(c) FT-SE index
This index (*The Financial Times* – Stock Exchange Index) is based on the 100 leading stocks and was based at 1000 on 1st January 1984. It is calculated continuously and forms the base for dealing in the FT-SE Traded Option and London Financial Future. It is known colloquially as the 'Footsie' index.

The index includes the largest 100 companies measured by Stock Exchange valuation, which account for nearly 70% of the total market value of quoted U.K. shares. Some companies with large market values have been omitted from the index for particular reasons.

The index is a weighted arithmetic index. The base values are re-calculated each quarter to reflect alterations in constituents and their market valuations. Changes to the index weights are made during a quarter for rights issues, or other changes in share capital of a company. No yield is published for the index.

(d) Fixed-interest indices
The objectives of these indices are somewhat different.

The first is to provide a description of the level and also the shape of the yield structure at a point in time and, following from this, a historic record of these items. Another objective is to provide a standard against which the portfolio performance of fixed interest investors can be measured. There are many other uses such as a comparison with the yields on ordinary shares to provide a measure of the 'yield gap' or the 'level of confidence'.

Two sets of indices are now available for the gilt-edged, debenture and preference share markets. One set provides a current and historical description of the market showing gross redemption yields, whilst the other set provides a standard for portfolio performance by giving a price for the fixed interest market together with ex-dividend adjustments to enable rates of return to be calculated.

For gilt-edged securities average gross redemption yields are given for the low, medium and high coupon categories, and further subdivided for 5-year, 15-year and 25-year redemption date yield points. A flat yield is also given for irredeemable stocks. The debentures and loan stocks yields are divided only by redemption date (again 5 years, 15 years and 25 years), and a flat yield is also shown for preference stocks. The index yields are derived by fitting a curve to the redemption yields for all stocks in the coupon band.

The price indices for gilt-edged securities are produced for All Stocks, Irredeemables, Under 5 years to maturity, 5 to 15 years to maturity and Over 15 years. These indices are arithmetically weighted gross prices (with accrued interest for short-dated gilts) weighted by market capitalization and represent the price performance for a holder of a uniform percentage of all the relevant issues. Separate figures are given on the ex-dividend adjustment so that rates of return can be constructed taking into account tax at the relevant rate. A single price index is calculated for Debentures and Loans and another for preference stocks. The mechanics of calculation are essentially the same as for the FT-Actuaries share index.

(e) Overseas indices

The quality and coverage of the FT-Actuaries indices for both shares and fixed interest assets is not to be found in many overseas countries. The Standard and Poors series of share indices in the U.S.A. are similar to those of the FT-Actuaries in the U.K., and there are overall market indices in a few other countries constructed in a broadly similar way. Sophisticated bond indices outside the U.K. and U.S.A. are rare. Investors wishing to use a consistent set of indices for stock markets in a number of overseas countries can use the Capital International Indices. A consistent weighted average method is used for calculation but the indices may be confined to market leaders rather than being a barometer of general stock market levels.

8.6 Investment performance measurement – portfolios

There are a number of reasons which can be advanced for performance measurement.

(a) To monitor the progress of investments

Institutional investors can use a wide range of investments, either directly, or indirectly through a unit trust or managed fund, where the future value of those investments cannot be determined at the outset. The investments may be held to meet certain liabilities and it will be necessary to chart the progress of the assets to ensure that the benefits can be paid as they fall due. Investment in certain types of asset will increase the likelihood of a greater overall return for the fund, but this will probably be accompanied by a higher chance of failing to secure the required level of return. Investors will therefore need to monitor the overall spread of investments, the return from each class of investment, and their associated levels of risk.

(b) To ascertain the relative performance

Institutional funds are generally managed by expert fund managers either employed directly or indirectly if the services of another institution are also used. It is necessary to ascertain whether the manager is doing a good, bad or indifferent job when compared with other managers of funds in a similar position.

(c) To analyse past performance and allocate future resources

The overall return on a fund will depend upon a number of factors such as the liability profile against which the investments are held and the tax position of the fund, but the return can usually be analysed between:

(i)   the strategy – the element due to the proportions held in each of the various asset categories (i.e. in equities, gilts, property etc.). and

(ii)   the securities – the returns on the actual assets held within each asset category.

If the contribution to the overall return is split between these two factors the investor can see the relative importance of each in the past and this should enable resources to be concentrated on the most important areas, and to facilitate corrective action where the performance is relatively poor. All too often meetings of trustees of pension funds and investment committees of life offices are dominated by a discussion of the relative merits of individual shares, and in many such cases it can be shown that the performance of the U.K. portfolio is closely in line with the market averages and has little effect on the overall result for the fund. It may well be better to allocate more of the meeting to discuss the strategy decision which has tended to be the main determinant of performance, and to let the individual manager use his expertise to pick individual shares.

(d) To identify managers with above-average track records

Performance measurement also enables investors to identify investment managers of the main institutions specializing in discretionary fund management with a good track record for the past, and to be aware of managers' characteristics, strengths and weaknesses before an appointment is made. When performance figures are requested nearly every prospective manager seems to be able to produce some statistics indicating an above-average past performance. The use of a consistent and objective basis for performance analysis provides a rational basis for assessing each manager's claims.

A life office has liabilities extending over a number of years and usually a proportion of these liabilities is fixed in monetary terms.

A pension fund has long-term liabilities (generally longer than those of a life office) and thus it is a continuing long-term exercise to determine whether the investments are achieving a satisfactory performance to enable the benefits to be paid when they fall due. The investment strategy followed by a pension fund or life office may be for the long term but in recent years many investment managers have tended to invest using a fairly short-term time horizon. This trend may be because of the view that the long term is a succession of short terms; the investment outlook is clouded with uncertainty; or because performance measurement services have, unfortunately, focused attention on short-term results.

Emphasis on short-term figures may discourage managers from taking remedial action which may be necessary for good long-term performance because they do not wish the expenses or size of any change to impair their short-term performance figures.

For most funds the short-term figures are not likely to be a good guide for the longer-term results and, unless the manager has disastrous results, his performance should be assessed over at least one stock market cycle. A stock market cycle varies in duration but does show how the manager copes in conditions of rising and falling security prices. This usually means waiting at least five years before reaching a firm conclusion about the manager's ability. A longer period may be necessary where an unconventional investment philosophy is used but because of the higher levels of risk often involved in these cases, an adverse situation cannot be left to continue indefinitely. Short-term figures for single quarters or single years may be useful to see trends established or to assess short-term market timing but the dangers of making firm conclusions from short-term figures should be avoided.

8.7 Investment performance measurement – the methods of measurement

There are many methods which can be used to measure the investment return on a fund and the appropriate method depends on the question that the calculations are designed to answer. For example, is the purpose to calculate the rate of return which has been earned on the pension fund or life office assets over a particular period, or is it to compare the performance of several different investment managers? Whatever the question, it is vital to have this clearly in mind when looking at the results.

The methods generally in use for pension funds assume that funds are investing to obtain the highest overall rate of return from income and capital combined, and take into account both income received and changes in market value. As funds generally have much more investment income and contributions than benefit outgo, it is assumed that there is no need to sell investments to pay benefits and no requirement for a specified level of current income. For life offices, the aim is usually to maximize the overall rate of return on the fund when tax and the liability structure have been taken into account. This may mean that a certain proportion of the assets is held in certain categories for 'matching' or income considerations.

Market prices midway between the buying and selling prices (mid-market prices) are generally used as the measure of the value of an asset at each point in time in performance assessment, even though funds could not necessarily sell their holdings at a price equal to this value. The price used is the same for all funds and enables the success of various alternative strategies to be determined, even though market prices are not necessarily relevant for funds that have no need to sell assets to pay benefits. The use of market values also provides a rate at which income can be exchanged into capital and vice versa.

(a) The money-weighted rate of return

If calculations are intended to measure the rate of return which has been earned in the assets of the fund then the money-weighted rate of return may be the appropriate measure. The money-weighted rate of return is that used in discounted cash flow calculations. The money-weighted rate of return is sometimes called the internal rate of return. This can be specified as follows:

If the initial market value of the portfolio is M_1, the final market value at time n is M_2 and C_j is the amount of the contribution made at time t_j before the end of the period, then the annual money-weighted rate of return i may be found from

$$M_1(1+i)^n + \sum_j C_j(1+i)^{t_j} = M_2$$

The rate of return i will be influenced by the timing and magnitude of the cash flows as can be seen from the following simplified and rather extreme example. Let us suppose that there are two funds A and B. The market value of both funds falls from 100 to 50 at the middle of the year and then fund B receives a cash injection of 100. Fund A now has assets of 50 and fund B of 150. During the second half of the year both funds double the value of their assets, so at the year end fund A has assets of 100 and fund B assets of 300.

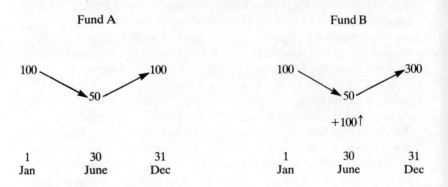

Fund A   Fund B

The money-weighted rate of return for Fund A is

$$100\,(1+i) = 100 \quad \underline{i = 0\%}$$

and for B is

$$100\,(1+i) + 100\,(1+i)^{\frac{1}{2}} = 300 \quad \underline{i = 69.7\%}$$

However, the manager of fund A has seen the value of his assets under management halve in the first half of the year and double in the second half. So has the investment manager of fund B. Although both managers achieve similar performances on the assets under management the money-weighted rates of return differ substantially because fund B was fortunate to receive some new money at the bottom of the market. The incidence and magnitude of new money flows are usually outside the control of fund managers and so any method which attempts to compare the performances of different managers should aim to eliminate the effect of new money flows.

(b) The time-weighted rate of return
The time-weighted rate of return method seeks to eliminate the distorting effect of new money flows by calculating the market value of the assets each time there is a cash flow and taking the product of the ratios of successive valuations. In other words, it examines the performance of a rep-

resentative slice of the fund. In the above example, the calculations of the time-weighted rate of return would be:

Fund A   Fund B

$$(1+i) = \frac{50}{100} \times \frac{100}{50}$$ $$(1+i) = \frac{50}{100} \times \frac{300}{150}$$

$$i = 0\%$$ $$i = 0\%$$

The rates of return in this example are now similar using this method but there is an additional problem in that the use of this method requires a valuation of the fund each time there is a cash flow. This is not a practical proposition for the vast majority of funds and some approximation is needed which will produce a close and, ideally, unbiased estimate of the true time-weighted rate of return. The method usually used is the 'linked internal rate of return'. Periods of one quarter of a year are used and the money-weighted rate of return is calculated for each quarter. The rates are then linked together so that if, for example, the calculated rates for four quarters were 1%, 2%, 3% and 4%, the linked internal rate of return for the year would be:

$$1.01 \times 1.02 \times 1.03 \times 1.04 = 1.104 \quad \text{i.e. } 10.4\%$$

Since only one quarter is considered at a time the importance of the new money relative to the money already in the fund is reduced considerably, but the procedure does not entirely eliminate the effect of new money flows. If periods shorter than one quarter are selected then a closer approximation to the true time-weighted rate of return would be achieved. The shorter the time period the more extensive the data and the number of calculations required; a reasonable balance should be obtained between increased administration and increased accuracy.

(c) The unit price method
The value of a holding in a unit trust or in an insurance company managed fund is obtained by dividing the value of the securities held by the unit trust or the managed fund by the number of units in issue to obtain the unit price. The unit price can form the basis of a performance measurement but it may not be answering the question of how well have the securities in the unit trust or managed fund performed. This is because the manager usually has some latitude for changing the basis on which the unit price is calculated relative to the value of the underlying securities, according to whether buyers or sellers of units predominate. Furthermore, the expenses

of participation in some managed funds may be dealt with before money is passed to the managed fund, whereas in others the expenses are taken from the fund. This latter problem may mean that two managed funds with identical securities and identical security performance would show different unit price changes, merely because one of the funds asks participants to pay its charges before investing and the other receives its remuneration from the managed fund itself.

8.8 Investment performance – complications from property

Market prices for Stock Exchange securities can be obtained easily on an objective and consistent basis, but property values are only available when valuations are carried out and even then contain a subjective element depending on the view of the valuer. Property cannot be instantly purchased or sold in the same way as Stock Exchange assets, and this, coupled with the variety of valuation frequencies and valuation methods in use, suggests that property performance should only be measured over lengthy periods (e.g. over five years or longer). Even then the margins of error in property return calculations are generally much higher than for Stock Exchange assets, and it is unlikely to be possible to be able to measure the relative abilities of a property manager. Despite these very real difficulties and the limitations of the returns, it is still all too easy to point to league tables of returns including property which appear to ignore all these problems. Returns on property assets should therefore be treated with great caution and, if conclusions are made, it is worth making sure that the conclusion can be substantiated from the system of measurement in use.

8.9 Investment performance comparisons

(a) Comparison with other pension and life office funds
Once returns have been calculated the next stage is to make some comparison between the returns and some yardstick. The choice of yardstick will depend to a great extent on the purpose of the calculations. When making comparisons it is necessary to compare like with like. Some of the problems associated with comparisons of returns on this basis were illustrated above and only limited comparisons are possible on a money-weighted basis. In general, most of the questions asked relate to the relative abilities of fund managers and hence it is normally appropriate to use the time-weighted rate of return or unit price methods.

The natural method of comparison is to compare the returns of a fund with those of other funds with similar characteristics. The characteristics could be those of size, level of cash flow, taxation position, nature of the liabilities, constraints on the investment manager and the level of risk. If pension funds were divided according to just these criteria, then it would only be possible to compare the returns for a fund with those of a few other funds. A large sample size would be much more desirable if it was still possible to maintain a like-with-like comparison. In the U.K. most self-administered pension funds have final-salary-type liabilities and, as mentioned above, are in the position of not having to realize assets for the foreseeable future. With the levels of inflation experienced in recent years and the uncertain investment conditions which have prevailed, funds have generally made little or no allowance for the maturity of their liabilities when framing investment policy. In addition, very few investment managers are hampered by investment constraints which cannot easily be changed by reference to the trustees, and most constraints are really better described as investment guidelines until the next trustees' meeting. Usually any actual constraints which are set down are to prevent trans-actions in the parent company's securities or possibly those of competitors, and this type of constraint is likely to have only a very marginal effect on investment performance. These considerations make it possible to sub-stantially enlarge the sample which can be used.

The sample size could be further increased if it was found that the returns were independent of the size of the fund and the level of the cash flow. The evidence available does not indicate a strong link between size and return, or, apart from short periods, between the cash flow of a fund and returns. The returns of final salary pension plans can therefore be compared together and the advantages of using larger sample size probably outweigh the disadvantages of combining funds with insignificant differences in characteristics.

The position is much more complex for a life office. Life offices generally have very different liability profiles and tax positions which make com-parisons between offices difficult, if not impossible. Comparison is possible for the unitized managed funds run by a life office, but not in general for the other assets. In theory if the life fund could be divided between that part invested on a 'matched' basis and that part invested to achieve the maximum overall rate of return commensurate with an acceptable level of risk, the task would be easier. In general performance assessment for life offices is at the more detailed level (i.e. measurement of the value added (or lost!) by the employment of an investment manager in equities over the passive or index alternative).

For unit trust managers a comparison of unit trust unit price changes must take into account the different investment philosophies and levels of risk undertaken. Conclusions should be made in the light of the possible

latitude for managers to alter their unit prices according to the predominance of buyers or sellers.

(b) Notional funds

A further yardstick for making comparisons is the notional fund. This is a
fund which is invested at some date in various sectors in certain specified
proportions and each sector performs in line with a stated index. For
example, a fund invested 60% in equities and 40% in fixed interest assets
may be used where a 60:40 ratio is considered to be a reasonable long-term
asset mix (or is the investment manager's current guideline) and the aim of
the investment manager is supposedly to outperform this notional fund.
Let us assume that at 1st January the notional fund is invested in 60:40 and
that equities subsequently rise in the first quarter of the year, so that the
ratio becomes 70:30. Does the notional fund now sell the better-per-
forming asset (i.e. equities) and purchase the other asset to maintain the
original 60:40 mix and, if it does so, are expenses to be taken into account?

The problem of rebalancing presents a fundamental difficulty to the
notional fund concept. If the notional fund does rebalance periodically it is
acting in an artificial way in that a real investment manager would be most
unlikely to follow this policy. If the notional fund is not rebalanced
periodically, the original 60:40 ratio may be changed over time into some
other ratio such as 80:20 and misleading conclusions can easily be drawn
from the 60:40 notional fund unless great care is taken to understand
precisely what it is. A more useful concept may be a notional fund which
does not rebalance but which was invested originally in the stated ratio (say
60:40) and invests new money received in the same ratio.

A 60:40 notional fund can therefore produce a wide range of results
depending upon the procedures for its calculation which need to be clearly
specified and understood. For a pension fund, however, it is difficult to see
what question can be answered by using notional funds which cannot be
more easily and satisfactorily answered by inter-fund comparisons on a
time-weighted rate of return basis. It is fairly rare to find a manager who
has constraints on his investment policy which cannot easily be altered by
reference to the trustees and there is little point in making a comparison
with a model fund invested in a similar way to the investment manager
guidelines. In any case, this certainly does not advise the trustees whether
the guidelines were correct, which is the question they probably should be
asking.

Because of the problems associated with inter-office comparisons, life
offices are forced towards the use of notional funds. Notional funds may
also be useful for short-term comparisons such as the analysis of performance between overall strategy and stock selection. There may also be

a place for the notional fund in single sector comparisons. For example, if the problem is to ascertain whether the stocks chosen within the U.K. equity portfolio have produced a higher or lower return than the stock-market as measured by the FT-Actuaries All Share Index, it is quite feasible to set up a notional fund with the same cash flows as the actual U.K. equity portfolio and to buy and sell units in this index. Here again, care needs to be taken to ensure that the calculations actually do answer the question being asked and that the problems associated with expenses have been considered.

(c) Expenses
The treatment of the expenses involved in managing the investments of a fund and those resulting from individual transactions need to be carefully assessed. It is again necessary to start by asking the purpose of the calculations which are to be made because in some circumstances it will be appropriate to make allowances for expenses and in other cases it will not.

(d) Risk
Measurement of rates of return should take into account the level of risk undertaken as there should be a trade-off between risk and return. Risk can mean different things to different people, and it is necessary to establish a nil risk position (or nearest practical alternative) against which the required definition of risk can be measured. In the U.S. risk is often used to mean the volatility of the price of a stock but price volatility may be unimportant to a pension fund investor whose liabilities are linked to salary levels and where there is no immediate prospect of selling assets to pay benefits.

Risk is usually related to the liability profile of a fund where it is measured but risk-adjusted performance figures are still uncommon in the U.K.

APPENDIX ONE

Settlement

U.K. background
Before TALISMAN the system for settling Stock Exchange business had operated unchanged for almost 100 years. As the market developed and volumes increased the arrangements gradually became excessively cumbersome and more complex to operate.

On the surface the old system was quite straightforward. The buying broker dealt with a jobber but, to avoid the cost and delays involved in registering the stock into the jobber's name, his bargain was usually linked for settlement directly with that of another broker who had dealt the other way in the same security. In most instances the buyer had dealt in a different amount of stock from the seller and this resulted in the need to split and certify transfers.

Something which was basically straightforward in theory became highly complicated in practice and at the end of a busy account there were up to half a million tickets and transfer forms passing round the market in order to link buyers and sellers, and effect the change of ownership. Volumes of that order, together with the inherent delays in preparing and passing tickets, meant that brokers' and jobbers' work was subject to sharp peaks around each Account Day. In addition to the huge number of ledger postings, most transfers had to be taken to the certification office and the stamp office before being delivered. When the stock was eventually received by the buying broker he was still faced with the task of registering it in the name of his client and obtaining a share certificate which finally provided evidence that the transfer of ownership was completed.

Against a background of increasing complexity and escalating costs the Stock Exchange began to look closely at the way in which technology could be used to alleviate the problems of a system which had operated almost unchanged since the nineteenth century. More importantly, continued dependence on an unreliable and outdated system created a risk which the Stock Exchange Council decided was unacceptable. They therefore approved the development of a radically new system, to be known as TALISMAN.

The process

The basis for TALISMAN is the operation of a Stock Exchange Nominee Company – SEPON Limited – with a single shareholding account in the register of every U.K. company whose shares are traded in the central market.

For all sales of securities, ownership is transferred from the sellers into the SEPON Accounts on the company registers, and for purchases buyers receive their shares by transfer from SEPON. Within each SEPON Account the central computer system maintains separate records for each jobber dealing in the stock and the movement of shares during the settlement process.

When the selling broker receives the share certificate and a signed transfer from his client he delivers them to the nearest centre, either in London or at one of the country offices. They are checked for good delivery and then the information is keyed into the computer system. The documents are then assembled with a computer-produced control schedule and passed to the registrar for registration from the client's name into the SEPON account. Within the computer system the sold stock is held in a suspense account and although legal title passes to SEPON on registration the effective control of the stock remains with the seller until delivery and payment on Account Day.

On Account Day ownership is transferred within the computer system from the seller's account to the jobber's account and the computer system automatically generates confirmation details of the transfer together with payment statements for the selling broker.

The stock in the jobber's account is then apportioned to purchasers automatically by the computer system. Once apportionment has taken place the computer generates transfers authorizing the removal of stock from the SEPON Account in the name of the buying clients whose details have been supplied to the central computer system on magnetic tape or through their terminals by the buying brokers. Bought transfers are then despatched, with the appropriate control documentation, directly to the registrar and upon registration out of SEPON legal title passes to the client and a new share certificate is issued.

The payments due to the Inland Revenue (and the Irish Revenue) for stamp duty are calculated automatically by the computer system and are collected directly from member firms when payment is made for the purchased stock. The payments due to and from member firms in respect of deliveries and apportionments are presented on a payment schedule and settled by cleared funds through a single account with the centre which acts as a clearing house.

An important feature for investors as well as member firms is in the area of dividends and rights where a centralized claiming and distribution service is operated. Under TALISMAN details of every bargain, including the dealing and registration dates, are held within the computer system which is therefore able to identify who is entitled to any benefit distribution. Benefits received by the centre arising from its SEPON holding are passed immediately to the entitled party. Where, through delays in registration, benefits are paid by the company to the wrong client the central computer system automatically generates the appropriate claim forms and passes these to the firms concerned so that benefits can be reclaimed and passed on to the entitled party.

In controlling the stock position with the SEPON account continual reconciliation is maintained between the central computer records and the SEPON holding on each company register. In the case of larger registrars this reconciliation is achieved through records passed on magnetic tape.

The dimensions
The whole process of settlement directly involves well over 200 member firms of the Stock Exchange, located in 65 cities and towns, over 400 registrars of companies, the Inland Revenue, the Irish Revenue, the major English and Scottish clearing banks, and over 700 institutional investors who have operating agreements with the Stock Exchange. Many thousands of other investors are involved by the completion of transfer forms designed especially for the system and incorporated in legislation by the application of a Statutory Instrument to the Stock Transfer Act 1963.

The future
The establishment of TALISMAN has provided a foundation for the introduction of further improvements to the settlement system on both a national and international basis. The lifting of Exchange Control regulations has led to a significant expansion in the trading of international securities and an increasing tendency to settle bargains in currencies other than sterling. In response to this trend, improvements were first made to enable settlement to be made in U.S. dollars and Irish pounds through the TALISMAN system. The service has been further extended to provide for the settlement of Australian, American and Canadian registered securities through TALISMAN.

TALISMAN represents one of the biggest computerized system developments ever undertaken in the U.K. and by any standard has been very successful. Looking to the future the Stock Exchange will be seeking to ensure that the U.K. securities market maintains its leading position within the securities industry of the world and that the Exchange itself continues to lead in terms of technological developments.

Gilt settlement

The Central Gilts Office Service

A computerized system for settling bargains in the gilt-edged market, known as the Central Gilts Office Service, is being developed jointly by the Bank of England and the Stock Exchange. Members of the Service will be able to settle transactions between one another in book entry form without the need for stock transfer forms, certificates or cheques. Initially the system will cover only stocks registered at the bank. The legal framework for the system will be provided by the Stock Transfer Act 1982 and related Statutory Instruments and the Bank of England will establish an office – the Central Gilts Office – to operate the system.

CEDEL

CEDEL, an independent company incorporated in Luxembourg, operates a securities and precious metals clearing, and safe custody system.

CEDEL clearing services are available for all fixed income securities traded in the international markets; Eurobonds (including DM denominated issues); Yankees, Samurais, Mexican Petrobonds, floating rate notes, convertibles; London, Singapore and Hong Kong tranche CDs; international equities in EDR, BDR and CDR form. CEDEL also offers safe custody and clearing services for gold bullion dealt in on the Luxembourg Stock Exchange.

With a single account number, a participant can settle transactions in 25 different currencies and in some 6000 securities issues. A securities account with CEDEL can be used on both a fungible and non-fungible basis. (Fungibility implies that certificate numbers are not available to the participant, whereas non-fungibility allows certificate numbers to be attributed to an account holding.) The non-fungible option is particularly welcomed by those institutions whose national legislation requires them to hold for their customers securities which can at any time be identified by numbers.

When two participants have agreed upon a trade and settlement date, the completion of this transaction is brought about by a security transfer from the seller's to the buyer's account and simultaneously a cash transfer from the buyer's to the seller's account. (A free transfer of securities is, of course, also possible.) These operations are fully computerized, with securities and cash entries processed simultaneously. The instructions are received from the participants, checked for correctness, matched with counterparty instructions and processed. The securities and cash positions are immediately available for chaining of transactions.

Securities held within CEDEL are lodged for safe-keeping with depository banks. All securities of one specific issue are deposited with one bank, usually a paying agent for this issue, thus minimizing the need for physical movement of securities. A permanent record is kept of all certificate numbers held on behalf of participants for safe-keeping in CEDEL. The certificate numbers of all lost or stolen bonds are also recorded in the system. Consequently, securities recognized to be of bad delivery are automatically rejected upon receipt into CEDEL.

Depository banks entrusted with the safe-keeping of securities held on behalf of CEDEL have a contractual obligation to insure for the replacement of security holdings in their safe custody. CEDEL's own global policy insures the replacement of certificates in case of a deficiency in the depositories' coverage. All physical movements and transfers of securities are fully insured on an individual shipment basis.

Cash balances of participants are placed only with leading institutions, and money-market-type rates are paid on participants' credit balances. The same rates are applied irrespective of the size or duration of the deposit. Coupon as well as redemption payments are credited to participants' accounts on the due date.

CEDEL also handles distributions of allotments in the primary market. Global bearer bonds representing an entire issue are accepted by CEDEL and allotted to every underwriting or dealing participant.

Facilities for bond lending are provided. Securities borrowed before 11.00 a.m. can be used to settle transactions on the same day. Automatic or case-by-case instruction to lend and/or borrow securities are accepted. Upon a participant's request, CEDEL will monitor his accounts for delivery commitments and automatically borrow securities to effect delivery and thereby avoid a 'fail' item.

CEDEL has 95 shareholders, all well-known international financial institutions, and serves approximately 1200 participants.

The service is fully computerized with a highly significant number of participants located in 53 countries, communicating with it through CEDCOM, a telecommunication link based on GEISCO, SWIFT and Telekurs/Investdata.

Euro-clear

The Euro-clear system is a clearance system for internationally traded securities, offering four interrelated services: settlement of trades, safe custody of securities, lending and borrowing of securities and cash transactions clearing. It is operated by Morgan Guaranty Trust Company from Brussels but makes use of the Company's offices throughout the world.

It accepts internationally traded debt securities, straight or convertible, in bearer or registered form, bearing fixed or floating rates of interest, and denominated in a wide range of currencies and composite currency units. Its services are also available for certain certificates of deposit and equities traded internationally in bearer or registered form. Securities are accepted in the form of definitive certificates, depository receipts or global certificates.

More than 80% of the securities' instructions are processed by book entry transfer, without physical movements of the securities. Participants have Securities Clearing Accounts and Cash Accounts. The buyer and the seller (both Participants) each provide an instruction on or before the settlement date. The instructions are compared and any differences between them reported to both parties. On the settlement date, subject to sufficient securities being available in the Securities Clearance Account of the seller, and provision for funds being available in the Cash Account of the buyer, the securities are debited to the account of the seller and credited to the account of the buyer. Simultaneously, cash is credited to the account of the seller and debited to the account of the buyer.

The securities settlement processing permits the buyer to use the securities, and the seller to use the proceeds from the sale, for the settlement of additional transactions on the same day.

Facilities are also available for the physical receipt and delivery of securities. A deposit of securities may be free of payment or against subsequent payment. Securities can be delivered free of payment out of the Euro-clear System and in certain locations, such as New York, can also be delivered against payment. In many other countries domestic clearance systems are used by depositaries of the Euro-clear system for the settlement of trades in domestic issues and, in an increasing number, delivery against payment is possible.

The underlying physical securities, some in global certificate form, are kept by major banks around the world who act as depositaries and paying agents, servicing the securities as necessary. The securities are insured against all risks, in transit or in the depository. The Lending and Borrowing service uses information from the daily securities settlement processing to measure borrowing needs and lending capabilities, allocate loans and borrowings of securities and make automatic reimbursements. It allows the Participants to lend securities, thereby increasing the yields on their portfolios. It enables Participants to borrow securities to settle transactions which they might not otherwise be in a position to settle immediately, avoiding the loss of interest that would be incurred on late settlement.

Lenders receive a fee, expressed as a percentage per annum of the market value plus accrued interest of the loaned securities, for the duration of the loan and borrowers pay a fee on a similar basis.

The service also includes New Issues. Subscription payments for a new issue are collected in collaboration with the lead manager in order to determine which allotments are to be delivered on the closing date. The new issue of securities is deposited at a depository of the Euro-clear System and credited to a special account. On the closing date, as instructed by the lead manager, the securities are transferred to the allottees by book entry transfer or by physical shipment.

Each Participant's Cash Account is divided into sub-accounts in each of the twenty currencies and composite currency units are accepted as settlement currencies in the Euro-clear System. Cash Accounts are used primarily for the settlement of securities transactions against payment and are in addition credited with the proceeds of coupons and redemption of securities. They may also be used for subscription for new issues or the exercise of warrants, instalment or other payments. All the activities are reflected in a daily statement of account which is produced for each currency.

Funds may be transferred by book transfer from one Participant to another, thus providing a multicurrency cash-clearing service for same-day execution and value, within the time frame of the Brussels working day. Funds may also be transferred by wire transfer to any bank for the account of the named beneficiary. Funds may be deposited for credit to a Cash Account at correspondents identified for each currency.

Euro-clear has 1300 Participations. It processes more than 12,000 securities instructions per day covering over 8000 different issues. Its turnover exceeds U.S.$500 billion annually. It operates a sophisticated computer communications system known as EUCLID and is linked to the SWIFT network.

APPENDIX TWO

A copy of this document, which comprises listing particulars with regard to St. Ives Group plc in accordance with The Stock Exchange (Listing) Regulations 1984, has been delivered for registration to the Registrar of Companies as required by those Regulations.

The directors of St. Ives Group plc named in "Directors and Advisers" below are the persons responsible for the information contained in this document. To the best of the knowledge and belief of the directors (who have taken all reasonable care to ensure that such is the case) the information contained in this document is in accordance with the facts and does not omit anything likely to affect the import of such information. The directors accept responsibility accordingly.

Application has been made to the Council of The Stock Exchange for the whole of the ordinary share capital of St. Ives Group plc, issued and to be issued, to be admitted to the Official List.

The application list for the ordinary shares now offered for sale will open at 10 a.m. on Thursday, 26th September, 1985 and may be closed at any time thereafter. The procedure for application, together with an application form, is set out at the end of this document. It is expected that renounceable documents of title will be posted on Wednesday, 2nd October, 1985 and that dealings will commence on Thursday, 3rd October, 1985.

ST IVES GROUP PLC

Offer for Sale by Tender

by

N. M. Rothschild & Sons Limited

of

2,267,000 ordinary shares of 10p each

at a minimum tender price of 290p per share,

the price tendered being payable in full on application

SHARE CAPITAL

Authorised		Issued and fully paid following the offer for sale
£825,000	ordinary shares of 10p each	£629,844.60

The ordinary shares now offered for sale rank in full for all dividends and other distributions declared, paid or made hereafter on the ordinary shares of St. Ives Group plc.

INDEBTEDNESS

Apart from intra-group liabilities, at the close of business on 23rd August, 1985, no company in the Group, as defined herein, had any loan capital (including term loans) outstanding, or created but unissued, or any outstanding mortgages, charges, debentures or other borrowings or indebtedness in the nature of borrowing, including bank overdrafts, liabilities under acceptances (other than normal trade bills) or acceptance credits, material hire purchase commitments, guarantees or other material contingent liabilities.

On 23rd August, 1985, the Group had bank balances, short term deposits and cash amounting to £941,782.

CONTENTS

DEFINITIONS

"St. Ives" or "the Company"	St. Ives Group plc or its predecessor company, as the context requires
"the Group"	St. Ives and its subsidiaries at the date of this document, together with Folio Holdings
"Severn Valley"	Severn Valley Press Limited and its subsidiary, Severn Valley Bindery Limited
"Kingsdale"	Kingsdale Press (a division of Severn Valley Press Limited)
"CB Dorey"	CB Dorey Limited
"Molyneux"	Molyneux Offset Limited
"Britannic"	Britannic Printing Supplies (London) Limited
"RJ Acford"	R.J. Acford (a division of Molyneux)
"Folio Holdings"	Folio Holdings Limited
"ordinary shares"	ordinary shares of 10p each in St. Ives
"the directors"	the directors of St. Ives

DIRECTORS AND ADVISERS

DIRECTORS	Robert Gavron *Chairman*
	Kenneth Peter Ladd FCA FCMA J Dip MA
	Peter Maxwell Woolley-Stafford
	Brian Charles Edwards FCA
	all of 47-58 Bastwick Street, London EC1V 3PS

SECRETARY AND REGISTERED OFFICE	Brian Charles Edwards FCA 47-58 Bastwick Street London EC1V 3PS
ISSUING HOUSE	N. M. Rothschild & Sons Limited New Court St. Swithin's Lane London EC4P 4DU
STOCKBROKERS	Rowe & Pitman 1 Finsbury Avenue London EC2M 2PA
AUDITORS AND REPORTING ACCOUNTANTS	Touche Ross & Co. *Chartered Accountants* Hill House 1 Little New Street London EC4A 3TR
SOLICITORS TO THE COMPANY	Titmuss, Sainer & Webb 2 Serjeants' Inn London EC4Y 1LT
SOLICITORS TO THE OFFER	Linklaters & Paines Barrington House 59-67 Gresham Street London EC2V 7JA
RECEIVING BANKERS	Ravensbourne Registration Services Limited 145 Leadenhall Street London EC3V 4QT
BANKERS	National Westminster Bank PLC 63 Piccadilly London W1V 0AJ
REGISTRARS AND TRANSFER OFFICE	Ravensbourne Registration Services Limited Bourne House 34 Beckenham Road Beckenham Kent BR3 4TU

KEY INFORMATION

The following information should be read in conjunction with the full text of this offer for sale.

BUSINESS

The Group is one of the leading quality colour printers in the United Kingdom, producing magazines, books and other publications for publishers and other commercial organisations. Its customers include Independent Television Publications (for which it prints parts of *TV Times*), Consumers Association (*Which* magazine), Morgan-Grampian, IPC Magazines, National Westminster Bank, British Telecom, Condé Nast (*Tatler*), Thomson Holidays and Oxford University Press.

TRADING RECORD

The Group's turnover and profit on ordinary activities before taxation are summarised below:

Years ended 31st July,	Turnover £'000	Profit before taxation £'000
1980	9,340	875
1981	9,867	758
1982	11,300	934
1983	12,446	1,748
1984	15,398	1,938
1985 (estimated)	18,300	2,500

The estimated results for the year ended 31st July, 1985 are based on audited accounts for the eight months to 31st March, 1985 and on unaudited management accounts for the four months to 31st July, 1985.

OFFER FOR SALE STATISTICS
BASED ON THE MINIMUM TENDER PRICE

Minimum tender price	290p
Market capitalisation	£18.26 million
Price earnings ratio based on estimated earnings per share for the year ended 31st July, 1985:	
of 24.5p after estimated actual tax charge	11.8 times
of 25.8p after notional 35 per cent. tax charge	11.2 times
Net tangible assets as at 31st March, 1985	£5.33 million
Net tangible assets per share as at 31st March, 1985	84.6p
Gross dividend yield based on the notional net dividend of 8p per share in respect of the year ended 31st July, 1985	3.9%
Dividend cover based on estimated profit on ordinary activities after taxation for the year ended 31st July, 1985 and the notional net dividend in respect of that year of 8p per share	3.0 times

Note: The financial information summarised above has been adjusted where relevant to reflect the acquisition of Folio Holdings, which is conditional on the admission of the ordinary shares to the Official List by the Council of The Stock Exchange.

INTRODUCTION

The business of the Group is printing and ancillary activities. The principal subsidiary of St. Ives is Severn Valley which is a medium and long-run web-offset printer of high quality magazines, brochures and books. Other activities of the Group include shorter-run web-offset printing, sheet-fed offset printing, book production, the provision of printing supplies and print subcontracting.

The Group has become one of the leading quality colour printers in the United Kingdom. Its growth has been based on a number of opportune acquisitions coupled with continuing and substantial investment in modern plant and equipment.

There are a number of special factors which the directors believe have contributed to the Group's successful profit record:

● The Group has built up an experienced and highly motivated management team. They are all shareholders in St. Ives and their remuneration is to a significant extent based on profit performance.

● Some 50 per cent. of the Group's turnover is accounted for by contract magazine printing. A further 30 per cent. consists of recurring orders from established customers. As a result, a high proportion of production can be planned several months in advance.

● The Group has a good reputation with its customers for providing quality and service at a sensible price. It has won a number of awards for the quality of its products.

● There has been continuing investment in modern machinery without any associated reduction in the workforce. Productivity is high by the industry's standards. Total capital expenditure incurred and committed on plant and machinery since 1st August, 1979 has been £10.2 million.

● Acquisitions have been carefully chosen to complement existing activities. Satisfactory manning levels have in each case been agreed in advance.

As a result of these factors, the financial performance of the Group has been impressive. Based on the most recent information available, Severn Valley's profit and capital employed per employee are amongst the highest of the major printing companies in the United Kingdom. The Group has no borrowings and, since 1979, all investment in plant and machinery has been financed from internally generated funds.

THE BUSINESS

DEVELOPMENT

St. Ives was formed by Robert Gavron in 1964 to acquire the CB Printing Group, a lithographic and letterpress printing company. He was joined by Kenneth Ladd in 1966 and, by 1968, following a period of rationalisation and modernisation which included the closure of its letterpress activities, St. Ives had become profitable.

Since then, St. Ives has grown as a result of the acquisition and subsequent development of a number of complementary businesses. Its first and most significant acquisition took place in 1972 when it bought the assets of a web-offset magazine printing business (then in receivership), which now trades as Severn Valley. Since the acquisition, there has been substantial investment in new printing and binding machinery culminating in the recent purchase and installation, at a cost of £3.7 million, of what the directors understand to be the most productive high quality colour web-offset press in the United Kingdom.

In 1976, St. Ives acquired H.P. Dorey & Co., a sheet-fed printing company with a modern factory and plant but with financial and marketing problems. Its business, which was merged with that of CB Printers, now trades profitably as CB Dorey from the original premises of H.P. Dorey & Co. in Romford, Essex.

The Group's activities were extended in 1979 with the acquisition from Reed International of RJ Acford, a book binder with some printing capacity, based in Chichester. Since the acquisition, there has been considerable capital expenditure, particularly to bring its printing capacity more in line with its book binding facilities.

In 1983, the Group acquired the assets of Kingsdale (then in receivership), a sheet-fed and web-offset printer of short and medium-run magazines and other publications.

PRINTING PROCESSES

There are three major commercial printing processes: letterpress, photogravure and lithography. Letterpress has largely been phased out apart from the printing of paperback books and some monochrome newspapers. Photogravure is characterised by very fast running presses but high set-up costs; it continues to be the most economical process for printing colour publications in very large quantities such as the Sunday newspaper colour supplements. In recent years, however, technical advances have led to lithography becoming predominant in the field of colour printing.

The Group uses only the lithographic process. Sheet-fed and reel-fed (web-offset) lithography is ideally suited to the printing of special interest and regionalised colour magazines, advertising brochures and books. This is largely due to moderate set-up costs, the ability to effect speedy changes from one job to another and reasonably high speed production.

THE BUSINESS TODAY

Severn Valley is the most important member of the Group, accounting for more than 70 per cent. of the Group's turnover and gross profit. Its principal production facility at Caerphilly, where some 180 people are employed, is equipped to print medium and long-run high quality colour magazines, brochures and books. A high proportion of the work is represented by contracts requiring production at regular intervals, usually weekly or monthly. These contracts may be ended on three to six months' notice but Severn Valley's experience is that, once obtained, they tend to continue. As a result, Severn Valley can project production schedules a number of months forward and, by obtaining additional orders, has achieved levels of plant utilisation close to total effective capacity.

The installation of the new Harris M850 eight unit press (referred to below) will increase capacity by more than 30 per cent. with the addition of very few extra staff. On the basis of forward orders already received, the directors are confident that Severn Valley will in due course be able to achieve a similar level of utilisation on the enlarged capacity.

Severn Valley also has a magazine binding and mailing facility which provides saddle stitching, in-line insertion, perfect binding, shrink wrapping and labelling. Paper required for the production of magazines under contract is generally purchased and supplied by the publisher. Turnover does not therefore include significant amounts of paper to be recharged to customers.

Kingsdale, a division of Severn Valley, operates from Reading. It specialises in the short and medium-run printing of magazines and other publications and its printing facility is therefore complementary to that of the Caerphilly factory.

CB Dorey is a sheet-fed offset printer principally engaged in the production of advertising and publicity brochures, folders and leaflets. Although orders are usually for a single print run, CB Dorey has a number of regular customers whose recurring orders account for a substantial proportion of its turnover.

RJ Acford undertakes book printing and binding and is more labour intensive than other parts of the Group. Prior to its acquisition by St. Ives, it was on the point of being closed and it has not yet performed to the satisfaction of the directors. Within the last year, however, there have been changes in management and significant capital expenditure on new equipment which should in due course enable it to make a useful contribution to the Group's results.

Molyneux and **Britannic,** which were part of the original CB Printing Group, are both located in the Group's head office building in London. Molyneux's activities include the subcontracting of specialist printing to companies both inside and outside the Group. It also provides a variety of print consulting services. Britannic provides printing inks and sundry supplies to the printing industry. Their activities contribute under 5 per cent. in aggregate of the Group's turnover.

It has been the Group's policy for some years to develop close relationships with a number of specialist sub-contractors in the labour-intensive areas of design, type-setting and colour separation. This has enabled the Group to offer its customers a complete and high quality service.

CUSTOMERS

The Group's business comes from a wide range of print users: magazine publishers, book publishers and large commercial organisations including banks, car and food manufacturers and tour operators.

The Group's customer list includes Independent Television Publications (for which it prints parts of *TV Times*), Consumers Association (*Which* magazine), Morgan-Grampian, IPC Magazines, National Westminster Bank, Condé Nast (*Tatler*), East Midland Allied Press, National Trust, Octopus Books, Thomson Holidays, Global Tours, Link House, Coats Patons, Peugeot Talbot, Citibank, Lloyds Bank, United Biscuits, Hamlyn Group, Oxford University Press, BBC Publications, British Telecom and many other household names.

RECENT INVESTMENT IN EQUIPMENT

The Group has made major investments in equipment, particularly at Severn Valley, where it now operates three fast running M850 Harris web-offset presses. In 1983 it purchased a five unit press capable of the simultaneous production of thirty-two A4 pages in colour and thirty-two in black and white per revolution at speeds of around 25,000 revolutions per hour. This press complements the four unit press acquired earlier which is capable of producing thirty-two colour pages. Most recently, Severn Valley has installed a new eight unit press which is capable of producing sixty-four pages in full colour at higher speeds than the other presses, giving customers total flexibility in the positioning of colour pages. This further improves productivity and expands capacity and enables Severn Valley to meet the increasing demand by magazine publishers for more colour.

In addition, over the last five years over £1 million has been spent on the installation of new binding equipment at Severn Valley, notably Muller saddle stitching machinery, perfect binding and mailing lines.

At RJ Acford the print department is being completely re-equipped. The first of two slow-running presses was replaced in July, 1983 by a new Crabtree press and the other is currently being similarly replaced. The higher speed and larger format of the new presses should substantially increase productivity and reduce the heavy overloading which has led to a considerable amount of work being sub-contracted; manning levels will remain unchanged.

DIRECTORS, MANAGEMENT AND STAFF

DIRECTORS

The board of St. Ives is responsible for the direction, supervision and co-ordination of all Group activities. All the main board directors are shareholders in St. Ives and their remuneration is linked to the profit performance of the Group.

Robert Gavron and Kenneth Ladd have each worked for the Group for some 20 years and Peter Stafford and Brian Edwards for 11 and 7 years respectively.

Robert Gavron (55) was called to the Bar after reading Law at Oxford. He has been in the printing industry for 30 years and founded St. Ives in 1964. He is chairman of St. Ives where he spends the majority of his time. He is a non-executive director of Octopus Publishing Group plc and of Electra Management plc. He is also chairman and controlling shareholder of Wardstock Limited which owns the book publishing companies, The Folio Society and Carcanet Press.

Kenneth Ladd (55) is Group financial director. After qualifying as a chartered accountant, he held a number of accountancy positions in industry before joining St. Ives in 1966 as Group financial controller. He was appointed Group financial director in 1967.

Peter Stafford (44) joined Metal Box as a graduate trainee after Oxford. He held various management positions before joining BPC as sales manager of a major subsidiary. He joined St. Ives in 1974 and was appointed managing director of Severn Valley in 1979. He was appointed to the Group board in 1981 and became Group managing director in 1985.

Brian Edwards (35) qualified as a chartered accountant in 1973. He worked for Touche Ross & Co. for four years before joining St. Ives in 1978. He was appointed to the board of St. Ives in 1981 and shares with Kenneth Ladd the responsibility for the Group's financial control. He is financial director of all the subsidiaries and is Group company secretary.

MANAGEMENT

The directors of subsidiary companies are given substantial autonomy and are responsible for clearly defined profit centres; a high percentage of their earnings is derived from bonuses related to the contributions of the profit centres for which they are responsible. They all own shares in St. Ives. In addition, St. Ives is introducing an executive share option scheme. Although there is no immediate intention to grant any options, this scheme will enable incentives to be offered to those existing senior employees who are not already significant shareholders in the Company and should help to attract new executives of high calibre.

In addition to the directors of St. Ives, the following are directors of subsidiary companies:

Peter Livermore (40) is sales director of Severn Valley. He started in the printing industry as a management trainee in 1961 and attended the London College of Printing. He joined the Group in 1977 and was appointed to his present position in 1978.

Trevor Blythe (38) is works director of Severn Valley. He worked with a number of printing companies before joining the Group in 1978 as a production manager. He was promoted to his current position in 1979.

William Carlisle (47) is managing director of CB Dorey. He joined HJ Heinz as a management trainee and, in 1962, moved to the printing industry. In 1969 he joined the Group and was appointed to his current position in 1982.

Michael Bigden (54) is sales director of CB Dorey. After five years in accountancy, he moved to the printing industry in 1958. In 1969 he joined the Group and was appointed to his current position in 1979.

Robert Beales (42) is production director of CB Dorey. He trained at the London College of Printing before holding positions with several printing companies. He joined the Group in 1979 and was appointed to his current position in 1984.

Jeremy MacLehose (38) was appointed managing director of RJ Acford on 1st July, 1985. He trained at the London College of Printing and has an MBA degree from Cranfield. He was managing director of Jolly & Barber, bookprinters, before joining the Group.

Peter Hassall (41) is sales director of RJ Acford. He worked in book production before joining RJ Acford in 1974 and was appointed to his current position in 1981.

Thomas Papworth (59) is a director of Molyneux. Prior to joining Molyneux in 1956, he held various positions in the printing industry.

Charles Imber (53) is a director of Molyneux. He started his career in printing in 1947 and joined the CB Printing Group in 1952.

STAFF

Staff numbers have increased with the overall growth of the Group. The average number of staff employed by the Group during the year ended 31st July, 1983 was 308. This had increased to 342 during the year ended 31st July, 1984.

The Group's staff as at 31st July, 1985, categorised by activity, was as follows:

Production	283
Sales and distribution	21
Administration	58
	362

The Group's productivity is amongst the best in the industry. Staff relations are good and there is a low rate of employee turnover.

The Group follows standard industry practice in its agreements with the trade unions (National Graphical Association and Society of Graphical and Allied Trades) in relation to pay awards and benefits.

All staff are covered by the State pension scheme. In addition senior executives make their own pension arrangements to which the Group contributes.

FOLIO HOLDINGS

The Group operates from freehold and leasehold properties in London, Caerphilly, Reading, Romford and Chichester. With the exception of the Reading property and certain rented warehousing in Caerphilly, all such properties are owned by Folio Holdings, at present a subsidiary of Wardstock Limited. St. Ives has agreed, conditional on the admission to the Official List of the ordinary shares, to acquire with effect from 1st August, 1985 all the issued share capital of Folio Holdings for a consideration of £1,518,000, which will be satisfied by the issue of ordinary shares at the minimum tender price. This corresponds to the value of the net tangible assets of Folio Holdings as at 31st July, 1985 and reflects Healey & Baker's valuation of the properties at that date (on an open market basis) of £1,515,000. As at the date of acquisition of Folio Holdings, its only material assets will comprise the properties referred to above. Details of the properties and of the acquisition agreement are set out in paragraphs 7 and 9(a)(i) respectively of "Statutory and General Information".

NET TANGIBLE ASSETS

The consolidated net tangible assets of St. Ives as at 31st March, 1985 (as shown by the Accountants' Report), adjusted to reflect the acquisition of Folio Holdings, were £5.33 million. On the basis of the number of ordinary shares in issue following the offer for sale, this is equivalent to net tangible assets of 84.6p per ordinary share.

FINANCIAL RESULTS

TRADING RECORD

The following table, which is derived from the Accountants' Report, summarises the results of St. Ives and its subsidiaries (on the historical cost basis), as adjusted to reflect the acquisition of Folio Holdings, for the five years ended 31st July, 1984 and the eight months ended 31st March, 1985:

	Years ended 31st July,					8 months ended 31st March,
	1980 £'000	1981 £'000	1982 £'000	1983 £'000	1984 £'000	1985 £'000
Turnover	**9,340**	**9,867**	**11,300**	**12,446**	**15,398**	**12,366**
Profit on ordinary activities before interest and taxation	888	711	837	1,637	1,845	1,569
Net interest receivable/(payable)	(13)	47	97	111	93	108
Profit on ordinary activities before taxation	**875**	**758**	**934**	**1,748**	**1,938**	**1,677**
Taxation on profit on ordinary activities	398	371	512	451	954	645
Profit on ordinary activities after taxation	477	387	422	1,297	984	1,032
Earnings per ordinary share	7.6p	6.1p	.6.7p	20.6p	15.6p	16.4p

Throughout the period covered by the table, Severn Valley has been the major contributor to the Group's turnover and profit, achieving significant profit increases in each year. For the Group as a whole, 1979/80 was a year of particular growth with profit before taxation almost double the £445,000 of the previous year; this was in part due to non-recurring benefits obtained from the advantageous terms upon which RJ Acford had been acquired in July, 1979. A strong performance by Severn Valley in 1981/82, a year in which it gained a higher proportion of contract work, was offset by a fall in CB Dorey's profitability. In 1982/83, the substantial increase in Group profit before taxation was due to further profit growth at Severn Valley, an increase in CB Dorey's profitability and some improvement at RJ Acford.

The Group's profit after taxation has followed a similar trend to profit before taxation with the exception of 1982/83 when the tax charge was particularly low. This resulted from the considerable capital expenditure incurred in that year and the consequential timing differences which are referred to in paragraph 5.3 of the Accountants' Report.

ESTIMATED RESULTS FOR THE YEAR ENDED 31st JULY, 1985

The directors estimate that, in respect of the year ended 31st July, 1985, the Group's turnover was £18.3 million, profit on ordinary activities before taxation was £2.5 million and profit on ordinary activities after taxation was £1.54 million. The improvement in profit before taxation of close to 30 per cent. was principally the result of high levels of plant utilisation at Severn Valley. On the basis of the number of ordinary shares in issue following the offer for sale, earnings per share are estimated to be 24.5p for that year.

These estimates are based on the audited consolidated accounts of St. Ives and its subsidiaries for the eight months ended 31st March, 1985 and on unaudited management accounts for the four months ended 31st July, 1985, both adjusted to reflect the acquisition of Folio Holdings. These adjustments will not be reflected in the audited accounts of the Group for the year ended 31st July, 1985 when they are published in due course since the acquisition of Folio Holdings will not have become effective until after the year end. The effect of these adjustments on profit on ordinary activities before taxation is an additional £186,000 and on profit on ordinary activities after taxation an additional £100,000.

DIVIDENDS

Had the ordinary shares of the Company been listed on The Stock Exchange since 1st August, 1984 and on the basis of the estimated results for the year ended 31st July, 1985, the directors would have recommended total net dividends of 8p per ordinary share in respect of that year. This would, at current taxation rates, represent a gross yield of 3.9 per cent. on the minimum tender price and would have been covered 3.0 times by the estimated Group profit on ordinary activities after taxation.

It is intended that, in future, dividend payments will be apportioned as to approximately one-third as an interim dividend payable in May and as to the balance as a final dividend payable in December of each year. The ordinary shares now offered for sale will first rank for the interim dividend payable in May, 1986; no dividend will be paid on the ordinary shares in respect of the year ended 31st July, 1985.

OFFER FOR SALE

The Group's development until now has come both from internally generated growth and from acquisitions. The directors consider that the Company is now of an appropriate size for its shares to be listed on The Stock Exchange. It is hoped that the listing, in facilitating the use of shares for expansion, will enable the Group to continue to grow at a fast rate. Although no specific acquisitions are planned, the directors believe that suitable opportunities will become available.

The offer for sale will enable existing shareholders to realise part of their shareholdings. No new money is being raised by the Group which the directors believe has sufficient funds to finance its present activities.

Following the offer for sale, Robert Gavron and his family interests will own in aggregate about 42 per cent. of the ordinary shares and the other directors, together with their family interests, will own in aggregate about 8 per cent. Excluding any shares which may be allocated to them in the offer for sale, employees will be interested in a further 4 per cent. of the ordinary shares.

PROSPECTS

The Group's contract printing operations allow it to anticipate a high proportion of its workload for the current year. Whilst it is inappropriate at this early stage in the year to make a forecast of profit, the directors believe that there will be a successful outcome. The installation of the new equipment at Severn Valley and RJ Acford should substantially improve productivity on existing contracts and also enable them to undertake a higher workload than in the past year when a substantial amount of printing had to be turned away or sub-contracted. It is therefore hoped that the additional equipment will improve both turnover and margins.

Over the five year period since the commissioning of its first Harris press at Severn Valley, the Group's profit before taxation has grown from £758,000 in 1980/81 to an estimated £2,500,000 in 1984/85, an average annual compound rate of 35 per cent. Whilst it must not be assumed that profit will continue to grow at this rate, it demonstrates the beneficial effect of installing modern machinery so long as suitable work can be obtained. Capital employed per employee and profit before taxation per employee at Severn Valley are among the best in the industry.

The directors believe that the growing number of trade and special interest magazines, together with the emphasis on flexibility in the printing and placing of colour pages within them, is likely to lead to an increasing demand for full colour web-offset printing. The Group has both the capacity to undertake increased workloads and also the ability to attract new contracts in this market. The significant increase in book sales in the United Kingdom in recent years is evidence of a vigorous market in which it should be possible to exploit the Group's increase in book production capacity. Demand for promotional and advertising material is expected to remain strong.

The directors intend to continue their policy of acquisition and investment, taking advantage of the greater range of opportunities available to a publicly listed company. They view the Group's future with confidence and believe that it has the necessary flair, managerial skills, capital equipment and financial resources to build on its recent growth.

LETTERS RELATING TO THE ESTIMATED RESULTS FOR THE YEAR ENDED 31st JULY, 1985

The following are copies of letters relating to the estimated results of the Group for the year ended 31st July, 1985:—

(a)   LETTER FROM TOUCHE ROSS & CO.

The Directors   Hill House
St. Ives Group plc and   1 Little New Street
N. M. Rothschild & Sons Limited   London EC4A 3TR

                                                 18th September, 1985

Gentlemen,

We have reviewed the accounting policies and calculations for the estimates of turnover, profit on ordinary activities before taxation and profit on ordinary activities after taxation of St. Ives Group plc and its subsidiaries (the "Group") for the year ended 31st July, 1985 as set out in the offer for sale document dated 18th September, 1985. The estimates are based on audited consolidated accounts for the eight months ended 31st March, 1985 and unaudited management accounts for the four months ended 31st July, 1985, both adjusted to reflect the acquisition of Folio Holdings Limited.

In our opinion, the estimates, for which the directors of St. Ives Group plc are solely responsible, have been properly compiled so far as the accounting policies, calculations and adjustments are concerned and are presented on a basis consistent with the accounting policies normally adopted by the Group.

Yours faithfully,

Touche Ross & Co.

(b)   LETTER FROM N. M. ROTHSCHILD & SONS LIMITED

The Directors   New Court
St. Ives Group plc   St. Swithin's Lane
                                                 London EC4P 4DU

                                                 18th September, 1985

Gentlemen,

We have discussed with you and with Touche Ross & Co. the estimates of turnover, profit on ordinary activities before taxation and profit on ordinary activities after taxation of St. Ives Group plc and its subsidiaries for the year ended 31st July, 1985 as set out in the offer for sale document dated 18th September, 1985. We consider that the estimates, for which the directors of St. Ives Group plc are solely responsible, have been made after due and careful enquiry.

Yours very truly,
for and on behalf of
N. M. Rothschild & Sons Limited

B. I. Myers   M. L. B. Emley
Director   Director

ACCOUNTANTS' REPORT

The following is a copy of a report to the directors of the Company and to N. M. Rothschild & Sons Limited made by Touche Ross & Co:—

The Directors
St. Ives Group plc and
N. M. Rothschild & Sons Limited

Hill House
1 Little New Street
London EC4A 3TR
18th September, 1985

Gentlemen,

We have examined the audited financial statements of St. Ives Group plc (formerly called St. Ives Group (1981) Limited) and its predecessor company, St. Ives Group Limited (together hereinafter called "the Company") and of their subsidiaries for the five years ended 31st July, 1984 and the eight months ended 31st March, 1985 ("the relevant accounting period"). The Company and its subsidiaries are hereinafter collectively referred to as "the Group". No audited financial statements have been prepared for the Group since 31st March, 1985.

We have acted as auditors to the Group throughout the relevant accounting period.

The financial information, which has been prepared under the historical cost convention, as modified by the revaluation of certain assets, is based on the Group's audited financial statements after making such adjustments, including those relating to the conditional acquisition of Folio Holdings Limited ("Folio"), as we consider appropriate. The net assets of Folio represent properties occupied by the Company and its subsidiaries. No account has been taken of any previous trading activities of Folio apart from those relating to the properties. The adjustments made comprise the elimination of the rents paid by the Group to Folio and the inclusion of the depreciation and the ground rentals relating to the properties owned by Folio, together with consequential taxation and other adjustments in the consolidated profit and loss accounts. These properties are included in the consolidated balance sheets as though they had been owned by the Group throughout the relevant accounting period.

In our opinion, the information in sections 1 to 5 gives a true and fair view of the profits and source and application of funds of the Group during the relevant accounting period and the state of affairs of the Group as at 31st July, 1980, 1981, 1982, 1983 and 1984, and as at 31st March, 1985.

1. ACCOUNTING POLICIES

The following are the principal accounting policies adopted in arriving at the financial information set out in this report:

1.1 Basis of consolidation

The Group financial statements consolidate the financial statements of the Company and all its subsidiaries for the relevant accounting period.

St. Ives Group plc was incorporated as St. Ives Group (1981) Limited on 23rd March, 1981. As part of a group reorganisation on 1st May, 1981, St. Ives Group plc acquired the business, undertaking and certain assets and liabilities of the company then known as St. Ives Group Limited ("the predecessor company"). The predecessor company was put into members' voluntary liquidation on 1st May, 1981 and, on 20th May, 1981, St. Ives Group (1981) Limited changed its name to St. Ives Group Limited (now St. Ives Group plc).

These financial statements reflect the transactions carried out by St. Ives Group plc, the predecessor company and their respective subsidiaries.

1.2 Tangible fixed assets

Depreciation is provided on cost in equal annual instalments over the estimated lives of the assets. The rates of depreciation are as follows:

Freehold buildings	2 per cent.
Long leasehold buildings	2 per cent.
Short leasehold buildings	Period of the lease
Leasehold improvements	20 per cent.
Plant and machinery	10 – 25 per cent.
Motor vehicles	20 – 33⅓ per cent.
Fixtures, fittings and equipment	20 per cent.

1.3 Stocks

Stocks are stated at the lower of cost and net realisable value. Cost represents materials, direct labour and appropriate overheads.

1.4 Deferred taxation

Deferred taxation is provided at the anticipated rate of corporation tax on the expected reversal of timing differences arising from the inclusion of income and expenditure in taxation computations in periods different from those in which they are included in the financial statements, except where reversals of timing differences are not anticipated in the foreseeable future.

1.5 Regional grants

Regional grants are provided for and amortised in equal annual instalments over the estimated lives of the assets to which they relate.

1.6 Provisions

Provision is made for repairs to plant and machinery and leasehold premises based on estimates of expenditure required to sustain the assets' operating capacity at present levels over their estimated useful lives.

1.7 Foreign currencies

Assets and liabilities in foreign currencies are translated into sterling at the rate of exchange ruling at the balance sheet date. Differences on exchange rates are included in profit on ordinary activities before taxation.

1.8 Profit taking

Income is accounted for when orders are completed and invoiced to customers.

2. CONSOLIDATED PROFIT AND LOSS ACCOUNTS

	Note	1980 £'000	1981 £'000	1982 £'000	1983 £'000	1984 £'000	8 months ended 31st March, 1985 £'000
				Years ended 31st July,			
Turnover	5.1	9,340	9,867	11,300	12,446	15,398	12,366
Cost of sales		7,300	7,884	8,889	9,236	11,619	9,290
Gross profit		2,040	1,983	2,411	3,210	3,779	3,076
Selling and distribution costs		466	527	515	517	562	408
Administrative expenses		893	945	1,185	1,185	1,451	1,161
Other operating income		(207)	(200)	(126)	(129)	(79)	(62)
		1,152	1,272	1,574	1,573	1,934	1,507
Profit on ordinary activities before interest and taxation		888	711	837	1,637	1,845	1,569
Interest receivable		57	87	97	111	93	108
Interest payable		(70)	(40)	—	—	—	—
Profit on ordinary activities before taxation	5.2	875	758	934	1,748	1,938	1,677
Taxation on profit on ordinary activities	5.3	398	371	512	451	954	645
Profit on ordinary activities after taxation		477	387	422	1,297	984	1,032
Dividends paid and proposed	5.4	28	25	14	45	169	147
Retained profit		449	362	408	1,252	815	885
Earnings per ordinary share	5.5	7.6p	6.1p	6.7p	20.6p	15.6p	16.4p

3. CONSOLIDATED BALANCE SHEETS

	Note	1980 £'000	1981 £'000	1982 £'000	1983 £'000	1984 £'000	1985 £'000
				31st July,			*31st March,*
Fixed assets							
Tangible assets	5.6	2,960	4,863	4,299	6,486	6,135	7,914
Current assets							
Stocks	5.7	384	626	455	559	828	926
Debtors	5.8	2,291	2,296	2,576	2,467	3,684	3,533
Cash at bank and in hand		680	341	960	992	1,198	1,274
		3,355	3,263	3,991	4,018	5,710	5,733
Creditors: amounts falling due within one year	5.9	2,752	2,973	3,059	3,629	4,787	5,019
Net current assets		603	290	932	389	923	714
Total assets less current liabilities		3,563	5,153	5,231	6,875	7,058	8,628
Creditors: amounts falling due after more than one year	5.10	(522)	—	—	(323)	(2)	(792)
Provisions for liabilities and charges	5.11	(904)	(1,063)	(939)	(1,706)	(1,567)	(1,967)
Accruals and deferred income	5.12	(335)	(388)	(318)	(552)	(517)	(538)
		1,802	3,702	3,974	4,294	4,972	5,331
Capital and reserves							
Called up share capital	5.13	5	5	5	4	5	5
Reserves	5.14	1,797	3,697	3,969	4,290	4,967	5,326
		1,802	3,702	3,974	4,294	4,972	5,331

4. CONSOLIDATED STATEMENTS OF SOURCE AND APPLICATION OF FUNDS

	Years ended 31st July,					8 months ended 31st March,
	1980 £'000	1981 £'000	1982 £'000	1983 £'000	1984 £'000	1985 £'000
Sources of funds						
Profit on ordinary activities before taxation	875	758	934	1,748	1,938	1,677
Adjustment for items not involving movement of funds:						
Depreciation	307	443	609	609	760	505
Amortisation of goodwill	29	—	—	—	—	—
	336	443	609	609	760	505
Total generated from operations	1,211	1,201	1,543	2,357	2,698	2,182
Funds from other sources						
Net book value of tangible fixed asset disposals	495	37	26	17	32	25
Regional development grants	320	120	16	310	51	79
	815	157	42	327	83	104
	2,026	1,358	1,585	2,684	2,781	2,286
Application of funds						
Purchase of tangible fixed assets	1,876	1,023	158	2,889	526	2,799
Taxation paid	19	16	40	117	200	45
Dividends paid	28	25	14	45	169	111
Redemption of share capital	—	—	—	800	—	—
Repayment of loan on property	138	413	—	—	—	—
	2,061	1,477	212	3,851	895	2,955
	(35)	(119)	1,373	(1,167)	1,886	(669)
Reversal of notional adjustments on properties owned by Folio	—	(45)	(238)	(228)	(228)	(151)
	(35)	(164)	1,135	(1,395)	1,658	(820)
Decrease/(increase) in working capital						
Decrease/(increase) in debtors	(941)	(5)	(280)	109	(1,217)	151
Decrease/(increase) in stocks	549	(242)	171	(104)	(269)	(98)
(Decrease)/increase in creditors and provisions	699	72	(407)	1,422	34	843
	307	(175)	(516)	1,427	(1,452)	896
Increase/(decrease) in cash at bank and in hand	272	(339)	619	32	206	76

5. NOTES TO THE FINANCIAL STATEMENTS

5.1 Turnover

The Group has only one class of business. Turnover, which has been exclusively within the United Kingdom, represents the net invoiced value of sales outside the Group during the relevant accounting period.

5.2 Profit on ordinary activities before taxation

Profit on ordinary activities before taxation is after charging/(crediting):

	Years ended 31st July,					8 months ended 31st March,
	1980 £'000	1981 £'000	1982 £'000	1983 £'000	1984 £'000	1985 £'000
Depreciation of fixed assets	307	443	609	609	760	505
Leasing and hire charges	7	5	5	1	—	2
Directors' emoluments	64	72	150	211	212	167
Auditors' remuneration	16	16	19	18	19	17
Interest on property loans payable within 5 years	70	40	—	—	—	—
Profit on sale of plant and machinery	(145)	(97)	(6)	(57)	(5)	(3)
Interest relief grant	—	(34)	(8)	(8)	(8)	—
Selective financial assistance	—	—	—	(10)	(10)	—
Regional development grant amortisation	(42)	(67)	(86)	(77)	(85)	(59)

5.3 Taxation

The taxation charge is made up as follows:

	Years ended 31st July,					8 months ended 31st March,
	1980 £'000	1981 £'000	1982 £'000	1983 £'000	1984 £'000	1985 £'000
United Kingdom corporation tax based on the profit for the year/period	(39)	141	706	(245)	1,098	341
Deferred taxation	437	230	(194)	696	(144)	304
	398	371	512	451	954	645

The taxation charge for the eight months ended 31st March, 1985 is based on the anticipated effective rate for the year to 31st July, 1985.

The actual taxation charge is reconciled with the anticipated charge as follows:

	Years ended 31st July,					8 months ended 31st March,
	1980 £'000	1981 £'000	1982 £'000	1983 £'000	1984 £'000	1985 £'000
Anticipated charge	455	394	486	897	937	727
Actual taxation charge	(398)	(371)	(512)	(451)	(954)	(645)
Difference	57	23	(26)	446	(17)	82
The taxation charge was reduced/(increased) by:						
Permanently disallowed expenditure and other differences	(45)	(45)	(10)	(17)	9	12
Prior year tax charges reallocated from subsequent years	1	(24)	7	28	14	—
Deferred tax adjustments	101	92	(23)	435	(40)	70
	57	23	(26)	446	(17)	82

The deferred tax adjustments arise primarily because taxation is provided at rates applying when reversals of timing differences are anticipated to take place rather than at current rates.

5.4 Dividends

No dividends have been paid in the relevant accounting period on ordinary shares. Dividends paid and proposed relate to the preferred ordinary shares of 10p each in issue during the relevant accounting period and the 'A' preferred ordinary shares of 10p each issued on 31st October, 1983 as follows:

	Years ended 31st July,					8 months ended 31st March,
	1980 £'000	1981 £'000	1982 £'000	1983 £'000	1984 £'000	1985 £'000
Preferred ordinary shares of 10p each	28	25	14	45	11	7
'A' preferred ordinary shares of 10p each	—	—	—	—	158	140
	28	25	14	45	169	147

5.5 Earnings per ordinary share

Earnings per ordinary share have been calculated on the profit on ordinary activities after taxation. Dividends paid in respect of the preferred ordinary and 'A' preferred ordinary shares have not been taken into account since all such shares will, on listing being granted, be converted into ordinary shares. The number of ordinary shares used in the calculation throughout the relevant accounting period is 6,298,446, being the number of ordinary shares which will be in issue following the offer for sale.

5.6 Tangible fixed assets

Tangible fixed assets at 31st March, 1985 comprised:

	Cost/ valuation £'000	Accumulated depreciation £'000	Net book value £'000
Freehold land and buildings	590	—	590
Long leasehold land and buildings	695	—	695
Short leasehold land and buildings	230	—	230
Leasehold improvements	136	102	34
Plant and machinery	7,202	3,426	3,776
Payments on account relating to plant and machinery	2,365	—	2,365
Fixtures, fittings and equipment	179	106	73
Motor vehicles	258	107	151
Total	11,655	3,741	7,914

Plant and machinery, fixtures, fittings and equipment include items, the costs of which have been fully depreciated, amounting to £1,179,000.

Freehold, long leasehold and short leasehold land and buildings will have been acquired by the Group through the conditional acquisition of Folio with effect from 1st August, 1985 and are included above at valuation. A professional valuation was undertaken by Healey & Baker as at 31st July, 1985.

5.7 Stocks

	31st March, 1985 £'000
Raw materials	531
Work-in-progress	414
	945
Less: payments on account	(19)
	926

5.8 Debtors

	31st March, 1985 £'000
Amounts due within one year:	
Corporation tax recoverable	58
Trade debtors	2,793
Bills of exchange	82
Other debtors	554
Prepayments and accrued income	46
	3,533

5.9 Creditors: amounts falling due within one year

	31st March, 1985 £'000
Trade creditors	2,051
Other creditors	979
Bills of exchange	415
Corporation tax	1,260
Other taxation	169
Social security	108
Dividends proposed	37
	5,019

5.10 Creditors: amounts falling due after more than one year

	31st March, 1985 £'000
Bills of exchange payable	792

5.11 Provisions for liabilities and charges

	31st March, 1985 £'000
Repairs to plant and machinery	260
Repairs to premises	71
Pensions	8
Deferred taxation	1,628
	1,967

The potential amounts of deferred taxation which have been fully provided are as follows:

	31st March, 1985 £'000
Capital allowances in excess of depreciation	1,744
Gains deferred by roll-over relief	41
Other timing differences	(138)
	1,647
Less: unrelieved advance corporation tax	(19)
	1,628

5.12 Accruals and deferred income

This comprises regional development grants which are amortised over the estimated lives of the fixed assets to which they relate.

5.13 Called up share capital

	31st March, 1985 £
Authorised	
10,500 'A' preferred ordinary shares of 10p each	1,050
9,500 preferred ordinary shares of 10p each	950
80,000 ordinary shares of 10p each	8,000
	£10,000
Allotted and fully paid	
10,500 'A' preferred ordinary shares of 10p each	1,050
2,000 preferred ordinary shares of 10p each	200
40,000 ordinary shares of 10p each	4,000
	£5,250

By or pursuant to resolutions passed on 11th September, 1985:

(a)   the authorised share capital of the Company was increased to £52,500 by the creation of 320,000 ordinary shares of 10p each, 10,500 preferred ordinary shares of 10p each and 94,500 'A' preferred ordinary shares of 10p each; and

(b)   a capitalisation issue was effected on the basis of 9 new shares of the relevant class for each ordinary, preferred ordinary and 'A' preferred ordinary share in issue.

By or pursuant to the Articles of Association of the Company (as amended) and resolutions passed on 17th September, 1985 and conditional on the ordinary share capital of the Company being admitted to the Official List by the Council of The Stock Exchange by 10th October, 1985:

(a)   the preferred ordinary and 'A' preferred ordinary shares were converted into ordinary shares of 10p each;

(b)   the authorised share capital of the Company was increased to £825,000 by the creation of 7,725,000 ordinary shares of 10p each;

(c)   47,586 ordinary shares in the Company were allotted, credited as fully paid, to Wardstock Limited as consideration for the acquisition of Folio. The effect of this transaction, had it been reflected in the financial statements at 31st March, 1985, would have been to increase the net current assets by £3,354, the issued share capital by £4,759, decrease distributable reserves by £628,550 and increase non-distributable reserves by £627,145; and

(d)   a capitalisation issue was effected on the basis of 10 new ordinary shares for each ordinary share in issue immediately after the satisfaction of the condition as to listing.

5.14 Reserves

(a) Distributable reserves

Profit and loss account:	Years ended 31st July,					8 months ended 31st March,
	1980 £'000	1981 £'000	1982 £'000	1983 £'000	1984 £'000	1985 £'000
Balance at beginning of year/period	948	1,797	2,314	2,614	2,962	3,667
Profit retained for the year/period	449	362	408	1,252	815	885
Folio properties at net book value	—	717	—	—	—	—
Less original carrying value in the Company	—	(674)	—	—	—	—
Adjustment to opening reserves for deferred taxation reallocated to prior years	400	—	—	—	—	—
Capitalisation issue of shares	—	—	—	—	(1)	—
Transfer from revaluation reserve relating to depreciation on revalued properties	—	—	28	28	28	28
Transfer to capital redemption reserve	—	—	—	(1)	—	—
Purchase of own shares	—	—	—	(799)	—	—
Reversal of notional adjustments on properties owned by Folio	—	112	(136)	(132)	(137)	(95)
Balance at end of year/period	1,797	2,314	2,614	2,962	3,667	4,485

(b) Non-distributable reserves

Revaluation reserve:	Years ended 31st July,					8 months ended 31st March,
	1980 £'000	1981 £'000	1982 £'000	1983 £'000	1984 £'000	1985 £'000
Balance at beginning of year/period	—	—	1,383	1,355	1,327	1,299
Revaluation surplus on properties owned by Folio arising on professional valuation undertaken in 1981	—	1,383	—	—	—	—
Revaluation deficit on properties owned by Folio arising on professional valuation undertaken as at 31st July, 1985	—	—	—	—	—	(431)
Transfer to profit and loss account arising on depreciation of revalued properties	—	—	(28)	(28)	(28)	(28)
Balance at end of year/period	—	1,383	1,355	1,327	1,299	840
Capital redemption reserve:						
Balance at beginning of year/period	—	—	—	—	1	1
Transfer from profit and loss account	—	—	—	1	—	—
Balance at end of year/period	—	—	—	1	1	1
Total non-distributable reserves	—	1,383	1,355	1,328	1,300	841
Total reserves	1,797	3,697	3,969	4,290	4,967	5,326

5.15 Capital Commitments

	31st March, 1985 £'000
Contracted for but not provided in the financial statements	1,413
Authorised but not yet contracted for	Nil

The amount contracted for relates to the three units of the Harris M850 eight unit press which had not been delivered as at 31st March, 1985.

Yours faithfully,

Touche Ross & Co.
Chartered Accountants

STATUTORY AND GENERAL INFORMATION

1. INCORPORATION AND SHARE CAPITAL

(a)   The Company was incorporated in England under the Companies Acts 1948 to 1980 on 23rd March, 1981 as a private limited company with registered number 1552113 under the name of St. Ives Group (1981) Limited in order to acquire the business, undertaking and certain assets and liabilities of the company then known as St. Ives Group Limited. On 20th May, 1981, the name of the Company was changed to St. Ives Group Limited and it was re-registered as a public limited company on 12th September, 1985 pursuant to a special resolution passed on 11th September, 1985.

(b)   On incorporation, the Company's authorised share capital was £10,000 divided into 90,000 ordinary shares and 10,000 preferred ordinary shares of 10p each ("preferred ordinary shares"). On 1st May, 1981, 40,000 ordinary shares and 10,000 preferred ordinary shares were issued credited as fully paid as consideration for the acquisition referred to in sub-paragraph (a) above.

(c)   On 3rd May, 1983, the Company purchased 8,000 preferred ordinary shares for a cash sum of £800,000 in accordance with section 46 of the Companies Act 1981.

(d)   On 2nd November, 1983, the sum of £1,050 (part of the revenue reserve) was capitalised and 10,000 new ordinary shares and 500 new preferred ordinary shares, credited as fully paid, were distributed to the holders of the ordinary shares and preferred ordinary shares respectively. The new shares were then converted into and re-designated as 10,500 'A' preferred ordinary shares of 10p each (" 'A' preferred ordinary shares").

(e)   On 14th August, 1985, conversion notices were sent by the Company converting all the preferred ordinary shares and 'A' preferred ordinary shares into ordinary shares on the basis of one ordinary share for each preferred ordinary share and one ordinary share for each 'A' preferred ordinary share, such conversion being conditional upon the ordinary shares being admitted to the Official List by the Council of The Stock Exchange.

(f)   By or pursuant to resolutions passed at an Extraordinary General Meeting of the Company and at separate class meetings of the holders of the preferred ordinary shares and the 'A' preferred ordinary shares held on 11th September, 1985:

(i)   the authorised share capital of the Company was increased from £10,000 to £52,500 by the creation of an additional 320,000 ordinary shares, 10,500 preferred ordinary shares and 94,500 'A' preferred ordinary shares; and

(ii)   360,000 ordinary shares, 18,000 preferred ordinary shares and 94,500 'A' preferred ordinary shares were allotted, credited as fully paid, by way of capitalisation of the sum of £47,250 standing to the credit of the revaluation reserve, *pro rata* to the holders of ordinary shares, preferred ordinary shares and 'A' preferred ordinary shares on the register on 10th September, 1985, such new preferred ordinary shares and 'A' preferred ordinary shares being subject to the conversion notices referred to in sub-paragraph (e) above.

(g)   By or pursuant to resolutions passed at Extraordinary General Meetings of the Company and at separate class meetings of the holders of the preferred ordinary shares and the 'A' preferred ordinary shares held on 17th September, 1985 and conditional on the ordinary shares being admitted to the Official List by the Council of The Stock Exchange by 10th October, 1985:

(i)   the authorised share capital of the Company was increased from £52,500 to £825,000 by the creation of an additional 7,725,000 ordinary shares of 10p each;

(ii)   the Company agreed to issue, credited as fully paid, 47,586 ordinary shares to Wardstock Limited as consideration for the acquisition of Folio Holdings pursuant to the agreement referred to in sub-paragraph 9(a)(i) below;

(iii)   5,725,860 ordinary shares were allotted, credited as fully paid, by way of capitalisation of the sum of £572,586 standing to the credit of the revaluation reserve (*pro rata* to their respective holdings) to the holders of the ordinary shares on the register immediately after the satisfaction of the condition as to listing (and therefore including the then existing holders of the preferred ordinary shares and the 'A' preferred ordinary shares and Wardstock Limited);

(iv)   the directors were generally and unconditionally authorised pursuant to Section 80(1) of the Companies Act 1985 to allot relevant securities (as defined in Section 80(2) of that Act) up to a maximum nominal amount of £195,155.40, such authority to expire on 16th September, 1990;

(v)   the directors were given power to allot equity securities (as defined in Section 94(2) of the Companies Act 1985) for cash as if Section 89(1) of that Act did not apply to the allotment, provided that such power, which was expressed to expire after the next Annual General Meeting of the Company, was limited to (a) the allotment of equity securities in connection with a rights issue in favour of ordinary shareholders where the equity securities attributable to the interests of all ordinary shareholders are proportionate (as nearly as may be) to the respective number of ordinary shares held by them and (b) the allotment (otherwise than pursuant to (a) above) of equity securities up to an aggregate nominal value of £41,250; and

(vi)   new Articles of Association were adopted.

(h) Following the offer for sale, the authorised share capital of the Company will be £825,000 divided into 8,250,000 ordinary shares of which 6,298,446 ordinary shares will be in issue and 1,951,554 ordinary shares will remain unissued. No issue of shares which would effectively alter the control of the Company will be made without the prior approval of the Company in general meeting.

(i) Following the offer for sale, no material issue of shares in the Company (other than to shareholders *pro rata* to existing holdings) will be made within one year without the prior approval of the Company in general meeting.

(j) The whole of the ordinary share capital of the Company is in registered form.

(k) The provisions of Section 89(1) of the Companies Act 1985 (which, to the extent not disapplied pursuant to Section 95 of that Act, confer on ordinary shareholders rights of pre-emption in respect of the allotment of equity securities which are, or are to be, paid up in cash) apply to the balance of the authorised but unissued share capital of the Company which is not the subject of the disapplication referred to in sub-paragraph (g) above.

(l) Save as disclosed in this paragraph 1 and save for intra-group issues, within the period of three years immediately preceding the date of this document no share or loan capital of any member of the Group has been issued or is agreed to be issued for cash or otherwise.

(m) No share or loan capital of any member of the Group is under option or is agreed conditionally or unconditionally to be put under option.

2. SUBSIDIARIES

The Company's operating subsidiaries following the offer for sale, all of which are or will be wholly owned, are listed below:

Company	Issued share capital
Severn Valley Press Limited	2,400 5 per cent. cumulative preferred shares of £1 each 17,700 6 per cent. cumulative preferred 'B' shares of £1 each 39,576 ordinary shares of £1 each
Severn Valley Bindery Limited	100 ordinary shares of £1 each
C B Dorey Limited	5,000 ordinary shares of 1p each 5,000 deferred shares of £1 each
Molyneux Offset Limited	100 ordinary shares of £1 each
Britannic Printing Supplies (London) Limited	100 ordinary shares of £1 each
Folio Holdings Limited	50,000 ordinary shares of 10p each 50,000 deferred shares of 10p each

The registered office of each of the above companies is 47-58 Bastwick Street, London EC1V 3PS.

3. MEMORANDUM AND ARTICLES OF ASSOCIATION

(a) The Memorandum of Association of the Company provides that the Company's principal objects are to acquire the shares or securities of any companies carrying on the businesses of printers and publishers and generally to carry on the business of a holding and investment company. The objects of the Company are set out in full in Clause 4 of the Memorandum of Association which is available for inspection as hereinafter provided.

(b) The Articles of Association contain, *inter alia*, provisions to the following effect:

(i) *Voting*

On a show of hands, every member who is present in person shall have one vote and, on a poll, every member shall have one vote for each ordinary share of which he is the holder, save that a member shall not be entitled to exercise such rights to vote if he, or any person appearing to be interested in shares held by him, has been duly served with a notice under Section 212 of the Companies Act 1985 and has failed to supply the Company with the requisite information within thirty days.

(ii) *Variation of Rights and Alteration of Capital*

(a) Whenever the capital is divided into different classes of shares, all or any of the rights or privileges attached to any class of share may, subject to the provisions of the Companies Act 1985, be varied or abrogated with the sanction of an extraordinary resolution passed at a separate meeting of the holders of the issued shares of that class, but not otherwise.

(b) The Company may by ordinary resolution increase its share capital, consolidate and divide all or any of its share capital into shares of a larger amount, sub-divide its shares into shares of a smaller amount and cancel any shares not taken or agreed to be taken by any person.

(c) The Company may by special resolution reduce its share capital, any capital redemption reserve, any share premium account and any other undistributable reserve in any manner subject to any authority and consent required by law.

(d) The Company may, subject, *inter alia*, to the provisions of the Companies Act 1985, purchase its own shares.

(iii) *Transfer of Shares*

The instrument of transfer of a share may be in any usual form or in such form as the directors may accept and shall be signed by or on behalf of the transferor and, unless the share is fully paid, by or on behalf of the transferee. The directors may in their absolute discretion and without giving any reason refuse to register the transfer of a share which is not fully paid or on which the Company has a lien. The Articles of Association contain no restrictions on the free transferability of fully paid shares provided that transfers are in favour of not more than four transferees.

(iv) *Entitlement to Profits and Surplus on Liquidation*

Subject to any special rights attaching to any shares or any class of shares issued by the Company, the holders of the ordinary shares are entitled *pari passu* amongst themselves, but in proportion to the number of ordinary shares held by them and the amounts paid up on them, to share in such profits of the Company as are paid out as dividends and the whole of any surplus assets in the event of the liquidation of the Company.

(v) *Directors*

(a) Unless otherwise determined by the Company in general meeting, the directors shall not be less than three in number; there is no maximum number of directors.

(b) Directors' fees shall be determined by the directors and such remuneration shall be divided between the directors as they may agree or, failing agreement, equally, except that any director who shall hold office for part only of the period in respect of which such remuneration is payable shall be entitled to rank in such division for a proportion of such remuneration related to the period during which he has held office. The directors may pay all reasonable expenses incurred by a director in attending and returning from meetings of the directors or committees of the directors or general meetings or otherwise in or about the business of the Company or in the discharge of his duties as director.

(c) Any director who holds any executive office (including for this purpose the office of chairman or deputy chairman whether or not such office is held in an executive capacity) or who serves on any committee or who otherwise performs services which in the opinion of the directors are outside the scope of the ordinary duties of a director may be paid such remuneration by way of salary, commission or otherwise as the directors may determine.

(d) The directors may from time to time appoint one or more of their number to be the holder of any executive office on such terms and for such period as they may determine.

(e) A director may be party to or otherwise interested in any transaction or arrangement with the Company or in which the Company is in any way interested and he may hold office in any company in which the Company is in any way interested and in any such case as aforesaid (save as otherwise agreed) he shall not be accountable to the Company for any benefit accruing to him thereunder or in consequence thereof.

(f) A director shall not vote in respect of any contract, arrangement or any other proposal whatsoever in which he has any material interest otherwise than by virtue of his interest in shares or debentures or other securities of or otherwise in or through the Company. A director shall not be counted in the quorum at a meeting in relation to any resolution on which he is debarred from voting but these prohibitions shall not apply to:

(i) the giving of any guarantee, security or indemnity to him in respect of money lent or obligations incurred by him at the request of or for the benefit of the Company or any of its subsidiaries;

(ii) the giving of any guarantee, security or indemnity to a third party in respect of a debt or obligation of the Company or any of its subsidiaries for which he himself has assumed responsibility in whole or in part under a guarantee or indemnity or by the giving of security;

(iii) any proposal concerning an offer of shares or debentures or other securities of or by the Company or any of its subsidiaries for subscription or purchase in which offer he is or is to be interested as a participant in the underwriting or sub-underwriting thereof;

(iv) any proposal concerning any other company in which he is interested directly or indirectly and whether as an officer or shareholder or otherwise howsoever provided that he (together with persons connected with him within the meaning of Section 346 of the Companies Act 1985) is not the holder of or beneficially interested in one per cent. or more of the issued shares of any class of such company (or of any third company through which his interest is derived) or of the voting rights available to members of the relevant company (any such interest being deemed to be a material interest in all circumstances);

(v) any proposal concerning the adoption, modification or operation of a superannuation fund or retirement benefits scheme under which he may benefit and which has been approved by or is subject to and conditional upon approval by the Board of the Inland Revenue for tax purposes; and

(vi) any proposal concerning the adoption, modification or operation of any scheme for enabling employees, including full time executive directors of the Company and/or any subsidiary, to acquire shares of the Company or any arrangement for the benefit of employees of the Company or any of its subsidiaries under which the director benefits in a similar manner to the employees and which does not accord any director as such any privilege or advantage not generally accorded to the employees to whom such scheme or arrangement relates.

The Company may by ordinary resolution suspend or relax the provisions of the Articles of Association referred to above to any extent or ratify any transaction not duly authorised by reason of a contravention of the relevant Article.

(g) No share qualification is required by any director.

(h) The statutory provisions relating to the appointment, retirement and re-election of directors who have reached the age of 70 years do not apply to the Company.

(vi) *Borrowing Powers*

The directors may exercise all the powers of the Company to borrow money and to mortgage or charge its undertaking, property and uncalled capital and to issue debentures and other securities whether outright or as collateral security for any debt, liability or obligation of the Company or of any third party.

(vii) *Unclaimed Dividends*

Any dividend unclaimed after a period of twelve years from its date of declaration shall be forfeited and shall revert to the Company.

(viii) *Pensions and Gratuities*

The directors may provide or pay pensions or other retirement, superannuation, death or disability benefits to any director or ex-director and for the purpose of providing any such benefits may contribute to any scheme or fund or pay premiums.

(ix) *Untraced Shareholders*

The Company may sell the shares of a member or person entitled on death or bankruptcy of a member if such member or person has not cashed warrants or cheques sent by the Company over a period of twelve years and the Company has, after giving notice in certain newspapers, received no notice either of the whereabouts or of the existence of the member or other persons. The Company shall be obliged to account to the person entitled thereto for the proceeds of sale.

4. EXECUTIVE SHARE OPTION SCHEME

On 17th September, 1985 the Company adopted an Executive Share Option Scheme ("the Scheme") conditionally on the ordinary shares being admitted to the Official List by the Council of The Stock Exchange by 10th October, 1985. The principal provisions of the Scheme, which is subject to approval by the Inland Revenue under Schedule 10 to the Finance Act 1984, are as follows:

(a) The directors may grant options to full time employees, including executive directors, employed by the Company or any of its subsidiaries. Options may be granted at any time within 42 days·after the announcement of the annual or interim consolidated results of the Group or within 42 days after approval of the Scheme by the Inland Revenue.

(b) The subscription price payable for an ordinary share on the exercise of an option will be not less than the higher of the nominal value and the average of the middle market quotations of an ordinary share, as derived from the Daily Official List of The Stock Exchange, for the three dealing days immediately preceding the date of the grant.

(c)   The number of ordinary shares over which options may be granted pursuant to the Scheme may not exceed 300,000 ordinary shares (being approximately 5 per cent. of the issued share capital following the offer for sale). This limit may be adjusted by the directors as appropriate (and as confirmed in writing by the auditors to be fair and reasonable and subject to the approval of the Inland Revenue) following any rights or capitalisation issue or any reduction, subdivision or consolidation of the share capital.

(d)   No executive may be granted an option if he is within two years of retirement or if the total amount payable on exercise of the option, taken together with the amount paid or payable on exercise of any other rights granted to acquire shares under any other scheme operated by the Company within the preceding ten years, would exceed four times his taxable emoluments (excluding benefits in kind) in the year of assessment in which the latest option is granted or the preceding year of assessment, whichever shall be the greater. An option is personal to the participant and is not capable of transfer or assignment.

(e)   No option may in any circumstances be exercised more than ten years after the date on which it was granted. An option may not generally be exercised within three years of the date of grant. However, options may be exercised:

(i)   within twelve months after the participant's death;

(ii)   in the event of a participant ceasing to be an executive for any reason other than death, to the extent that the directors may determine in their absolute discretion, in which event it must be exercised, if at all, within six months after the later of the date of cessation and the third anniversary of the date of grant;

(iii)   within 42 days after any general offer for shares in the Company becomes unconditional; and

(iv)   if notice is given of a resolution for the voluntary winding up of the Company (unless the winding up is for the purposes of a reorganisation or reconstruction which makes provision for the adjustment or cancellation of options confirmed by the auditors to be fair and reasonable) at any time until the commencement of the winding up.

(f)   Ordinary shares issued under the Scheme will rank *pari passu* with the other ordinary shares then in issue except as regards dividends and other distributions payable to the holders of ordinary shares on or by reference to a date prior to the exercise of the option.

(g)   The Scheme is governed by rules and will be administered by the directors. The directors may not alter the Scheme to the advantage of participants or executives without the prior consent of the Company where the alteration relates to the definition of "executive", "option price", "participant", "relevant emoluments" or "relevant amount" or the rules relating to the limitation on the size of the Scheme, the limitations on individual participants, the ascertainment of the subscription price, the conditions of options, the prohibition against exercising an option when the participant has such an interest as is referred to in paragraph 4(1)(b) of Schedule 10 to the Finance Act 1984, the obligation on the Company to apply to the Council of The Stock Exchange for admission of the shares the subject of an option to the Official List and the ranking of such shares *pari passu*, the rules relating to take-overs and amalgamation, variation of capital, liquidation, administration and amendment of the Scheme. Subject thereto, the directors may amend any provision of the Scheme. The Scheme may not be amended in any respect without the prior approval of the Inland Revenue.

5. DIRECTORS' AND OTHER INTERESTS

(a)   Following the offer for sale, the interests of the directors in the ordinary shares of the Company, as they will be shown in the register of directors' interests maintained under the provisions of the Companies Act 1985, will be as follows:

Director	Beneficially	%	As Trustee	%
R. Gavron	2,472,377	39.3	201,300	3.2
K. P. Ladd	178,750	2.8	—	—
P. M. W. Stafford	173,250	2.7	—	—
B. C. Edwards	173,250	2.7	—	—

None of the directors will be applying for shares in the offer for sale.

The aggregate holdings of the directors immediately following the offer for sale will amount to 50.7 per cent. of the issued ordinary shares.

(b)   Save as aforesaid, the directors are not aware of any shareholding which, following the offer for sale, will represent five per cent. or more of the Company's issued ordinary shares or of any other person who, directly or indirectly, jointly or severally, exercises or could exercise control over the Company.

(c)   There are no outstanding loans granted by any members of the Group to any of the directors nor any guarantees provided by any member of the Group for the benefit of such directors.

(d) R. Gavron and his family interests own all the issued share capital of Wardstock Limited which is the vendor of Folio Holdings under the agreement referred to in sub-paragraph 9(a)(i) below. He is or was therefore directly or indirectly interested in all the contracts set out in paragraph 9 below. The directors are parties to the offer for sale agreement and the deed of indemnity referred to in paragraph 8 below. Printing is carried out by the Group on an arm's length basis for Octopus Publishing Group plc (of which R. Gavron is a non-executive director and shareholder) and for The Folio Society Limited (of which he is the chairman and, through Wardstock Limited, the controlling shareholder). Save as disclosed herein, no director has any interest in any transaction which is of an unusual nature, contains unusual terms or which is significant to the business of the Group and which was effected by the Company during the current or immediately preceding financial year or which was effected during any earlier financial year and remains in any respect outstanding or unperformed.

6. DIRECTORS' EMPLOYMENT ARRANGEMENTS

(a) On 17th September, 1985, P. M. W. Stafford and B. C. Edwards each entered into a service agreement with the Company (approved by the ordinary shareholders) for seven years from 18th September, 1985 at an annual salary of £42,000, subject to annual review, together with a commission as mentioned in sub-paragraph (b) below. The agreements may be terminated by either party by not less than six months' notice expiring on or at any time after 18th September, 1992.

(b) Each of the directors is entitled to a commission at the rate of 1.5 per cent. on the annual profit on ordinary activities before taxation of the Group in excess of £1.5 million. The base profit level is subject to adjustment to take account of, *inter alia*, inflation and any further issues of share capital.

(c) The aggregate remuneration (including benefits in kind) of the directors for the year ended 31st July, 1985 is estimated at £255,000, including £90,000 in respect of commissions based on the estimated profit on ordinary activities before taxation for that year. For the year ending 31st July, 1986, the aggregate remuneration (before commissions based on profit) will be approximately £177,000.

(d) There is no arrangement under which any director has agreed to waive future emoluments nor has there been any waiver of emoluments during the financial year immediately preceding the date of this offer for sale.

7. PREMISES

The following is a summary of the Group's properties:

Property	Occupier	Area	Tenure/term	Rent	Rent review dates
1. Light industrial premises and offices at 47/58 Bastwick St., London EC1	The Group	18,000 sq. ft.	Leasehold–150 years from 25th December, 1960	£1,000 p.a.	25th March, 1990 and every 30 years thereafter
2. Industrial premises at Pontygwindy Industrial Estate, Caerphilly, Mid-Glamorgan	Severn Valley	45,750 sq. ft.	Leasehold–999 years from 20th December, 1966	£585 p.a.	20th December, 2046 and every 80 years thereafter
			Leasehold–99 years from 12th June, 1970	£130 p.a.	12th June, 2020, 2041 and 2062
3. Industrial premises at Pontygwindy Industrial Estate, Caerphilly, Mid-Glamorgan	Severn Valley	20,750 sq. ft.	Leasehold–5 years from 1st September, 1984 with option to renew for a further 5 years unless the landlord wishes to occupy the premises	£38,000 p.a.	1st September, 1987 and every three years thereafter

Property	Occupier	Area	Tenure/term	Rent	Rent review dates
4. Industrial premises at Unit A3, Imperial Way, Reading, Berkshire	Kingsdale	10,450 sq. ft.	Leasehold–25 years from 24th June, 1982. Tenants may terminate as at 24th June, 1988	£37,150 p.a.	24th June, 1988, 1992 and every five years thereafter
5. Industrial premises at Faringdon Avenue, Harold Hill, Romford, Essex	CB Dorey	33,000 sq. ft.	Leasehold–62 years less 7 days from 25th December, 1971	£10,900 p.a.	25th December, 1986 and every fifteen years thereafter
6. Industrial premises at Terminus Road, Chichester, West Sussex	RJ Acford	57,550 sq. ft.	Freehold Leasehold–42 years from 25th December, 1969	— £2,300 p.a.	— 25th December, 1990 and every seven years thereafter

Note:
The properties referred to under 3. and 4. above have not been included in Healey & Baker's valuation.

8. OFFER FOR SALE ARRANGEMENTS

(a) By an agreement dated 18th September, 1985 ("the Offer for Sale agreement") between (1) the Company, (2) the directors, (3) certain shareholders in the Company ("the Vendors") and (4) N. M. Rothschild & Sons Limited ("Rothschilds"), Rothschilds has agreed (conditionally, inter alia, on the admission to the Official List of all the ordinary shares by 10th October, 1985) to purchase a total of 2,267,000 ordinary shares from the Vendors at a price per share equal to the striking price under the offer for sale, less 2 per cent. of the minimum tender price plus value added tax, if applicable, on such 2 per cent. Rothschilds has agreed to offer for sale by tender all such shares to the public. Warranties and indemnities have been given to Rothschilds by the Company and the directors jointly and severally and by certain of the Vendors on a several basis. Rothschilds will pay underwriting commissions of $1\frac{1}{4}$ per cent. of the minimum tender price and a fee of $\frac{1}{4}$ per cent. of the minimum tender price to Rowe & Pitman (together with value added tax where applicable). The Company has agreed to pay all the costs and expenses of the application for the ordinary shares to be admitted to the Official List and other costs including the fees of its legal advisers and of the reporting accountants and the costs of printing, advertising and circulating the offer for sale document (together with value added tax where applicable). The Company will also pay an amount to Rothschilds to the extent that interest earned on application moneys is less than Rothschilds' agreed fees and expenses.

(b) The Vendors and the number of ordinary shares being sold under the Offer for Sale agreement are summarised as follows:

Vendor	Ordinary shares
R. Gavron, his family and related interests	1,658,827
K. P. Ladd, his family and related interests	124,520
P. M. W. Stafford	57,750
B. C. Edwards and related interests	57,750
Staff (12 employees)	89,978
Morgan Nominees Limited	168,410
MGX Nominees Limited	96,140
The Trustees of the Company's Share Incentive Scheme*	13,625

*The Share Incentive Scheme was set up in 1972 to enable staff to acquire shares in St. Ives. Its residual holding of ordinary shares is being sold. The trustees have resolved to wind up the scheme and to remit the net proceeds to the Company in accordance with the rules of the scheme.

(c) By a deed of indemnity dated 18th September, 1985 between (1) the directors, (2) certain of the Vendors, (3) Rothschilds and (4) the Group, the directors and certain of the Vendors have given indemnities in respect of taxation in favour of the Group.

(d)   All the existing shareholders have undertaken that they will not (without the prior written consent of Rothschilds) dispose of any ordinary shares prior to the publication of the annual accounts of the Company for the year ending 31st July, 1986. The undertakings of R. Gavron and K. P. Ladd and certain of their related interests extend until after the publication of the accounts of the Company for the year ending 31st July, 1987. In addition, P. M. W. Stafford and B. C. Edwards have given undertakings to Rothschilds that, having agreed to sell 25 per cent. of their existing holdings of 231,000 ordinary shares each under the offer for sale, they and their related interests will each be entitled to sell only one-tenth of such holdings following the publication of the accounts of the Company for each of the years ending 31st July, 1987 to 1991 inclusive but will not otherwise dispose of any shares until after the publication of the accounts of the Company for the year ending 31st July, 1992. Other senior employees of the Group have agreed to similar restrictions for varying periods.

9.   MATERIAL CONTRACTS

(a)   The following contracts, not being contracts in the ordinary course of business, have been entered into by St. Ives and its subsidiaries within the two years immediately preceding the date of this document and are or may be material:

(i)   an agreement dated 17th September, 1985 made between (1) Wardstock Limited and (2) the Company whereby Wardstock Limited agreed to sell to the Company all the issued share capital of Folio Holdings for the sum of £1,518,000 to be satisfied by the issue, credited as fully paid, of 47,586 ordinary shares. (These ordinary shares rank in full for the capitalisation issue referred to in sub-paragraph 1(g) above). Wardstock Limited has agreed to refund to the Company in cash the difference between the value of such shares (and the related capitalisation shares) at the striking price and £1,518,000. The agreement is conditional upon the admission of the ordinary shares to the Official List by the Council of The Stock Exchange by 10th October, 1985 and completion will take place forthwith thereafter; and

(ii)   the Offer for Sale agreement and the deed of indemnity, both dated 18th September, 1985, referred to in paragraph 8 above.

(b)   In addition, the following contracts, not being contracts in the ordinary course of business, have been entered into by Folio Holdings within the two years immediately preceding the date of this document and are or may be material:

(i)   a transfer dated 15th January, 1985 made between (1) R. Spooner and P. G. D. Curzon, (2) C. L. Corman and P. B. W. Hamlyn and (3) Folio Holdings whereby White House Cottage, Millfield Lane, London N6 was acquired by Folio Holdings for the sum of £150,000 in cash;

(ii)   a transfer dated 31st July, 1985 made between (1) Folio Holdings and (2) Wardstock Limited whereby White House Cottage, Millfield Lane, London N6 was sold to Wardstock Limited for the sum of £151,773 in cash;

(iii)   an agreement dated 7th October, 1983 made between (1) D. J. Frost and D. R. C. Heymans and (2) Folio Holdings whereby Folio Holdings agreed to purchase 11 Holly Mount, London NW3 for the sum of £118,000 in cash;

(iv)   an agreement dated 14th May, 1985 made between (1) Folio Holdings and (2) L. A. Albin and T. J. Watson whereby Folio Holdings agreed to sell 11 Holly Mount, London NW3 for the sum of £157,500 in cash;

(v)   an agreement dated 31st July, 1985 made between (1) Folio Holdings and (2) Wardstock Limited whereby Folio Holdings agreed to sell to Wardstock Limited all the issued share capital of The Folio Society Limited for the sum of £874,550 in cash; and

(vi)   a transfer dated 31st July, 1985 made between (1) Folio Holdings and (2) Wardstock Limited whereby all the issued share capital of Carcanet Press Limited was sold to Wardstock Limited for the sum of £20,000 in cash.

10. TAXATION

(a)   The directors have been advised that the Company is a close company as defined in the Income and Corporation Taxes Act 1970 but should cease to be a close company following the allocation of ordinary shares to applicants under the offer for sale.

(b)   Shortfall clearances under paragraph 18 of Schedule 16 of the Finance Act 1972 have been obtained for the Company and its subsidiaries in respect of their accounting periods to 31st July, 1984 and for Folio Holdings in respect of its accounting periods to 31st August, 1984. Indemnities have been given by the directors and certain of the vendors under the deed of indemnity referred to in paragraph 8 above in respect of possible shortfall apportionments of the income of any member of the Group and in respect of capital transfer tax liabilities of the Group.

(c) When paying a dividend the Company has to remit to the Inland Revenue an amount of advance corporation tax at a rate which is related to the basic rate of income tax and is currently three-sevenths of the dividend paid. Accordingly the advance corporation tax related to a dividend currently equals 30 per cent. of the sum of the cash dividend plus the advance corporation tax. For shareholders resident in the United Kingdom the advance corporation tax paid is available as a tax credit which individual shareholders who are so resident may set off against their total income tax liability or in appropriate cases should claim in cash. A United Kingdom resident corporate shareholder will not be liable to United Kingdom corporation tax on any dividend received. Other persons who are not resident in the United Kingdom should consult their own tax advisers as to whether they are entitled to reclaim any part of the tax credit, the procedure for claiming payment and what relief or credit may be claimed for such tax credit in the jurisdiction in which they are resident.

11. WORKING CAPITAL

The directors consider that, having regard to the bank facilities available, the Group has sufficient working capital for its present requirements.

12. GENERAL

(a) No member of the Group is engaged in any litigation or arbitration proceedings and no litigation, arbitration or claim is known to the directors to be pending or threatened against any member of the Group which may have or has had during the twelve months prior to the date hereof a significant effect on the Group's financial position.

(b) Save for the conditional acquisition of the shares of Folio Holdings referred to in sub-paragraph 9(a)(i) above, there has been no significant change in the financial or trading position of the Group since 31st March, 1985 other than in the ordinary course of business.

(c) Touche Ross & Co. have given and not withdrawn their written consent to the issue of this document with the inclusion herein of their letter and report and the references thereto and to their name in the form and context in which they appear.

(d) N. M. Rothschild & Sons Limited has given and not withdrawn its written consent to the issue of this document with the inclusion herein of its letter and the references thereto and to its name in the form and context in which they appear.

(e) The valuation of the properties owned by Folio Holdings has been carried out by Healey & Baker, International Surveyors, Valuers and Auctioneers, 29 St. George Street, Hanover Square, London W1A 3BG, who have given and not withdrawn their written consent to the issue of this document with the inclusion herein of the references to their name and to their valuation in the form and context in which they appear.

(f) The costs to be borne by the Company in connection with the offer for sale are estimated at £395,000 (exclusive of value added tax).

(g) N. M. Rothschild & Sons Limited, merchant banker, is registered in England (No. 925279) and its registered office is at New Court, St. Swithin's Lane, London EC4P 4DU.

(h) The principal place of business of the Company is at 47-58 Bastwick Street, London EC1V 3PS.

(i) The financial information set out in this offer for sale document does not comprise full accounts within the meaning of the Companies Act 1985. Full accounts for the periods ended 31st July, 1980, 1982, 1983 and 1984 have been delivered to the Registrar of Companies.

Following the liquidation on 1st May, 1981 of the predecessor company to St. Ives, no statutory consolidated accounts for the predecessor company were required to be delivered to the Registrar of Companies for the year ended 31st July, 1981. However, non-statutory consolidated accounts were produced for the year ended 31st July, 1981 which reflected the transactions carried out by the predecessor company, St. Ives and their respective subsidiaries and, on that basis, were reported on by the auditors without qualification. Similarly, non-statutory consolidated accounts for the year ended 31st July, 1982 were reported on by the auditors without qualification apart from the reference to the non-inclusion of current cost financial statements as indicated below. These accounts for the two years ended 31st July, 1982 form the basis of the financial information for those years reported on by Touche Ross & Co.

The statutory consolidated accounts of St. Ives for the period from its incorporation on 23rd March, 1981 to 31st July, 1982 were delivered to the Registrar of Companies and were reported on by the auditors with the following qualification:

"It has proved impractical to carry out procedures to verify the fair value, as determined by the directors, of the assets and liabilities acquired by the holding company from the predecessor at 1st May, 1981.

As stated in note 1 to the financial statements, the directors have not included in the consolidated profit and loss account the results of the subsidiary companies for the period from 1st May, 1981 (the date of acquisition) to 31st July, 1981".

The qualification arose because an audit was not undertaken of the assets and liabilities of the predecessor company at 1st May, 1981 prior to their acquisition by St. Ives. Since these statutory accounts do not form the basis of the financial information presented in this offer for sale document, this qualification has no effect on that financial information.

The statutory consolidated accounts of St. Ives and its subsidiaries for the periods ended 31st July, 1982, 1983 and 1984 were qualified in that they did not include current cost financial statements as then required by Statement of Standard Accounting Practice No. 16 which is no longer operative.

The statutory consolidated accounts of St. Ives and its subsidiaries for the year ended 31st July, 1983 were qualified in that they did not include a Source and Application of Funds Statement as required by Statement of Standard Accounting Practice No. 10. A Source and Application of Funds Statement for that year has been included in the financial information presented in the Accountants' Report.

13. DOCUMENTS FOR INSPECTION

The following documents or copies thereof may be inspected at the offices of Linklaters & Paines, Barrington House, 59-67 Gresham Street, London EC2V 7JA during normal business hours on any week day (Saturdays and public holidays excepted) for a period of fourteen days following the date of publication of the offer for sale:

(a)   the Memorandum and Articles of Association of the Company;

(b)   the audited consolidated accounts of the Company and its subsidiaries for the two years ended 31st July, 1984 and the eight months ended 31st March, 1985;

(c)   the audited accounts of Folio Holdings for the two financial periods ended 31st August, 1984 and the eleven months ended 31st July, 1985;

(d)   the written consents referred to in paragraph 12 above;

(e)   the report and letter of Touche Ross & Co. set out herein, together with their statement of adjustments;

(f)   the letter of N. M. Rothschild & Sons Limited set out herein;

(g)   the report of Healey & Baker setting out the valuation of the properties owned by Folio Holdings;

(h)   the rules of the Executive Share Option Scheme referred to in paragraph 4 above;

(i)   the service agreements referred to in paragraph 6 above;

(j)   the material contracts referred to in paragraph 9 above; and

(k)   the undertakings referred to in sub-paragraph 8(d) above.

18th September, 1985

TERMS AND CONDITIONS OF APPLICATION

1. Acceptance of applications will be conditional upon the ordinary share capital of the Company being admitted to the Official List of The Stock Exchange by 10th October, 1985. Until then, application moneys will be kept by Ravensbourne Registration Services Limited ("Ravensbourne") in a separate bank account and, if listing is not granted, will be returned (without interest) by crossed cheque in favour of the person named in box 5 through the post at the risk of the applicant(s).

2. Subject as contained herein, applications will be accepted on the following basis:—

    (i)   all ordinary shares for which applications are wholly or partly accepted will be sold at the same price ("the striking price"), which will not necessarily be the highest price at which applications (including applications at higher prices) are received for the total number of ordinary shares offered under the offer for sale. In deciding the striking price and the basis of allocation, N. M. Rothschild & Sons Limited ("Rothschilds") will have regard, *inter alia*, to the need to establish a satisfactory market in the ordinary shares;

    (ii) applications for ordinary shares at less than the striking price will receive no allocation; and

    (iii) if applications are received for less than the total number of ordinary shares offered, the striking price will be the minimum tender price.

3. Rothschilds reserves the right to present all cheques and banker's drafts for payment on receipt, to retain letters of acceptance and surplus application moneys pending the clearance of all cheques and to accept in part only or to scale down or reject applications and, in particular, multiple or suspected multiple applications at any one price. If any application is not accepted in whole or is accepted in part only or is scaled down, the application moneys or, as the case may be, the balance thereof, will be returned (without interest) by crossed cheque in favour of the person named in box 5 through the post at the risk of the applicant(s).

4. By completing and delivering an application form, you (as the applicant(s)):—

    (i)   offer to purchase the number of ordinary shares specified in your application form (or such smaller number for which the application is accepted) on and subject to these terms and conditions and subject to the Memorandum and Articles of Association of the Company;

    (ii) authorise Ravensbourne to send a letter of acceptance for the number of ordinary shares for which your application is accepted, and/or a crossed cheque for any moneys returnable by post, at the risk of the person(s) entitled thereto, to your address (or that of the first-named applicant) as set out in the application form and to procure that your name (together with the name(s) of any other joint applicant(s)) is/are placed on the register of members of the Company in respect of such ordinary shares the entitlement to which has not been duly renounced;

    (iii) agree that, in consideration of Rothschilds agreeing to consider applications upon the terms and subject to the conditions set out in the offer for sale document relating to the Company dated 18th September, 1985, your application may not be revoked until after 10th October, 1985 and that this paragraph 4(iii) shall constitute a collateral contract between you and Rothschilds which will become binding upon despatch by post to or, in the case of delivery by hand, receipt by Ravensbourne of your application;

    (iv) agree that completion and delivery of an application form shall constitute a warranty that your remittance will be honoured on first presentation and further agree that any letter of acceptance and any moneys returnable to you may be retained by Ravensbourne pending clearance of your remittance;

    (v)   agree that all applications, acceptances of applications and contracts resulting therefrom under the offer for sale shall be governed by and construed in accordance with English law;

    (vi) warrant that, if you sign an application form on behalf of another person, you have due authority to do so; and

(vii) confirm that, in making an application, you are not relying on any information or representation in relation to the Group other than as contained in the offer for sale document and you accordingly agree that no person responsible solely or jointly for the offer for sale document or any part thereof shall have any liability for any other information or representations.

5. Acceptance of applications will be effected by announcement of the basis of allocation to The Stock Exchange.

6. Up to 5 per cent. of the ordinary shares being offered for sale will in the first instance be made available at the striking price to meet applications from employees of the Group, if made on the special pink application forms made available to them. In the event of excess applications from employees of the Group, the basis of allocation will be decided by Rothschilds in consultation with the Company.

7. No person receiving the offer for sale document, or an application form, in any territory other than the United Kingdom may treat the same as constituting an invitation or offer to him, nor should he in any event use such form unless, in the relevant territory, such an invitation or offer could lawfully be made to him or such form could lawfully be used without contravention of any registration or other legal requirements. Any person outside the United Kingdom wishing to make an application hereunder must satisfy himself as to full observance of the laws of any relevant territory in connection therewith, including obtaining any requisite governmental or other consents, observing any requisite formalities and paying any issue, transfer or other taxes due in such territory.

AVAILABILITY OF OFFER FOR SALE DOCUMENTS

Copies of the offer for sale document and application form can be obtained from:—

N. M. Rothschild & Sons Limited
New Court
St. Swithin's Lane
London EC4P 4DU
 and
3 York Street
Manchester M2 2AW

St. Ives Group plc
47-58 Bastwick Street
London EC1V 3PS

Rowe & Pitman
1 Finsbury Avenue
London EC2M 2PA

Ravensbourne Registration
Services Limited
Bourne House
34 Beckenham Road
Beckenham
Kent BR3 4TU

LISTING AND DEALING ARRANGEMENTS

The application list will open at 10 a.m. on Thursday, 26th September, 1985 and may be closed at any time thereafter. The striking price and the basis on which applications have been accepted will be announced as soon as possible after the application list closes. It is expected that letters of acceptance will be posted to successful applicants not later than Wednesday, 2nd October, 1985 and that dealings in the ordinary shares will commence on Thursday, 3rd October, 1985. Any dealings in the ordinary shares following the announcement of the basis of allocation and prior to the receipt of letters of acceptance are at the risk of the applicant so dealing.

The ordinary shares now offered for sale will be registered by the Company free of stamp duty and registration fees, in the names of purchasers or persons in whose favour letters of acceptance are duly renounced provided that, in cases of renunciation, letters of acceptance (duly completed in accordance with the instructions contained therein) are lodged for registration by 3 p.m. on Friday, 1st November, 1985. Share certificates will be despatched on or about Friday, 29th November, 1985.

PROCEDURE FOR APPLICATION OVERLEAF

PROCEDURE FOR APPLICATION

The following notes should be read in conjunction with the application form.

1. Insert in box 1 (in figures) the number of ordinary shares for which you are applying. **Applications must be for a minimum of 100 ordinary shares** or in one of the following multiples:—

   —for not more than 1,000 ordinary shares, in a multiple of 100 ordinary shares

   —for more than 1,000 ordinary shares but not more than 5,000 ordinary shares, in a multiple of 500 ordinary shares

   —for more than 5,000 ordinary shares but not more than 10,000 ordinary shares, in a multiple of 1,000 ordinary shares

   —for more than 10,000 ordinary shares in a multiple of 5,000 ordinary shares.

2. Put in box 2 (in figures) the price you are willing to pay for each ordinary share. Applications must be made either at the minimum tender price of 290p or at any higher price which is a multiple of 5p.

3. Put in box 3 (in figures) the amount you pay, which is the number of ordinary shares inserted in box 1 multiplied by the price per share inserted in box 2.

4. Sign and date the application form in box 4.

   The application form may be signed by someone else on your behalf (and/or on behalf of any joint applicant(s)) if duly authorised to do so, but the power(s) of attorney must be enclosed for inspection. A corporation should sign under the hand of a duly authorised official whose representative capacity must be stated.

5. Put your full name and address in BLOCK CAPITALS in box 5.

6. You must pin a separate cheque or banker's draft to each completed application form. Your cheque or banker's draft must be made payable to "Ravensbourne Registration Services Limited" for the amount payable on application and should be crossed "Not Negotiable".

   No receipt will be issued for your payment, which must be solely for this application.

   Your cheque or banker's draft must be drawn in sterling on an account at a branch (which must be in the United Kingdom, the Channel Islands or the Isle of Man) of a bank which is either a member of the London or Scottish Clearing Houses or which has arranged for its cheques and banker's drafts to be presented for payment through the clearing facilities provided for the members of those Clearing Houses (and must bear the appropriate sorting code number in the top right hand corner).

   Applications may be accompanied by a cheque drawn by someone other than the applicant(s), but any moneys to be returned will be sent by crossed cheque in favour of the person named in box 5.

7. You may apply jointly with other persons.

   You must then arrange for the application form to be completed by or on behalf of each joint applicant (up to a maximum of three). Their full names and addresses should be put in BLOCK CAPITALS in box 7.

8. Box 8 must be signed by or on behalf of each joint applicant (other than the first applicant who should complete box 5 and sign in box 4).

   If anyone is signing on behalf of any joint applicant(s), the power(s) of attorney must be enclosed for inspection.

9. You must send the completed application form by post, or deliver it by hand, to Ravensbourne Registration Services Limited, 145 Leadenhall Street, London, EC3V 4QT so as to be received not later than 10 a.m. on Thursday, 26th September, 1985. Photostat copies of the application form will not be accepted.

   If you post your application form, you should use first class post but you do so at your own risk. You should in any event allow at least two days for delivery.

APPLICATION FORM

The application list for the ordinary shares now being offered for sale will open at 10 a.m. on Thursday, 26th September, 1985 and may be closed at any time thereafter.

ST IVES GROUP PLC

Offer for Sale by Tender
by

N. M. Rothschild & Sons Limited

of 2,267,000 ordinary shares of 10p each at a minimum tender price of 290p per share, the price tendered being payable in full on application

I/We hereby offer to purchase the number of shares shown in box 1 at the price per share shown in box 2, on the terms and subject to the conditions set out in the offer for sale document dated 18th September, 1985, and I/we attach a cheque or banker's draft for the amount shown in box 3.

1	2	3
Number of ordinary shares applied for	*Price per share	Amount of cheque/banker's draft attached
	p	£

*The price per share at which application is made must be indicated here and must be either at the minimum tender price of 290p or at a higher price which is a multiple of 5p.

UNLESS THIS APPLICATION FORM IS PROPERLY COMPLETED IN ACCORDANCE WITH THE PROCEDURE FOR APPLICATION SET OUT IN THE OFFER FOR SALE DOCUMENT DATED 18TH SEPTEMBER, 1985, IT MAY BE TREATED AS INVALID.

Dated 1985	Signature	4

FOR OFFICIAL USE ONLY

1 Acceptance number

2 Shares allocated

3 Amount received

£

4 Amount payable

£

5 Amount returned

£

6 Cheque number

PLEASE USE BLOCK CAPITALS

Mr. Mrs. Miss or Title   Surname
Forenames in full
Address in full
Postcode

5

→ ☐ Pin here your cheque/banker's draft for the amount in box 3.   **6**

Fill in the section below only when there is more than one applicant. The first or sole applicant should complete box 5 and sign box 4. Insert below only the names and addresses of the second and subsequent applicants, each of whose signatures is required in box 8.

PLEASE USE BLOCK CAPITALS

Mr. Mrs. Miss or Title Surname	Mr. Mrs. Miss or Title Surname	Mr. Mrs. Miss or Title Surname	
Forenames in full	Forenames in full	Forenames in full	
Address in full	Address in full	Address in full	7
Postcode	Postcode	Postcode	

Signature	Signature	Signature	
			8

Printed by Williams Lea a member of the Ⓦ Ⓛ Ⓖ Williams Lea Group   023957

GLOSSARY

Gross Domestic Product (GDP) – the total value of all goods and services produced within the particular country concerned. Income from overseas is not included and no deduction is made for depreciation or a reduction in capital stocks. GDP may be calculated at constant prices, at market prices or at factor cost.

Gross National Product (GNP) – the total value of all goods and services produced within the particular country concerned plus the net income from overseas. GNP is calculated without taking any deductions for depreciation or any reduction in capital stocks. GNP may be calculated at constant prices, at market prices or at factor cost.

Public Sector Borrowing Requirement (PSBR) – this is basically derived as the total Government expenditure less the total Government revenue, but also takes into account the borrowing requirements of local authorities and public corporations. PSBR equals central Government borrowing requirement
    less central Government lending to local authorities,
    less central Government lending to public corporations,
    plus local authorities' borrowing requirements,
    plus public corporations' borrowing requirements.

BIBLIOGRAPHY

The following bibliography covers those works which the authors have used extensively or which are of value in extending coverage of topics. The abbreviations JIA, TFA and JSS are used for references to papers in the *Journal of the Institute of Actuaries*, the *Transactions of the Faculty of Actuaries*, and the *Journal of the Institute of Actuaries Students' Society* respectively.

Chapter 1   The economic framework

The most recent review of the role of institutions in the U.K. is the Wilson Report. The papers by Arthur and Hall are useful essays describing institutional investment in a more reflective context.

1 *Report of the Committee to Review the Functioning of Financial Institutions*, Cmnd 7939 (*The Wilson Report*), HMSO 1980.
2 *Economics, Institutional Investment, and the Common Good*, T. G. Arthur, Transactions of the 22nd International Congress of Actuaries, 1984.
3 *The Role and Responsibilities of the Institutional Investor*, L. G. Hall, Transactions of the 22nd International Congress of Actuaries, 1984.

A number of publications by the Bank of England are helpful in understanding the role of the authorities in the financial markets. The following three are very relevant to Chapter 1.

4 *The Measurement of Capital*, Bank of England, September 1980.
5 *The Measurement of Liquidity*, Bank of England, July 1982.
6 *Monetary Statistics*, Bank of England Quarterly Review, December 1982.

The Central Statistics Office produces monthly digests of financial and other statistics.

Chapter 2   The capital markets

In order to keep pace with the changes taking place currently in the City of London and in capital markets generally it is essential to keep abreast of articles in newspapers and other periodicals. The Stock Exchange is one of the Self Regulatory Authorities and publishes developments in its Year Book and in its Quarterly bulletin.

Chapter 3   Types of security

Our book replaces Volume 1 of *Institutional Investment* by Gilfrid Day and Andrew Jamieson. More extensive coverage of the various types of security is given in the other volumes of their work.

7 *Institutional Investment, Volume II Gilt Edged Securities*, J. G. Day and A. T. Jamieson, Institute of Actuaries 1980.
8 *Institutional Investment, Volume III Other Fixed Interest Securities*, J. G. Day and A. T. Jamieson, Institute of Actuaries, 1980.
9 *Institutional Investment, Volume IV Equity Investment*, J. G. Day and A. T. Jamieson, Institute of Actuaries, 1980.
10 *Institutional Investment, Volume V Property*, J. G. Day and A. T. Jamieson, Institute of Actuaries 1980.
11 *Institutional Investment, Volume VI Overseas Investment*, J. G. Day and A. T. Jamieson, Institute of Actuaries 1980.
   The following two works are more recent in their approach.
12 *Inside the Gilt-Edged Market*, F. P. S. Phillips, Woodhead-Faulkner, 1984
13 *Trading in Options*, G. Chamberlain, Woodhead-Faulkner, 1982.

Chapter 4   Elements of accounts for investors

For further reading the following references are short in number and reasonably comprehensive of the whole subject.

14 *How to Understand and Use Company Accounts*, R. Warren, Business Books Ltd, 1983.
15 *Interpreting Company Reports and Accounts*, G. Holmes and A. Sugden, Woodhead-Faulkner, 1986.
16 *The Debate on Inflation Accounts*, D. Tweedie and G. Whittington, CUP, 1984.
17 *A Chronology of the History of Inflation Accounting*, R. D. Clark, Accountancy Magazine, 1985.
18 *The Lessons to be Learned from the Development of Inflation Accounting in the U.K.*, C. A. Westwick, Accountancy and Business Research.
19 *Accountancy for Changing Prices: How We Got Here and Where We go Next*, I. F. H. Davidson, Inaugural Arthur Anderson Lecture at University of Aston, 16th February, 1984.

Chapter 5   New issues

As with the chapter on capital markets innovation and general progress in the market place requires the serious practitioner to maintain reading of official publications, and of less formal reviews of developments in the USM and OTC markets.

Chapter 6   Portfolio theory and planning

The list below is by no means comprehensive but does cover diverse articles of actuarial thought.

20 *Review of the Principles of Life Office Valuations*, F. M. Redington, JIA 78, 286.

21 *The Financial Structure of a Life Office*, A. T. Haynes and R. J. Kirton, TFA 21, 141.
22 *The Evaluation of Ordinary Shares using a Computer*, D. Weaver and M. G. Hall, JIA 93, 165.
23 *The Matching of Assets to Liabilities*, A. J. Wise, JIA 111, 445.
24 *Immunized and Dedicated Bond Portfolios for U.K. Pension Funds*, G. M. Morrison, JSS 28, 135.
25 *A Mathematical Model for the Gilt-Edged Market*, R. S. Clarkson, JIA 106, 85.
26 *A Market Equilibrium Model for the Management of Ordinary Share Portfolios*, R. S. Clarkson, JIA 110, 17.
27 *Some Applications of Stochastic Investment Models*, A. D. Wilkie, JSS 29, 25.

MTP has been covered very briefly in the text and the interested reader is directed to the following for more comprehensive treatment.

28 *Investments*, W. F. Sharpe, Prentice Hall, 1978.
29 *Modern Developments in Investment Management*, J. Lorie and R. Brealey (Editors), Dryden Press, 1978.
30 *Modern Portfolio Theory and Investment Analysis*, E. J. Elton and M. J. Gruber, John Wiley & Sons, 1981.
31 *Implications of Modern Portfolio Theory for Life Assurance Companies*, A. J. Frost, JSS 26, 47.
32 *Modern Portfolio Theory and the Measurement of Risk*, P. G. Moore, Transactions of the 22nd International Congress of Actuaries, 1984.

Chapter 7   Investment in inflationary conditions

The seminal works in this area are contained in the references to the authors' paper on this subject which form the basis for this chapter.
33 *Investment in Inflationary Conditions*, A. J. Frost and D. P. Hager, Transactions of the 22nd International Congress of Actuaries, 1984.

Chapter 8   Practical portfolio management

The development of performance measurement has been a significant event in the last decade. There are now many articles and books being published on the subject, publicly and privately.
34 *Measurement of Pension Fund Investment Performance*, D. P. Hager, JSS 24, 33.

INDEX